THE NEW ESCAPE TO PARADISE

Our Experience Living and Retiring In Panama

Richard Detrich

August 2015

4

The cover photo was taken on our back porch just before I
hopped into the spa. The mountain is Volcan Baru and the
orange juice is our own, home grown.

Photographs throughout were either taken by the author, or
Rebecca Detrich, or are credited unless they are in the public
domain and/or from the U. S. government..

Comments NEW ESCAPE TO PARADISE

"**Richard tells it exactly like it is ... how I wish this wonderful tool were available before we moved here.** It would have saved a lot of frustration trying to figure it all out for ourselves." *Kathy Donelson*

"**A pragmatic and thought-provoking guide. If you seriously contemplate moving to a new land** you certainly should be prepared with this book!" *James Fletcher*

"**This is a comprehensive, boots on the ground book about what it is like to live in Panama.** I can't think of anything Richard didn't cover." *Judy Sacco*

"I enjoyed reading your book! It's **very illuminating and entertaining.** You have an ability to communicate and have an enjoyable writing style." *Doug Tyler*

"**Down to earth, no sugar coating, Richard gives both the good and not so good of living in Panama.**" *Steve McVicar*

"*The New Escape to Paradise* **is a must read for anyone thinking/dreaming about retiring to Panama.** This book is highly informative, current, and down to earth. Richard tells it like it is about retirement in Panama." *Allison Guinn*

"Part philosopher, part psychologist, part historian, part travel guide, and part economist, all describe Richard Detrich as he weaves his tale of life in Panama. He tells it 'like it is' without the hype. *The New Escape to Paradise* **is a must read for anyone who is considering relocating to another country whether it's Panama or somewhere else.** " *Kristin Stillman*

Comments ESCAPE TO PARADISE

"**This book is a must read! Not only is it filled with information, it is very enjoyable to read, as well.** Richard obviously loves living in Panama but doesn't hesitate to point out the negatives." *Debbie Curtis*

"Richard's book is full of helpful information about what to consider when moving to another country. Most of the questions I had about Panama were answered. **His writing style is friendly and I felt like I was listening to a friend sharing his experiences.**" *Peggy Archambault]*

"**Best book on Panama I have read.**" *Antoinette Jackson*

"Detrich tells you the good and the bad and debunks a lot of what you read on the Internet that is old and out of date. **Very easy to read. Well written.**" *Sarah Reynolds*

"I recommend this to anyone thinking that moving outside the United States is the answer to your dreams or problems. You need Richard's checklists. **Your expectations need to be challenged to see if they are real..**" *Colin "Soup" Campbell*

"**Honest and helpful**. I am glad this book has inspired me to be adventurous and to consider this relocation." *Linda and Bob Little*

"Your book ... is entertaining, informative, and a quick read. **Once I started reading it, I found it difficult to put down.**" *Harry Kooiman*

"**If anyone is considering 'the move' this book should be required reading.** I found it very realistic and thought provoking, as well as helping you look at your dreams. Detrich helps you look at your reasons for moving abroad in a logical, no-nonsense manner. All this introspection has helped me make my decision to relocate based on hard fact not pipe dreams." *Penny Sloan*

"**Written in a style which captures the reader's imagination and makes one want to read it in one sitting,** Detrich's book presents the challenges, joys and often frustrating aspects of navigating life in Panama. An experienced expat who is living the reader's dream reveals in an unbiased fashion what to expect of Panamanian living." *Denise Visci*

"This book is not only informative, but well written, funny and keeps your attention. Richard doesn't sugarcoat the problems you'll find in Panama, but he also helps you feel comfortable about making the move. Go in with your eyes open and you should have a good experience." *Bill Hazel*

" I really enjoyed making the list of 15 things we wanted in our place of residence. Great exercise! **This has honestly been more helpful to me than any other expat book I've read."** *Lusk Meierl*

"It's about time! **Of all the articles and books I have researched this one tells it like it really is with no personal axes to grind.** He answers questions that the other literature I read failed to ask, much less answer. His approach is far from lofty or detached. It's like you're both sitting at the breakfast table sharing conversation with a little wit here and an off-hand comment there: none of it a waste, but a nice easy way to give you the information." *Bob Little*

"Moving to another country is a big decision but Richard's book helps you think through all the benefits of moving to Panama. *Escape To Paradise* **is the best information I have found anywhere about relocating to Panama."** *Jackie Lange]*

"We gathered several publications, attended a conference and been to Boquete twice, but *Escape To Paradise* **is by far the most useful book we have read so far."** *Bob Milligan*

Contents

Introduction

$\mathcal{P}$eople kept asking the same questions over and over: why we moved to Panama[1] and what life was like. So I decided to write a book, *Escape to Paradise*, not really expecting many people would buy it. I was wrong! A lot of folks are very interested in escaping to paradise!

After ten years living in Panama with all the changes, I felt it was time to rework the book, hence *The New Escape to Paradise*.

In my academic and professional career I've learned to write many different ways. There were dreaded term papers in high school, one short story a week in my freshman college English course, writing sermons for oral presentation in seminary, a PhD thesis, business writing, and web copy. Through it all I've learned that the best way to communicate is to write the way you talk[2]. So I'm always pleased when reviewers say the book is "like talking to Richard over breakfast," and less pleased when others want to pick things apart, pointing out flaws in grammar. Most folks don't worry much about grammar when they talk with friends.

This book is about Panama, although I will share with you how we sorted through several countries before choosing Panama. Of course this book is based on our own personal experience in Chiriqui, the province where Boquete is located.

Regards, Richard
Boquete, Chiriqui, Panama
August 2015

1. Why Panama?

"*I* am probably the only *gringo* in Panama who ever moved here because of the Embera Indians[3].

Originally, I knew really nothing about Panama. Yes I knew it had a Canal. When we had travel agencies I used to send people on cruises through the Canal and had been through myself on cruise ships during the Noriega years, or as the locals refer to it, "the dictatorship." Back then, as we slipped through the Canal the shore looked totally foreign, and threatening, evoking much the same feeling that Cuba was supposed to evoke for Americans from the United States.

I had waded through David McCullough's book, *The Path Between The Seas: The Creation of The Panama Canal 1870-1914*, about the Panama Canal. But in terms of modern Panama my only impressions had come from the movie *Tailor of Panama*. Although the only major motion picture actually filmed in Panama, I would eventually come to realize its highly inaccurate depiction of Panama.

Not only was Panama not on the list of countries that my wife and I were considering, we'd never even thought of Panama.

I was serving as a volunteer Protestant chaplain on a cruise ship that was cruising in the Caribbean and sailing into the Canal, turning around in Gatun Lake, and returning to Florida. The ship turned out to offer a stop in Panama, providing opportunity for passengers to disembark in Gatun Lake if they were taking one of a handful of shore excursions.

One of the shore excursions offered was a trip in a dugout

canoe to an "Authentic Embera Indian Village." My wife thought it sounded fantastic and jumped at the opportunity. At almost $100 a head, I thought it sounded expensive and I was sure it would be a hokey rip-off aimed at tourists, not that any cruise line would ever offer a "hokey rip-off" shore excursion. Nikki went on the tour and I took advantage of my chaplain status to go ashore to the "Gatun Lake Yacht Club" for the day – not a yacht or marina in sight, but it was a chance to actually set foot in Panama.

An Embera group from another village had been recruited by the tour operator to provide local, mostly naked, color. Bare-breasted girls and men in nothing but red loin cloths met the passengers disembarking the ship's tenders for the obligatory port disembarkation photos. To my knowledge this is the first time cruise ship photos had ever featured bare-breasted girls, so of course it was a big hit with the passengers, if exploitative.

There was nothing at the Gatun Lake Yacht Club. This truly was a hokey tourist rip-off. I guess to compensate, the tour operator of the "yacht club tour" was offering free beer. There was a group of Embera women selling baskets. I looked at the baskets then walked across the lawn where the men were sprawled out. One young guy was sitting at a cement picnic table, all alone, and appeared to either be stoned, drunk, or sleeping. Another Embera was sitting at another table watching me closely, since most of the ship's passengers were huddled together by the dock and the beer. He said something to me in Spanish, and I stumbled to reply which pretty much exhausted my Spanish. Somehow I managed to ask if this kid at the table was drunk or stoned. He laughed and said the guy was his brother, and he was just tired from the all-night trip in from their jungle village. He yelled for his brother to come over and join us. Poor guy had obviously been in the middle of a very erotic dream, and he wandered across, half asleep but obviously aroused, not easy to hide in a loin cloth, and so this provoked a lot of good-natured laughter and teasing from the other guys.

The guy I was talking to was Erito and eventually I met all his brothers and it wasn't long until we are all sitting at a cement table deep into conversation, truly amazing given my halting and very limited Spanish.

It turned out that Erito was the head of his village. His uncles had worked for the U. S. Army teaching the early astronauts and Green Berets jungle survival, so Erito knew a few words of English. About this time I got the idea of going over to where the tour operator was serving free beer, and bringing back beer for everyone . Of course, with the beer, the group of my new Embera friends continued to grow. I met Auselio and his girl friend, Erito's wife, Fernando and everyone else.

Auselio was in love and he wanted a picture taken of him and his beautiful bare-breasted girl friend. He gave me a *regalo* or gift of a beaded necklace, and I, with nothing else to give, gave him the 24 Hour Fitness shirt from off my back. Auselio said that he couldn't wait to get back to the village to get his girl friend to put on the shirt so, as he put it, she'd "look sexy like American[4] girls." I patiently explained that in the United States the object was to get the T-shirt *off* the girl,.

They wanted to know what I did for work and since my job was director of e-commerce for 24 Hour Fitness at the time, I told them "Internet." Auselio's eyes lit up and he said, "Internet!" I thought to myself, "Oh, no, they have a website and he's the webmaster." That wasn't the case, but I began to realize that these guys, although committed to preserving a lifestyle, were very intelligent, articulate, and very aware of technology and what was happening in the rest of the world.

By this time, two hours into the conversation, we were attracting the notice of the tour operator's personnel, and I guess, we were consuming a lot of beer. One of the tour operator's guys began serving the beer so I didn't have to keep jumping up for more, and bringing fruit punch for the Embera women. I wanted to take a swim in the Canal, but these guys who live in jungle huts, told me it was "too cold." I called them a "bunch of pussies" and then had to explain the term – gales of more laughter. I gave them my 24 Hour Fitness gym bag. They almost got my shorts, which was all I had left, but I figured the sight of a drunken chaplain wearing a red loin cloth re-boarding the ship might not go over too well with the cruise line, so I kept the pants on. When it was time for the Embera culture and dance show for the passengers, I was escorted to a plastic chair in front of the ship's passengers and told that this performance was for me.

I was told by Erito, and this was later confirmed by the ship's staff, that I was the first passenger she'd seen who really connected and entered into this kind of interaction with the Embera. Erito invited me to come back and visit his village and stay in his home. Five hours later, Nikki got off the motor coach from her trip to the Embera village (a nearer and different village than Erito's), and was greeted by her husband and all the Embera shouting, *"Esposa! Esposa!"* ("Wife! Wife!")

Let it be said that the Embera village trip was the highlight of Nikki's cruise. I have worked on ships transiting the Canal in the years since and I can tell you that every time we send groups out to the Embera village, people come back to the ship saying, "Richard, that was the best tour ever."

Back on the ship the shore excursion manager, who'd been observing this scene from a distance, commented on my unique experience. The Embera and passengers usually kept a discrete distance from one another. She promised that if I sent a package to the ship in Florida, she would see it got to Erito on the next Canal voyage.

I decided to send them a package that included a booklet of the pictures I had taken of our time together, along with pictures of my family and home in Ventura, California. I went to Joann Fabrics to buy the wildest fabrics I could find to send the guys for loin cloths. It was the first week of December and I was standing in a long line of women at Joann Fabrics waiting for my fabric to be cut and measured. I had a pile of wild fabric in my arms and this old lady in front was determined to make conversation. "My, what an interesting assortment of fabric: what are you making?"

Just wanting to escape Joann Fabrics, I said, "Oh, you'd never guess."

"A clown costume?"

"Hardly. But, if you must know, loin cloths for Embera Indians in Panama!" That, I thought, would end the conversation.

To which she replied, "The Embera! My daughter lives in Panama City and knows the Embera and collects and sells their baskets." Now what were the chances?

So I sent the package to the ship and got an email back from the ship saying, "The guys loved the package! There was much laughter and celebration. Erito wants to know when you are coming to visit."

So that began the process of searching online for anything that I could find out about the Embera and Erito's village of San Juan de Pequini. It truly is a small world on the Internet. Online I found pictures that tourists had taken of Erito and his village. But the more I searched online for stuff about the Embera and Panama the more sites I discovered about Panama in general and about retiring, moving and living in Panama. This was interesting. And the more I read the more interested I became.

So, thanks to Erito, Auselio, and the Embera of San Juan de Pequini I discovered Panama and it made it to our short list. Many Latinos are very surprised at this story and our relationship with Erito and his family. Most Panamanians only know the Indians who work for them, generally not the Embera. Although they have considerable political power, in the Panamanian social structure the Indigenous are at the bottom of the totem pole, often treated as if they don't exist. We have been fortunate to continue our relationship with our Embera friends. Erito and his family have visited with us several times in Boquete and I have been able to continue to visit their village with tours from the ships and with just my family.

A postscript about Auselio: today Auselio has "filled out" and looks like an ex-US Marine. He has two lovely children and is a leader in his village. When I went to visit the Embera village, Auselio was concerned that I not flash the picture around that I had taken of him as a teenager with his girlfriend at Gatun Lake. It seemed he'd fallen in love with and married another girl.

"Why Panama?"

Diversity

Panama is known to the world for its Canal, being the flag of registry for many of the world's ships, an international banking and business center, and the crossroads of the world and hub of the Americas. Panama's population is around 3.7 million people, about 1.6 million of whom live in and around Panama City.

Where we live, the province of Chiriqui, is far from the skyscrapers of Panama City. Home to David, the second largest city in Panama, Chiriquí's main industry is still agriculture. Chiriqui provides most of the country's dairy cattle, beef cattle, vegetables, citrus and bananas. Our particular town, Boquete, provides some of the world's finest high-altitude, shade-grown, Arabica coffee. Each year there is a "cupping" where major coffee buyers from all over the world come to sample and bid at auction for coffee. Consider that in Panama there are:

- 4,414 kilometers [1,500 miles] of coastline
- 940 bird species
- 10,000 species of plants
- 200 species of mammals
- 200 species of reptiles
- Nesting homes to four species of sea turtles

- Mountain peaks from which you can see both the Pacific and Caribbean
- Rivers where rafters can ride 20 sets of rapids in a single afternoon
- 1,518 islands
- More deep-sea fishing records off the Pacific coast of Panama than anywhere else in the world
- Seven Indigenous Indian cultures
- 30 percent of the country is set aside for conservation
- 125 animal species found nowhere else in the world
- Variety of ecosystems including tropical rain forests, grasslands, mountain forest, cloud forests, mangroves and deserts
- Two national marine parks, one of which, Parque Nacional Marino Golfo de Chiriqui, is just a short boat ride from Boca Chica, the tiny fishing village where our casita is located

You can have a morning swim in the Pacific and the same afternoon sip cocktails in the Caribbean. How's that for diverse?

Because I'm on the ship about half of the year, when I'm home in Boquete, my idea of a good time is sitting by the fire with my wife and dogs, eating dinner on the couch, and watching TV. Since I "eat out" every night on the ship, I'm not very interested in going out when I'm home. So I'm generally not really social when I'm home, but this has been a busy week. Sunday we were invited to a potluck lunch and there were expats[5] from Canada, United States, England, South Africa, Holland, Spain, Italy, France and Hong Kong, plus Panamanians. It was a fun afternoon with a neat and diverse group of people.

Thursday we had a bunch of people over for a wine and cheese party that went from 4:30 p.m. until 9:00 p.m. One of our neighbors is a professional Poker player and his partner is from Taiwan. Friday we were invited over to a gay couple's house down the road for dinner. They've been together for 20 years and could maybe teach a lot of straight folks something about "family values." Saturday night we went to a French restaurant in town for a five-course dinner with five different French wines ($90 for two, including tax and tip) and at our table were a retired race car driver, a horse trainer, a Canadian, a Brit, a Panamanian, and a few Americans like us. It is a very diverse, interesting and fun group.

Panamanians themselves are a historically diverse group with strains of Indigenous cultures, and Spanish ancestry. There are many people in Boquete who have English surnames going back to early English settlers who intermarried with Panamanians. Jews, Greeks, Chinese, West Indian Africans, French, North Americans, and others all were involved in the Canal and entered into the mix. The result is that Panamanians are a mixed and beautiful group of people. When you throw an innate friendliness, politeness, and a lot of patience into the mix, you get a really great group of people.

Officially Panama is a Roman Catholic country, although religious freedom is encouraged. Catholicism is the largest religious group, but slowly declining. The fastest growing group is evangelical charismatic churches. "Hosanna!" is an Assembly of God church in Panama City that started in a storefront. Today 14,000 worship every Sunday at three services in a sanctuary that seats 5,000. The church runs a medical center, TV, radio stations, and has planted numerous daughter churches around the country.

You find Seventh Day Adventists, Mormons, and Muslims. There are mosques in many of the larger cities, including David. My background with Muslims was largely influenced by Black Muslims in New York, so I'm often a bit taken aback seeing a Panamanian Muslim woman in the grocery store dressed modestly and appropriately, but looking like she just stepped off the runway of a Paris fashion show.

There is a Mormon Temple in Panama City and perched high above the city on a mountain called, *la montaña del Dulce Canto* ("the mountain of Beautiful Singing") overlooking the city, is the Baha'i mother temple for Latin America.

Again, in all ways, this is a very diverse country.

One of the things we've enjoyed over the years is just to jump in our 4X4 and explore. This weekend we headed off to Puerto Armuelles, formerly home to Chiquita Banana. Faced with labor problems, the banana plantations went elsewhere and for many years Puerto Armuelles has been an economically depressed area. Now with a new four lane road between the town and the Pan American Highway, and with some new beachfront development, and the promise of new deep water port facilities, Puerto Armeulles may be on the verge of a comeback. But we ended up hopelessly lost in an old banana plantation area with nary a *gringo* in sight, yet everyone was friendly and eager to be helpful, even to two lost *gringos*.

Beauty

Panama is a gorgeous country in addition to the beauty and diversity of the people.

Because the country isn't that big, in a single day you can drive from the Pacific to the Caribbean, from the *frontera* at the Costa Rican border to the edges of the Darien jungle, almost from one end of the country to the other. In a single afternoon you can pass through a half dozen eco systems. Coral reefs, deserted beaches, mangrove swamps, grasslands, ranches, pine-covered mountains where you feel like you've been dropped into the Alps, cloud forests, tropical rainforests, small Central American villages, and a vibrant Miami-like Central American city – it's all here, and it's all waiting to be discovered.

With over 1,500 islands, there is almost an island for everyone! And the weather is beautiful too! At nine degrees from the equator, there are hot and humid regions, but there are also mountain towns like Boquete, where the temperature year round is a near-perfect 18 to 27 degrees Celsius [65 to 80 degrees Fahrenheit]. Even in many of the warmest areas there are ocean breezes that mitigate the temperatures.

In California we had four seasons: earthquake, fire, rain, and mudslide – take your pick. Panama has three seasons: rain, rain, and rain. Well, not really. Summer, the dry season, is much like Southern California with little rain from mid-December to mid-April. Winter, the rainy season, or the "green season" as the tourist people prefer, runs from May to November. The months of June and July are kind of a Panamanian version of the North American "Indian summer." So, how much rain? How much rain depends on where you are in Panama. Boquete gets moisture even in the "dry season." In the late afternoon a *bajareque* mist moves in over the mountains. Barely enough to wet the ground, it creates spectacular rainbows throughout the valley and the mountains. Boquete averages as much rain in a month as Ventura, California receives in an average year. Even in the rainy season it rarely rains all day. Usually mornings are bright and pristine and everyone is up, out, and taking care of business. About 2:00 p.m. the clouds start to move in and generally there will be an afternoon storm, sometimes continuing into the night. It can be a drizzle, or you can get five inches in a few hours in a tropical downpour. But, with the possible exception of October, the worst month of the rainy season, it never feels oppressive.

The Caribbean side, and the area around Bocas, receives the most rain, up to 3,500 millimeters per year. That's about 10 feet, but who's counting? With that much water you can make your own wet T-shirt contests without even going to a bar.

Panama is not only beautiful, it is also clean.

Many Caribbean islands are gorgeous, if you can overlook overflowing, stinking trash bins, beaches littered with plastic bottles and bags, and roadsides covered with trash. Once you are away from the city, Panama is pretty clean. People are proud and make a conscious effort to keep things nice and clean. You'll find less trash along major roads than in California. And because Panama doesn't have the strong gang culture of the States, there is very little graffiti. Where you do find graffiti it is mostly an expression of a current political grievance.

Now I hasten to add that in North America and Europe many of us have a compulsion about trash and properly disposing of everything. It took me months before I felt comfortable throwing a banana peel into the forest, but my Indigenous friends lectured me on how everything returns to the ground and gives nourishment. I have traveled around the world several times with groups of mostly North Americans. We've visited the Taj Mahal, the Pyramids and Angkor Wat. Wow! And what do people talk about when we get back to the ship? Trash!

Many parts of the world do not view trash and litter the same way as we do. People are different and cultural attitudes are different. In many parts of the world folks are too concerned with where the next meal is coming from to worry about trash.

Panama is clean, relatively clean. Are roadsides perfect? No, but compared to many tropical, Latin American countries, Panama is clean. Just like in North American cities you can find filthy corners and freeway intersections.

Economics

Panama's currency is called the "Balboa" but it is in fact the U. S. dollar. Since 1904 Panama, except for one week, has used the U. S. dollar, so, even if you aren't from the States, you pretty much know what something costs. You don't have to wonder, "How much is that in real money?" Panamanian coins are in the same denominations as U. S. coins, in fact they have the same size and weight and coins are used interchangeably. You can put a Panamanian quarter in a vending machine in Miami just as you can put a U. S. quarter in a Panamanian machine. Due to the short life-span of $1 paper bills and the high cost of shipping worn out paper bills back to the U. S. Treasury, Panama has introduced a one

Balboa coin which is equal in value to the dollar and looks and feels a little like a one Euro coin.

Because Panama's currency is the U. S. dollar, the rampant inflation that plagues many South and Central American countries and "Banana Republics" is not a problem. Panama's currency is as strong as the U. S. dollar. When the U. S. dollar is weak against major world currencies the price of many things we import goes up in Panama just like it does in the United States.

As the U. S. Treasury Department continues to print massive amounts of currency to pay for U. S. wars [War on Drugs, War on Terrorism, Afghanistan, Iraq] as well as for bailouts of giant corporations with high-paid lobbyists and executives, the U. S. dollar has become devalued. The U. S. dollar is now worth less and buys less, which has led to inflation, not only in the United States, but also in places like Panama and Ecuador which use the U. S. dollar.

Panama is one of the world's "sit up and take note" economies and the booming economy has also contributed to inflation.

- Panama has a robust service industry. It is a major center for off-shore banking and corporations.

- Many of the ships in the world fly the Panamanian flag, although Panama has no navy.

- The Canal goes cha-ching, cha-ching, cha-ching twenty-four hours a day. Although it is an independent agency, it plows money into the country. The Canal makes a direct contribution to the government of over $1.25 BILLION a year plus indirect contribution in the form of taxes, social security payments, etc. The Canal is completing a $6 billion dollar expansion and already is starting work on plans for yet another expansion to handle even larger ships.

- The Chinese are expanding their massive harbors at the ends of the Canal and the Canal has plans underway to develop a massive LNG terminal.

- The Trans-Panama oil pipeline transports oil from Alaskan supertankers that dock at Puerto Armuelles, across the Isthmus since the supertankers don't fit through the existing Canal.

- Panamanian coffee shows up in Starbucks and other coffee blends around the world and is exported to Japan, Scandinavia, Germany, Italy and Taiwan.

- Bananas, melons, pineapples and beef are exported.

- Panama is currently the site of the development of what will be the second largest copper mine in the world as well as a gold mine. With the high cost of gold, the precious metal represents the highest dollar-value export of the country.

- The Colon Free Zone is the second largest free zone in the world, second only to Hong Kong. Panama has created an additional free zone at Panama Pacifico, the planned community on the site of the former Howard Air Force Base. Other free zones are planned for Aguadulce and David.

- Panama has announced the creation of a new harbor in Aguadulce that will handle giant tankers and cruise ships. The new harbor in Aguadulce is mandated as Panama becomes the logistics center for Latin America.

- Tocumen International Airport cannot expand fast enough to keep up with the demand. Panama is indeed the crossroads and hub of the Americas and the hassles that have been created in the United States by TSA and other supposed "cures" for terrorism, have led many to choose to connect in Panama.

Unlike some of its neighbors, Panama has a comparatively diverse economy. The standard of living in Panama and the average income, although low by North American standards, is the highest in Central America, and yet the cost of living in Panama overall is less than in North America and Europe.

Depending on where you are from you can live better for less in Panama. Our overall cost of living in Boquete is still about one third of what it would be today in Ventura, California, where we used to live. . We'll talk more about this in the chapter on "Running the Numbers," but it is amazing how much your money can buy in Panama.

Traditionally banking in Panama has been very private, although after a full court press by the United States to break bank secrecy and holding a Free Trade Agreement hostage, the United States has managed to break down the bank secrecy in Panama the same way it did in Switzerland and elsewhere. Over 200 international banks have a presence in Panama, although because of Panama's banking laws, you need to open different accounts in Panama even if it's the same bank you use back home.

There are, of course, fees when you transfer money between countries, or currencies and it's not quite as simple as it looks in movies, but it does work. With the new Free Trade Agreement and FATCA[6] , the United States has imposed a lot of additional bookkeeping and reporting duties on Panamanian banks, so you may find banks who don't want to be bothered with U. S. citizens as new clients.

A lot of people assume that Panama is a "tax-free" haven -- not exactly. There is no Panamanian tax on income that is earned outside Panama. And there is no Panama tax on interest earned from bank deposits in Panama. If you are U. S. citizen you owe the government a "pound of flesh" regardless of where you live in the world or where your money comes from: there is no escaping U. S. tax if you have a U. S. passport.

If you are a U. S. citizen and your permanent residence is outside the United States, i.e. you are not in the United States or its airspace or territorial waters, for over 30 calendar days a year, you, and your spouse should you have one, can each deduct up to $100,800 [2015] of *earned* income. Earned income does not include passive income like income from investments, pensions, Social Security, royalties and the like. If you have questions you will need to talk to a Panamanian and U. S. tax attorney. The United States now has far more IRS agents at the Embassy in Panama City than FBI agents, which tells you the priority. And everyone knows that if you ask two IRS agents the same question you will get two different answers and neither agent accepts any responsibility, nor does the IRS, for the misinformation you are given. So good luck with that.

Don't think that Panama is tax-free! There is a value added, ITBS tax of seven percent on almost everything except food, including on services. There are property taxes, although there are some exemptions, and taxes on corporations and foundations even if you don't make money, as well as lots of fees.

Location

Panama's location, the Isthmus bridging North and South America, nine degrees north of the equator, is one of the ideal locations in the world, not just because of the ideal weather, but also because of its strategic location.

Even if it wasn't home to the Canal, Panama would be a strategic center of world commerce. Vasco Nunez de Balboa and Christopher Columbus both put into Panama long before a Canal was even conceived. Sir Frances Drake and Henry Morgan both sacked Panama, proving that piracy in Panama is nothing new, except that today's pirates are more likely to be fly-by-night, mostly North American, real estate developers than sea-farers.

One of the major benefits of Panama's location is that it lies outside the hurricane belt. Anyone who has witnessed the devastation of South Florida or the Caribbean by a hurricane will immediately appreciate the importance of living outside of the hurricane belt. Tropical depressions can cause lots of rain, particularly on the Caribbean side, which can produce local flooding at times, but … no hurricanes.

Panama has no currently active volcanoes unlike other Central American countries. Volcan Baru towers above my home town of Boquete rising 11,407 feet [3,478 meters] above sea level. It doesn't "look" like a volcano because some 50,000 years ago much of the volcano collapsed. Today it has not just one, but seven craters. On a clear day from its summit, you can see both the Pacific and Caribbean.

In Panama, like back in California, we occasionally do rock and roll. Although near the intersection of several major tectonic plates out in the Pacific Ocean, unlike California we do not sit on top of the major fault. Largely as a result of fairly recent quakes – a 6.3 quake on Christmas Day in 2003 killed two people in Puerto Armuelles – seismic building codes have been updated and careful attention to seismic engineering is an essential part of building a home in Panama. Although at times we have lots of tremors as the plates move, most of these quakes are hardly felt or noticed. All the little quakes are actually good as they relieve pressure bit by bit. When quakes are noticeable, they generally aren't the rolling variety like we experienced in California, but it feels more like someone backed a car into the corner of the house.

Infrastructure

Panama, in part due to U. S. influence through the Canal years, has the best infrastructure of any Central American or Caribbean nation. And face it, no matter how romantic your dreams, if you're going to live someplace, infrastructure is important. But the infrastructure is far from perfect. Under the current government massive amounts have been invested in new roads, bridges and infrastructure. Panama City now even has a Metro. So, although improving, the infrastructure is far from perfect.

Water

Panama has tons of fresh water. Coming from Southern California, where my water and sewage bill ran as high as $160 a month, I still find it disconcerting to pay only $7.50 a month for water, no matter how much I use. Where we live, just above Boquete, our water is piped down from high up on the volcano. It's the same volcanic water you buy in the store. Plus I have my own well which taps into an underground stream, flowing from way up on the volcano. In most of Panama you can drink the water, although, particularly when you are acclimating to a new area, it might be advisable to boil your water initially.

Sewage

In Panama City and Colon heavy rains can cause drainage systems and sewers to overflow, and raw sewage makes its way into the bays or oceans. Panama City is in the middle of building a major new sewer system, aided by grants from Japan. It is a challenging project because of the continuing growth of the Panama City metropolitan area. The goal is for the Bay of Panama to once again be enjoyed as a seaside playground.

Outside of the city most homes in Panama use septic tanks. Some of the coastal Indians have traditionally used the ocean as a sewer. In rural areas sometimes people just throw trash in the rivers, counting on the river to carry their garbage into someone else's backyard. As Panama becomes more and more "first world" it struggles with the challenges of dealing with waste and initiating programs of recycling. Panama City, which still uses an old, traditional "dump" is moving toward programs of recycling and building modern facilities to recycle waste and use what is left over to generate electricity.

Roads

Panama has some of the best roads in Central America. In Panama much of the Pan-American Highway is already four lanes, and most will be four or at least three lanes when the current construction is completed. Main roads in Panama are generally quite good. When you get off the beaten track, however, as we frequently do while exploring, anything goes. On side roads and out-of-the-way places it can get quite rough. It used to be that unless a former politician happened to live in the area, the road would remain rough. Now with money flowing in from the Canal and the government committed to improving infrastructure, even rural roads are being paved. But a four-wheel drive vehicle still makes a lot of sense.

Many Panamanian drivers aren't quite as good as the roads. Driving in Panama City is a never-to-be-forgotten experience! Many expats will not drive in Panama City and instead hire drivers when they go to town. As an ex-New Yorker I find driving in Panama City chaotic, but a challenge and refreshing in the sense that other drivers do not use the standard, offensive New Yorker hand signals, and people occasionally actually will let you into a stream of traffic, particularly if you close your eyes and just go. Panama cities don't always have one-way street signs since generally everyone knows which streets are one-way and which way they go, and if you don't, lots of people on the sidewalks will remind you.

Since many roads are only two lanes, you may need to brush up on your passing skills. The rules here, in practice at least, are different. A double yellow line used to mean that it might be a good idea to at least look before passing, but as the money flows in Panama things are becoming more and more regulated. Transitos, the traffic police, now have radar guns that work. Laws regarding speed, use of seat belts, and non use of cell phones are increasingly being enforced with large fines for violations. U-turns are generally prohibited everywhere and you can get a hefty fine even if you do a "semi-legal" U-turn pulling off the main road and turning.

Our friend, and the builder of our first house, Jeff Daugherty, has lived all over the world building for Chevron. When we came to Panama he advised us that no matter where in the world you live, even if it is infested with terrorists, the single most dangerous thing for Americans abroad is driving. Folks will stop or pull into traffic without warning, and make left hand turns without signaling, which is especially fun if you've just pulled out to pass!

The key to driving and surviving in Panama is to expect the unexpected. Driving on California freeways may seem a nightmare to non-Californians, but basically you sit bumper-to-bumper and creep, or you zoom along at 90 miles an hour bumper-to-bumper. Both are hazardous but you know what to expect. In Panama a horse, cow, or Indian may suddenly appear in the road. The guy with his right turn signal on may end up turning left. Or the truck full of cows up ahead may be stopping without any lights. In rural areas like Chiriqui, old farm pickups may or may not have working brakes. Driving in Panama you always need to be alert.

Public Transportation

In Panama City the city has completed the first line of a new Metro system and developed a city bus system to replace to previous system of independent bus operators using old school buses imported from the States. Because the old buses were sometimes in poor repair, and some of the drivers proudly advertised that they were high on pot most of the time, there were lots of accidents and the buses become known as the "Red Devils." There are two explanations for the name. One is that they ended up in so many accidents and spilled so much blood on the city streets, and the other is that if and when the drivers were killed, they went straight to hell. The new public system is still working out some of the kinks, but it is greatly improving traffic flow.

Taxi cabs are plentiful in Panama City and fares are more-or-less regulated. Locals know what the fare should be but tourists often end up paying more than they should. Cab

drivers are pretty much the same all over the world.
When you get outside Panama City there is an amazing
network of private buses serving almost every place in the
country. Frequently these are old school buses, crowded with
locals and often with luggage and chickens strapped on top of
the bus. And there are yellow cabs, privately run but
requiring a government license, everywhere. Usually you will
share a taxi ride with others.

Phones

Panama thinks it has reasonably good telephone service, but
based on my personal experience I would disagree. It is now
almost impossible to get a land line so you are largely
dependent on cellular service. There are several cellular
services that spend a great deal splashing their colors of paint
all over the country and advertising signals they claim to be
fantastic. Like many people we find it necessary to have two
of the three services, separate phones, and even then calls are
continually dropped and often we cannot get a decent signal.

Everyone, well almost everyone, has at least one cell phone. I
joke that Panamanian babies come out of the womb equipped
with a cell phone in hand. According to a recent study of cell
phone penetration, Panamanians have 1.9 cell phones per
person!

Monthly cellular plans seem much more expensive than in the
States, so most people use pre-paid phone cards. To call our
families in the States from Panama costs about the same as it
did from California, but like most folks we use Skype and call
for free. Often I will have to use Skype to even call for a small
cost within Panama because the cell signals are so poor.

Mail

Mail service in Panama is nothing like the States. For one
thing we don't have addresses. Really. Even in Panama City
addresses will describe an area, and the name of the street,
and the name of a building, and if necessary where that

building is in relation to a larger, better-known building. People who demand my street address and don't understand that we don't have such a thing, at least as they expect, look bewildered when I tell them, "on the road to the cemetery the driveway before the *beneficio*". Alternatively, you can just ask for "The *gringos* with the two Dalmatians." So without addresses and no mail delivery, you pick up your mail at the post office in town. When we first came to Panama there weren't enough mail boxes to go around so we had to use general delivery. Every time we saw a funeral procession we'd rush to the post office to see if we could get the postal box of the deceased.

Some expats use a Miami post office box and a courier-forwarding service. This can get expensive, particularly when the credit card providers and other junk mail producers get your Miami PO Box address and all the junk mail comes to Panama. You can either get a subscription to such a service, paying a small monthly fee, or use providers like Mail Boxes, Etc. to forward occasional packages.

I regularly order books from Amazon or my publisher and have had them sent by regular mail without problem. Generally an order takes twelve to seventeen days to arrive by regular mail. The catch is if the Panamanian customs people decide to check the package and hold it in David at the main post office. To retrieve it requires a trip to David, standing in line, and paying a few cents a day "storage" fee because you didn't drop everything and run into David. With a book, and books are exempt from duty, it is a real pain driving to David, signing forms and getting them rubber stamped (two different windows and two different stamps of course!) and then paying storage fees for a book on which there is no duty anyway. But, as we often say to one another, "Welcome to Panama!"

Internet

Much of Panama is wired. There are Internet cafes with rates ranging from sixty cents to a dollar an hour and the government is committed to making the Internet universally available. In many communities they have opened public Internet centers where the first hour is free, and then you pay something like twenty-five cents an hour. Some areas, like the main Plaza in downtown Boquete, have free Wi-Fi ... when it is working.

Our personal Internet connection has been a nightmare. When we first moved to Valle Escondido they promised "high speed Internet" which it never was until we moved to our farm and then Valle Escondido got cable TV and the fastest Internet in town. Where we are now living we have no choice but to use a wireless service which runs around $65 a month for 1 Meg. Some folks just use their smart phone as a hotspot if they a service provider with a tower nearby.

Internet connectivity is not as reliable as it is in much of the world. When our service is spotty, which it often is during rain storms or heavy fog, I remind myself that at least it is better than it is on the ship.

The former administration promised, but was unable to deliver, free Internet for everyone. Now, Facebook founder Mark Zukerberg has partnered with the current administration again promising free Internet access.

Supplies

It's important to be able to have a good source of supplies wherever you choose to live. As a general rule in Panama we have found that, "You can find anything you want in Panama City, anything you need in David." *Find* is the operative word. You're going to have to look for things and learn, largely from others, where to find certain things, but for the most part, it's here. You may not find the brand you are used to, and it may be packaged differently, but in all likelihood it's available somewhere in Panama City.

In the eight years we have been in Panama we have seen huge changes in David. Anything you need is pretty much available in David. We've seen new malls with department stores and home improvement stores. No Home Depot, Bed Bath & Beyond or Walmart – yet. But we do have PriceSmart, from the folks who brought you the original Price Club in California. The variety and prices aren't nearly as advantageous as Price Club/Costco/Sam's Club and there isn't something new to tempt you every time you visit, but for us there's a certain comfort in shopping at PriceSmart. And no, we don't have Walmart but there are four huge supermarkets in David, and four smaller ones in Boquete. In Volcan there are two supermarkets.

When we came to Panama we brought a forty-foot container because we had a lot of furniture we liked and things that were important and meaningful to us, like my wife's grand piano. We know other folks who sold everything before leaving the States, came down with a suitcase, and furnished their entire homes very nicely with what they purchased in Panama. So it's really a matter of choice. If you have a lot of patience you can get wood, metal and rattan furniture hand-crafted. All you need is a photo or sketch of what you want. It's easier to get old overstuffed furniture re-upholstered, provided you can find fabric you like, than it is to find new overstuffed furniture that suits American preferences for style and comfort.

We had seen an armoire we liked in a shop in Santa Barbara before we left California. It was about $8,000. I took a picture and showed it to a woodworker who make the same armoire for me in Panama for $750. I give my metal worker a rough sketch of railings, a hanging light, whatever and in a few days he comes back with a more detailed sketch and a price. A light that might cost $200 in the states, is hand-made for $70.

Propane

Like most of the world there is no natural gas service in Panama, so you have to adjust to living with propane. It's easy to get propane but "developing nation" propane tends to be dirtier and not as hot or efficient as propane in the States.

Folks who know about such things tell me it is really butane not propane. Many Panamanians do not have hot water heaters or use so-called "suicide" shower heads – plug in electrical units attached to the shower head. The "dirty" propane is hard on traditional tank water heaters, so most expats are going to on-demand hot water systems, either electric or propane. Yet the propane on-demand hot water systems, most of which are made in China, don't work after two years either and need replaced, and even the electric units, some of which are actually made in the U. S., aren't much better.

Electricity

Beware of property that doesn't have electrical service. Putting in electrical lines can cost a small fortune. Generally the electric company will provide only 100 meters [around 328 feet] of connection.

Considering all the hydroelectric power generated in Panama, particularly in Chiriqui, you'd think electricity would be a bargain. It should be, but it isn't. Private companies provide electricity and happily sell the surplus to Costa Rica while charging customers more than in most Latin American countries. In Boquete we don't need air conditioning or heating, but during the rainy season dehumidifiers can consume a lot of power. Electrical service is generally reliable … most of the time. There are outages which usually are only a few minutes or a few hours. Some people have put in back up generators but generally we don't mind burgers on the grill with a romantic candlelight dinner. Beware if your neighbor has a giant generator that roars to life automatically, even in the middle of the night, every time the lights flicker.

Because power frequently goes on and off, you should equip your house with whole house surge protectors. In addition we use individual power surge protectors on computers and televisions. During the rainy season when we get spectacular electrical storms we generally disconnect computers and televisions to avoid surges from nearby lightening strikes.

Things are certainly improving and most of our experience has been outside of Panama City. In Panama City things are more dependable and most large buildings have back up generators.

Lifestyle

One of the things I like best about Panama is that we enjoy a better lifestyle for a lot less money.

Living in Panama is for the most part far healthier. Traffic accidents are probably a push, but the air in Boquete is crisp and clean and unpolluted. And you should see the stars at night! The food is far better. Meat is all locally grown in Chiriqui province and is not force-fed on feedlots or loaded with hormones. Vegetables and fruits are locally grown on small family farms and there are several small organic growers. Carrots, potatoes, onions are fresh from the farm, and haven't been around for months in warehouses being treated with who-knows-what to keep them looking edible. We have an abundant supply of inexpensive tropical fruit and grow our own oranges and bananas. The pineapple and melons grown in Panama are the sweetest imaginable.

The bread, if you so choose, is freshly baked. Bread is more expensive than other food items because the climate and soil in Panama is not conducive for growing wheat.

The water we drink in Boquete comes from the volcano and is like what we bought in bottles for $2.50 a liter back in California. In fact Boquete water is bottled and sold throughout Panama.

We don't have the temptation of fast food. Yes, if you get desperate, there is a McDonald's and Kentucky Fried Chicken, Subway, Pizza Hut and TGIF Friday's in David, and every franchise under the sun in Panama City, but for the most part we eat healthier.

The thirty to forty-minute trip to David once a week used to be trying at times, but now with a new four lane highway it is a lot easier and less frustrating, but at its worst it was nothing like the 101 Freeway. I'm not spending 10 percent of my life stuck in Southern California traffic.

In many ways life in Boquete is like life was in the States in the fifties. Real family values dominate. The family is all-important. The work week is Monday through Saturday at noon. Saturday evenings and Sunday afternoons you will see entire families, dressed in their best, coming to town to shop, treat everyone to an ice cream cone, and go to church. Many of the Indians live in what we in the States would, in exercise of our cultural imperialism, term "hovels," yet when they come to town they are wearing spotless clothing, their hair is slicked back, and the children walk obediently with their parents. There is little smoking in Panama. The government has outlawed smoking in all public buildings, restaurants, bars, hotels, on the street and in parks, but even at eighteen or twenty cents a cigarette, it is an expensive habit for people who may only make $15 a day.

Aside from occasional political comment, there isn't a lot of graffiti. Outside of the big cities, trash isn't strewn about. There is no prevalent gang culture. There isn't the same oppressive police presence or climate of fear as in the States. Police are being better paid, trained, and slowly more effective. National Police, like city cops in the United States, now carry little hand-held computers which link them immediately not only into national computers, but into Interpol as well. So if you are on the lam from the law and come to Panama you will get caught.

Even the Transitos, the traffic police, similar to California Highway Patrol in the States, operate in a very civilized manor. Their cars and motorcycles are well marked and always parked very visibly next to the highway in the same way. Transitos used to wear fluorescent red reflective vests, good for both safety and also Transito-spotting, but they seem to have gotten the message about "visibility," so the vests are gone. Safety versus revenue … it's a tough choice. More and more now have radar, radar that now works, but not to worry – a dozen motorists coming in the opposite direction will flash their lights indicating you should slow down either for an accident ahead or a Transito. Besides, most Transitos seem preoccupied on their cell phones and the hassle of hanging up on their girlfriends, putting on helmets, and hopping on motorcycles, well, it's a whole lot of hassle when the Transito's role seems mostly to remind good people by their presence to slow down and obey the law.

Occasionally you will run into an entrepreneurial Transito who needs your help with shoes for his kids or lingerie for his mistress, but as Panama becomes more organized and computerized he or she is more likely to have a working radar gun and a hand-held computer that once he starts the ticket, there is no turning back and you are nailed.

The incessant U. S. demand for illicit drugs and Panama's proximity to Colombia creates an enormous problem. Weekly, you read about huge seizures of literally tons of cocaine that the Colombian drug cartels are trying to smuggle through Panama. Until the United States takes the profit incentive out of the drug trade by decriminalizing and regulating all drugs all of Latin America will be plagued by drug cartels with seemingly unlimited amounts of money.

Panama produces both rum and the more popular local alcohol, called *seco*, a clear liquor which like rum is brewed from sugar, but *seco* is sold at seventy proof. Although the tax has increased, alcohol is still relatively cheap and it can be a problem. Sunday morning after payday it's not all that unusual to see Indians sleeping it off in the street. When the sun comes up the police rouse them awake and send them home.

I see lots of young people wearing caps and shirts with pot leaves, but this may be more an aping of North American culture, which Panamanians love to do, rather than a commitment to being a "pot head." I don't see a lot of stoned kids or obvious stoned-kid behavior. Some of my expat contemporaries, products of the sixties ... well, you've got to wonder. I suspect that the biggest consumers of marijuana in Boquete are sixty-something expats.

But, unlike the Ventura-Oxnard area of Southern California, you don't open the paper every other day to read about kids killing kids because they wear the wrong color shirts, or just to prove they can kill someone, or cops killing suspects because they are suspects and the cops can, or gangbangers shooting cops because they are cops. In fact in Panama in general and in our area in particular, there seems to be very little killing, which is refreshing.

Panama isn't perfect and like any place it struggles with problems.

Long noted for corruption, the present government struggles to create an environment with "0% Percent Corruption" as did the previous government. Every election season the party in power is accused of massive corruption, just like the current party in power accused the last party in power.

Is there injustice in Panama? Certainly but Panama, having lived through the agonizing years of "the dictatorship," doesn't pretend to be the "shining light" and has never set itself up as the be-all and end-all and the ultimate standard of a just society. Panama doesn't pretend to know what's best for the rest of the world, and even if it did, doesn't have a military to impose itself on the rest of the world.

Panamanians have a laid-back and hassle-free attitude towards life, which taken on the whole leads to a more relaxed life. Adjusting to "Panamanian time" is difficult, but not impossible. Things will get done, it just might take longer than you would expect or like. When I first came to Panama and was being frustrated by the seemingly impossible task of getting things finished, I received some important advice. The first was from a *gringo* who had happily adjusted. His advice was just one word: "Surrender!" If you don't worry about it, it's not a problem. The other advice came from my banker, "Don't stress: live long!"

Overall, the cost of living in Panama is far less than in the North America. How much less will depend on you, what your standard of living was in your home country, and what you want your standard of living to be in Panama.

Because we "cashed out" when we sold our home in California, and then purchased our home in Boquete for cash, we don't have to cope with a mortgage which was always one of our retirement goals. My Social Security combined with my wife's pension and Social Security is about one-third what our income was in California, but in Panama we live comfortably and enjoy a better lifestyle without having to work, without the stress of Southern California life, albeit still with nothing left over at the end of the year.

Prices have increased in Panama, no question, but they have also dramatically increased in the States as well. So our cost of living with today's dollars and costs is still about forty percent of what it would be in the States, and we live better.

One of the unfortunate things about the web is that a lot of people accept anything they read online as the gospel truth. Not so! Another unfortunate thing is that most stuff on the web is not dated, so there is a lot of outdated cost information on the web about Panama. A lot of real estate listings, still on the web as if they were current, were sold years ago. The fact that Panama used to give you a "*Pensionado*" or retirement visa if you could prove you have $500 per month pension or $600 per couple, implied that you could live on $600 a month in Panama. The truth is you can certainly live on $600 a month and many Panamanian retirees live on far less. But that Panamanian minimal retirement lifestyle isn't what most Americans have in mind.

Bananas, should you not be growing your own, are two for 15 cents. Fresh bread is sixty cents a baguette. A deliciously ripe pineapple is $1.50 *gringo* price, 75 cents for Panamanians.

Along with a booming economy comes inflation, so food prices are increasing in Panama. Cereals, Pam, Kleenex and all the other "essentials" of American life that have to be imported cost about the same as or slightly more than they do in North America.

We discovered that we don't really pay that much less for food partly because we still like some of the things we enjoyed in the States and like to buy some things that are partially prepared. Eating out, because the cost of labor is low in Panama, can still be a bargain compared to Southern California. $3 for my haircut and $6 for my wife to have her hair cut … real bargains compared to the States. My daughter from the Bay Area, who happens to be visiting right now, paid $90 for a hair cut before she left San Francisco! Granted, San Francisco isn't cheap, but … in Seattle when my wife was visiting my other daughter earlier this year, it was $35 at Supercuts. Local residents get massages for $40 midweek, and a manicure and pedicure runs $13-$26, which compared to an hour massage in the States or on a ship for $90-125 is a real deal.

How much can you live on? Well, how much can you live on in Southern California? It depends. Less if you live in Bakersfield, more if you live in Beverly Hills. It just depends. There is no hard and fast rule. To find out what you can live on, you'll need to do your homework on both ends, spend time, and do your own research.

Incentives

Panama expat retirees receive the same *Pensionado* or retiree benefits as are granted to Panamanian retirees. Why? A few years back Valle Escondido estimated that each expat who retired to Boquete spent about $250,000, including land, home, car, furnishings and legal fees for immigration. According to Valle Escondido, "Because the amount of money is significant and coming from a foreign source, the expat also becomes a foreign investor. These additional foreign investors become very significant in financial terms. In the case of Valle

Escondido they alone represent about $50 million in initial investment. The average retiree has about $2,000 a month in expendable income. This represents another $6 million a year in spending on food, maintenance, and travel. In addition to these expenditures, each retiree has an average of three visitors per year who come as guests and consequently tourists." Since this report was issued prices have gone up considerably.

Pensionado Visa

The big benefit of a *Pensionado* visa is the right to permanently live in Panama and the right to come and go from Panama. The *Pensionado* visa represents a big welcome mat. You can't work for anyone with a *Pensionado* visa, but you can invest in your own business or consult.

Other benefits to *Pensionados* include an Import tax exemption of up to $10,000 on household goods and discounts on many services, such as:

- 50% off on movies, recreational, and sports events
- 50% off on hotels Monday through Thursday, 30% on Sunday
- 30% off on public buses and trains
- 30% off on boat and ship transportation
- 25% off on national airline flights
- 25% off in restaurants
- 25% off on telephone land lines and water
- 25% off on electricity if under $50 a month
- 20% off on prescription drugs
- 20% off on doctor visits and surgery
- 15% off in fast food restaurants
- 15% off in hospitals without insurance
- 15% off on dental work
- 15% off on optometrist visits

That sounds great, but often actually getting the discounts is another story. It's the law, yes, but there are a lot of restaurants and others who simply decide not to offer the discounts. Some restaurants seem to work overtime to avoid giving the *descuento*. The Thursday night all-you-can-eat rib special is a "special" so no discount. Increasingly restaurants will have a note on their menu reading, "*Pensionado* discount is already included in our prices." Illegal, yes, but most of these places are owned by *gringos*.

Some drugs have a minimal mark up so, no discount.

Book an international airline flight roundtrip from Panama and you will pay a little less than the standard senior rate.

Book your hotel online, no discount. Have a special rate, other than the "rack rate," no discount. As an example of how the game is played, small bed and breakfast in Boca Chica offers online Internet rates, available to everyone, of $165-185 a night. They explain their *Pensionado* rate as follows: "Panamanians and residents age 55 for women and 60 for men, pensioners and retirees receive a minimum discount of the regular prices of hotels, motels, and pensions of 50 percent from Monday to Thursday and 30 percent from Friday to Sunday. Retiree's discount is taken off the regular bungalow rack rates shown above, and may not be combined with our internet discounted rates or any other promotional offers or discounts." The "regular" rate is $300-330 a night (as if anyone would actually pay that!), so the discounted *Pensionado* rate, assuming a 50 percent discount, is actually $30-40 less than the rate offered to everyone. While any discount is nice, it certainly is not what most people think of when the benefits of Panama's *Pensionado* program are touted as fifty percent off hotels Monday through Thursday.

You see how the game is played. If you happen to get the discount, nice, but ... **In my opinion the *Pensionado* discounts are highly over-promoted and overrated.**

Supposedly an additional *Pensionado* benefit is tax exemption to import a car every two years. On the surface this looks good, but in some cases it's cheaper, and far easier, just to buy a car in Panama. Everyone knows car importing horror stories. You can end up paying more to import your car than it would cost new in Panama. It's still difficult to get parts for makes and models of cars that are not common in Panama. On the other hand my attorney purchased a Hummer in Kansas, imported it, and saved $30,000 over what it would have cost in Panama, but that is the exception rather than the rule. Check everything out carefully before you decide to import a car. And remember, some of the costly required equipment, like catalytic converters, that are required in many countries are not required in Panama. Of course that also applies to some safety features which we assume are standard in the States, little things ... things like air bags.

There are visa options other than the *Pensionado* visa, some of which offer the opportunity to work in Panama. I'll talk more about these in the chapter on "Legalities."

Foreign Ownership of Real Property

There is no problem with foreigners owning property in Panama, a big benefit compared to some other Central American countries.

In the past in most cases, land was purchased using an "S. A." or *sociedad anónima* corporation. Here the corporation owns the land and the actual owners of the corporation, the holders of the stock, are anonymous in the public record. This is one way of protecting and shielding assets, and was all very legal. Whoever actually has the shares in their hand, owns the company, which owns the land, making it simple and easy to pass on assets to your heirs or transfer property. Now Panama wants more "transparency" of ownership so they can collect taxes on transfers. And the United States which wants to control all information in the 21st century world and doesn't like anything they can't "see" has pushed Panama to make S. A. corporations less than truly anonymous. It appears that S. A. corporations will continue, but that the owners of the stock will need to be listed, anonymous to the average person, but accessible to government agencies or with a court order.

Property Tax Exemption

As an incentive to develop property, Panama has granted
various real estate tax exemptions depending on the value of
the improvement. Originally these were for twenty years of no
property tax, and those benefits are transferred when a
property is sold. So there are still properties on the market
with portions of the twenty-year exemption. Under the new
law there is still a property tax exemption for new
construction, but it is not as generous and decreases as the
cost of construction increases, thus offering the greatest
exemption to the least expensive properties of the poorest
people which probably makes sense. It should be noted that
the tax exemption is on improvements and does not include
the land. You pay taxes on the land when the value goes over
$30,000, but most land is undervalued because properties are
sold using a recorded contract which undervalues the land,
and a "private" contract showing the actual purchase price.
Sooner or later properties will be revalued.

Condominium developments pay taxes on the value of the
land from the start.

Agricultural land is generally not taxed.

Not Taxed

Panama has a territorial tax code, meaning only income
generated in Panama is taxed. Income from foreign sources is
not taxed, and filing income tax forms for income earned
outside of Panama is not required. So if you are a *Pensionado*
and receive Social Security and/or other income from the
United States, this income is not taxed in Panama. You do,
however, have to file United States income taxes if you are a
U. S. citizen. Interestingly interest from deposits in a
Panamanian bank is not taxable in Panama.

Might this ever change? Might Panama decide to tax all
income regardless of source, meaning expats would start
paying Panamanian income tax on income from *outside* of

Panama? Certainly! Anything can change. In fact, in the closing days of 2013 the Panama Assembly passed a bill that would have required everyone to pay tax on all income, wherever it was generated. The Assembly was clearly aiming a loaded gun at their feet! Fortunately, legislators took another look, and repealed the bill.

Things can change. Government policies can change, even on things people like to pretend are sacrosanct. It happens everywhere. Since the U. S. Independence, habeas corpus, the requirement that a person under arrest be brought before a judge or into a court, has been assumed to be a "right." Yet after 9/11 this "right" was been suspended in the name of an on-going "national emergency." Historically in the name of "national emergency", or even just to balance the budget, governments have made all kinds of changes. There are no guarantees in Panama or anywhere else.

If you live permanently outside the United States (and you have to prove you've not been in the United States more than thirty days a year) you can exempt around $100,800 [2015] per person of your *earned* [not income from pensions, Social Security, royalties, investments] foreign income. Check with your accountant.

Foreign Investment

Panama offers numerous schemes to encourage foreign investment including tax concessions and even, under certain scenarios, Panamanian passports. There are incentives for starting businesses, for tourist business in certain designated areas, for reforestation projects, and the like. Panama has several free zones to encourage manufacturing activity.

Action Items and Points to Ponder

If we were talking face-to-face we'd be interacting and you'd be peppering me with questions and I would be asking you some important questions. "Action Items" are important questions and/or activities that will help you crystallize your thinking about relocating to Panama, or in many cases, anywhere else.

STOP. Get a sheet of paper and do your homework. Write down your answers and notes, if not now, then later.

1. Which benefits of Panama do you find interesting and why?

2. What are the elements of your current lifestyle that you like and what are the elements you dislike?

Culturally relevant. If you live in the steaming Chagres jungle it makes a lot of sense to wear less. Our friends, Zuleika, Katrina and Erito, at the "stairway" to their house at Embera Puru. Erito has fewer problems with his house than I do.

This picture 2015 shot of Erito, Zuleka and family was taken when I took 90 people from the ship to the village. Katrina, the toddler above, is front row on the left, *Abuela* is on the right, and Yetsibel has just graduated from university.

2. Dare to Dream

I was turning 60. As usually happens, life hadn't turned out exactly the way I had planned when I was in my 20s. I was becoming less and less sure I wanted to work until I dropped as I thought when I was in my 20s. Retirement, forced or voluntary, was looming and I began to seriously look at how we were going to survive retirement.

It was actually because of my daughter, Noelle, and her husband, George. They had taken a cruise vacation and fallen in love with the little, and relatively unknown, Caribbean island of Dominica. What others may have seen as a dirty and impoverished island, these sun-starved kids from the Pacific Northwest saw as paradise. George was growing restless at his job and Noelle was looking for her first teaching job. They stumbled on a website of properties in other countries and found a fledgling marina/bar operation for sale in Dominica and they started to dream. Naturally, they wanted us to go online and check it out and that's what started us looking at the idea of escaping abroad.

Who of us has not at sometime in their life just wanted to run away from it all and ... escape?

Our kids eventually settled down to reality; we, however, kept fantasizing.

Over the years we had spent a lot of time in the U. S. Virgin Islands. We had friends who lived in St. Thomas and we were the ones who encouraged them to move to the Virgin Islands in the first place.. Over eleven years we visited St. Thomas annually. As chaplain on cruise ships and later as owner of travel agencies, I frequently visited the Virgin Islands and the rest of the Caribbean. In the back of my mind I had always dreamed of someday living on St. John overlooking Pillsbury Sound.

If money were no object, what was it that we really wanted?

So we began to dream. If money were no object – a big IF by the way – and if we could live anywhere we wanted ... what was it that we wanted?

My wife and I each began by making lists of the qualities our ideal nirvana would need. We each had the task of coming up with 15 things we were looking for in an ideal paradise. The lists intentionally were made independently without consultation. Then after each of us had finalized our own list we sat down together.

This is what we came up with.

Nikki's Top 15 List:

1. Breezes to mitigate heat and humidity
2. Warm (but not over 85 degrees Fahrenheit or 29 degrees Celsius)
3. Good medical care
4. Ocean view
5. Clean
6. Smaller town
7. Basic dependable utilities including Internet
8. Availability of supplies
9. Lower cost of living
10. Clear title and ownership
11. Near a nice beach
12. English widely accepted as second language
13. Diverse, accepting, open, tolerant
14. Ample water supply
15. Stable currency and low inflation

Richard's Top 15 List:

1. Warm
2. Lower cost of living
3. Breezes to mitigate heat and humidity
4. Basic dependable utilities including Internet
5. Ample water supply
6. Clean
7. Near a nice beach
8. Clear title and ownership
9. Good medical care
10. Availability of supplies
11. Stable government
12. English widely accepted as second language
13. Ocean view
14. Stable currency and low inflation
15. Opportunity for business, investment, owner working

Amazingly, and perhaps not so amazingly after 30 years of marriage, our lists were remarkably similar. So we pulled our lists together to get one "Top 15" list. Now we knew what we wanted, *if* it were available somewhere, and *if* money was no object.

It doesn't hurt to dream!

The MBA in me forced yet another exercise to further refine our dream. If we had 100 points, and only 100 points, with which to assign value, how would we assign those points? We needed to further refine our wish list. After much discussion, here's what we ended up with relative value to the items on our wish list:

- Lower cost of living - 30 points - We knew we couldn't make it without lowering our cost of living.

- Good medical care - 20 points – Like it or not, someday we were going to be "seniors."

- Warm – 15 points – We remembered those cold

Michigan and Wisconsin winters.

- Opportunity for investment, business or working – 15 points – No matter what, we wanted an additional income stream.

- Basic dependable utilities, including Internet – 10 points – How great could life be without drinking water or the web?

- Availability of supplies - 5 points – It was too late in life to start a subsistence lifestyle.

- Clean – 5 points – We had seen a lot of beautiful beaches on islands that were trashed.

There you had it – the weighted list. The other wants were still important; niceties, but not absolutely essential. If we could have it all, great, but these were our "must haves." Others of course may have other choices.

Knowing what we wanted, unfettered by restrictions of budget or reality, we began to dream and to think of places we'd been, or heard of, or read about that might prove our nirvana. We scoured the web, and kept dreaming of running away from it all. It's not that we were actually planning to retire; dreaming was just good therapy.

What is it that you would like to do today?

It's not just where you dream about living, but what you dream about doing. What is it that you would like to do today?

If you are at the point where you wake up and can't wait to get to work, as I was when I was with 24 Hour Fitness, you're not ready for this book. Enjoy your work. Put this book on the shelf and come back when things change. But if you dream about walking an endless beach, sailing the Caribbean, exploring jungles, or teaching kids to read in the South Bronx, now is the time to explore your dreams and give them definition.

We ended up in Panama in large part because of those Embera Indians I met on my Panama Canal Cruise.

The Embera and Wounaan Indians together are estimated to have a population in Panama of around 30,000 to 60,000, but nobody knows for sure since the Embera live deep in the jungle in tiny villages and survive on subsistence farming, hunting and fishing. The men have generally replaced their traditional loincloths with shorts for daily wear, but many women still wear only skirts. All have rich tattoo-like body decoration made from the juice of the *jagua* fruit. Aside from being decorative it protects them from mosquitoes and ultraviolet rays.

As I mentioned, I met an Embera Indian, Erito Barrigon, while on a Panama Canal cruise. Lubricated by lots of Atlas beer, I became fast friends and *hermanos* with Erito and his brothers. They invited me to visit their village which is about an hour's drive from Panama City and then another 45 minutes by dugout canoe across a lake and up a jungle river. It was in researching the Embera, so I could fulfill my promise to visit, that I accidentally discovered the retirement benefits of Panama.

When my wife and I came to "check out" Panama and I wanted to visit Erito's Embera village and spend the night. It seemed a little wiser to let Nikki stay at the hotel while I went off to who knows what in the jungle.

I distinctly remember Erito and his brothers picking me up at a tiny hamlet on the edge of Madden Lake. We loaded up their dugout canoe, or *piragua*, with supplies including three cases of Atlas beer. I thought this strange since I knew at the time alcohol was not permitted in the village. I quickly learned the plan: Erito, his brothers and I would drink all the beer before getting to the village, thus, although arriving very relaxed, not offending anyone. It worked! Although I confess, it's not easy to take a pee from a dugout canoe.

We crossed the lake, and were making our way up the Río de Pequini to their tiny village of San Juan. We were deep in the jungle and well-brewed, and I remember leaning back in the boat, looking up at the jungle canopy covering the river and thinking ...

"This is not the 101 Freeway! This is adventure! I can die now and know I've lived!"

That was the moment I knew for certain that it as time for a change.

Action Items and Points to Ponder

We've sometimes seen couples who visit Panama with the idea of living here. One loves Panama, and the other dislikes it. Did they really sit down beforehand and discuss what each considered important and what each wanted? We've seen couples sell everything in the United States and move here only to become disillusioned or realize that they didn't want to give up all the comforts of life in Miami, Los Angeles or wherever. This book is designed to help you think through what it is that you want before you make a major change in your life. I want you to do your homework and make a choice that works for you.

1. So, assuming money was no object and you could live anywhere you wanted ... what is it exactly that you want? Come up with your own "Top 15" lists.

2. OK, now discuss your lists and come up with a joint "Top Fifteen" list. Have fun!

3. What do you dream of doing? Get a pad and pencil and spell it out. Go ahead – money is no object here, dreams are free!

Panama City is a hip, Latin American capital city where over a third of the country's population lives, but is only one aspect of Panama.

With 2,414 kilometers [1,500 miles] of coastline on two oceans, there are lots of places where you can stroll alone along the beach.

3. Finding Paradise

$\mathcal{N}$ow that you know what you're dreaming of, how do you find it? Where in the world would you like to live?

Maybe, just maybe, you already have found it. Maybe you're *already* living in the perfect place.

Our home was in Ventura, California, right on the Pacific coast, about halfway between Los Angeles and Santa Barbara. We lived on a hillside overlooking the Pacific Ocean. I woke up to the view of the sun rising over the Santa Monica Mountains sparkling off waves rolling in on Ventura beach. I could look out the window and know if the surf was up, if it was a good day for ocean kayaking, or if a storm was brewing. I could sit in my spa at night, sipping wine, and see the famed stone arch at the end of Anacapa Island. At night I looked out over the twinkling lights of Ventura. Ventura was the only place we ever lived in Southern California where we actually knew our neighbors and they were the best. Property values were soaring. I was a Realtor so I didn't have to commute anywhere. Compared to most of Southern California the crime rate was relatively low. And Ventura's weather, except for the summer fog, is probably the finest in the continental United States. What was there not to like? Ventura was damn near perfect.

So when you're looking for Paradise, be sure to include the place you already live. It's a good reality check and a good comparison. And maybe, just maybe, you've already found the perfect place.

So, how do you go about finding your Paradise?

1. Make a list.

We started sitting down one evening by the fire with a bottle of good chardonnay, a world map, and a pad of paper. We talked about places that sounded interesting and places where we'd been on trips. Even places we'd seen in movies. Any place that even sounded remotely interesting was fair game.

In our case that gave us:

> Greek Isles
> Thailand
> Polynesia
> Hawaii
> Key West
> Virgin Islands – United States and British
> Dominica
> Costa Rica
> Belize
> St. Martin
> St. Lucia

And on our list, we included the place we already lived, Ventura, because maybe we had already found paradise and just didn't know it. Interestingly Panama, the place we ended up, never appeared on any of our early lists.

I had a file folder for each of the destinations on the list. Notes, thoughts, information, interesting property listings I found online, photos ... everything got stuck in a file folder.

2. Visit a good bookstore.

Next I'd suggest that you start spending a few evenings at a good bookstore. Get a latte and start browsing the travel section, scanning guidebooks from destinations that look interesting. At this point just browse, don't buy. If you feel guilty for making the bookstore your public library just keep buying cappuccinos. Of course there is the public library, but in most cases you'll find more of what you want at the bookstore, it will be more current, and the library generally doesn't offer cafe mochas.

Don't forget the magazine section. You'll find some great travel magazines, some with features on your areas of interest. Check out calendars as well, since, like magazines, they are a good source of pictures.

While we were in this research stage I had pictures of dozens of beaches and islands stuck on the refrigerator. My screen saver was a collection of photos I'd found online of places that looked interesting. There is nothing like looking at a picture to help you escape work and start dreaming. Pictures help you vicariously try a place on for size to see if it fits.

3. Go online.

The Internet is the best resource in the world but be forewarned that anyone can put anything on the Internet. Just because you found something online doesn't mean it's true. The biggest plague of the Internet is that much of the information isn't dated. People are notorious about not removing outdated information from the web, particularly specifics like prices and cost of living. Unless a web page is actually dated, and not with the applet that automatically gives today's date, implying it's current even although it may not be, it's not very helpful.

Don't forget to search for pictures as well. An interesting side note: we ended up retiring in Boquete, Panama. Do a picture search on Google for "Boquete" with your "safe" filter turned "off" and you will be shocked. You'll find pictures of our tiny little town, pictures of rainbows, flowers, mountains and coffee, but you'll also find ... let's just say that Boquete, like my nickname, has multiple meanings and in Brazilian Portuguese it means something all together different. When I work with crew members on the ship from Brazil and tell them where I live they almost choke!

I collected images online and downloaded them into my own

PowerPoint presentation so I could develop a digital file of my research. I had maps, scenic views, stories, and a regular presentation on potential areas ... it was a great tool for dreaming.

It may be a lot of work, but that is the point. You need to do a lot of work and analysis before you pick up and move to Panama or anywhere else in the world.

Don't forget the news groups, bulletin boards, and discussion forums. You'll find all kinds of postings from expats online. Use email. You'll find a lot of expats are more than happy to respond to emails and answer knowledgeable questions. What's a knowledgeable question? I got an email from a man in Minnesota who wrote – I kid you not! – "I'm interested in retiring to Panama. What should I do?" Not knowledgeable. A lady wrote, "We're falling in love with Boquete. What is the school situation? Is there an American or international school in Boquete or David? I can't find anything online." That was a knowledgeable question which I could answer.

If you are lucky enough to know Spanish or other languages, include in your search criteria sites in languages other than English. If you're interested in Latin or Central America you'll find a wealth of additional information on the Spanish websites.

4. Keep your eyes and ears open.

It's amazing how sometimes you never see something, until you're looking for it. You've driven down the same road scores of times and have never noticed a particular shop, until one day you're looking for it. Or you've shopped in the same grocery store and never noticed a particular item, until the day you're looking for it, and there it is.

Once you're thinking in terms of particular destinations, you'll be surprised at connections that pop up. A co-worker's parents are retiring there, or your neighbor's kids just got back from backpacking in a country you've found interesting, or the gas station attendant was born there. Check out newspaper articles, books, magazines, even movies.

A quick word about movies: movies are movies. You know better than to think that every North American lives the way they are portrayed in movies. You know that just because a movie is set in a particular location, doesn't mean that the location is portrayed accurately. Los Angeles isn't really like it's portrayed in the movies, and it may not even be Los Angeles that you're seeing in the movie.

John Travolta's movie "*Swordfish*" was actually filmed in downtown Ventura. The old section of downtown was closed off for two months and became downtown Los Angeles. Our old two-story Bank of Italy[7] building became a Los Angeles skyscraper. And when the bomb supposedly went off, our little downtown corner of Ventura looked like a war zone. Movies are fun, but basically make-believe.

I mention all this because the movie "*Tailor of Panama*" helped create a negative impression of Panama that almost kept Panama off our short list. Yes, the movie was actually filmed in Panama. It was the first major motion picture to be filmed in Panama and the government went all out, even giving movie makers access to the Presidential Palace of The Herons. Because movie making wasn't a Panamanian business at that time there weren't companies to provide hundreds of extras, so the extras were actually recruited right off the streets, no SAG card required. But when the movie came out, people were shocked. The movie, although fun and interesting, bore absolutely no resemblance to the reality of Panama.

5. Use your vacation time.

Depending on your timeline, use your vacation time to explore. Visit some of the places on your list that you find interesting. Aside from having a great time, you can start to get the feel of a place and know if you want to consider it as a place to live. Granted, being on vacation in a place is VERY different than living there, but it's a start.

Go beyond the tourist hot spots. Invest in a good map. This will come in handy, not only on your vacation, but also later. Rent a car and drive around. Get off the beaten path and see if it feels comfortable. Chat with the locals, especially the ones not connected with the tourist trade or real estate sales, and find out about their experiences. Search out expats already living there, buy them a drink or two or three, or take them out for dinner, listen and ask questions. If I'm having coffee or in a store and a visitor wants to ask me questions about life in Panama, I'm more than happy to share. Tune into some of the local gossip. Pick up the local papers, even if you don't really know the language.

Visit the local supermarkets. Identify products similar to those you buy at home and jot down the prices. What are the items you think you couldn't do without? Are they available? If they have "big box stores" visit them. When we first visited PriceSmart in David we realized it wasn't Costco, but it was comforting for us to know it was there, had a similar look and feel to the way were used to shopping, and at least some of the familiar products were available.

Talk to some real estate agents. Understand that in most countries real estate practice is very different than in the United States, so go in with eyes wide open. Be upfront, and don't forget that you're not here to buy, just to learn. A good real estate agent will be happy for the contact that may eventually turn into a sale, but don't expect a free tour or hours of time. Get away from the timeshare-type folks and get a feel for the prices of homes that are the type of home in which you could imagine yourself living.

As you visit places you want to ask yourself this basic question, "Can I see myself living here?" There are many places in the world that I love – Amsterdam, the Greek Isles, Menorca, Tuscany, even Alaska – but I don't see myself living in these places on a permanent basis. Nice to visit for vacation, maybe even an extended vacation or a couple month home exchange, but not permanently.

And just doing the vacation research, even if you don't book the trip, is valuable. You'll pick up a lot of information and travel brochures are a great source for the pictures to decorate your cubicle or office.

Of course all information you pick up on your trip, or researching a trip, ends up in the relative destination folder.

6. Develop a short list.

As you go through the research process, you're going to find yourself eliminating some destinations. "Forget that!" As you do, cross them off your list and trash the folder. Eventually you want to weed the list down to four to eight destinations in which you are really interested, including, of course, where you already live.

In our case we ended up with six destinations, including Ventura. We already knew what we wanted (Remember Chapter 2, "Dare to Dream?") … lower cost of living, good medical care, clean, warm, opportunity, dependable basic utilities and supplies.

Our short list ended up with:

- Ventura – Pretty close to paradise in the United States and the stuff of movies and dreams.

- Costa Rica – We had heard it was a great U. S. retirement destination and had visited San Jose and along both coasts on a couple of cruises.

- Panama – Panama was a long shot that wasn't even on our initial list. We had stopped in Panama on a cruise, found a lot of interesting information online, and eventually went back for two weeks to either rule it out or keep it in.

- St. Thomas, U. S. Virgin Islands – Over the years we'd spent a lot of time in St. Thomas. We'd seen cruise ships change Charlotte Amalie from being a sleepy little Caribbean town to a gridlock of ships, taxicabs, tourists, and shops, but we also knew there were areas of the island that were still remote and beautiful. Because we knew the USVI, and we knew the islands were different, we included each island separately.

- St. John, U. S. Virgin Islands – I will always love St. John. Much of the island is National Park and Cruz Bay still retains a little of the charm that we found in St. Thomas before the cruise ship invasion.

- St. Croix, U. S. Virgin Islands – The biggest of the three Virgin Islands, and although we'd visited it several times on cruises, it was the one we knew the least.

7. Now's the time to buy some books.

You want to go back to the bookstore and buy some of the guidebooks that seemed most helpful and start to really research and study. Be sure to check out Amazon.com: often books are out-of-print and you can often find these books being resold on Amazon.

Get some maps. When we were researching we found it almost impossible to get a good map of Panama. Now, National Geographic publishes a wonderful map of Panama. If you were wise, and if you've already had an opportunity to visit the places on your short list, hopefully you picked up maps while you were there.

8. Analyze the short list.

OK, maybe the MBA in me got carried away. But the best way I knew to analyze and compare was to make a list of all the things that were important to us, rank them, assign values, and see where we ended up. One of Bill Gates' great gifts to mankind is the computer spreadsheet program, Excel. If you know Excel, it is relatively easy to create a spread sheet that will let you make the comparisons.

You've already identified what's important to you -- now expand that list. Understanding that no one place can provide everything you want, you still need to expand that list. Say you find a place that looks like paradise, but there is a coup every two years, or inflation is 40 percent a year – how great is paradise going to be? What if every five years a hurricane wipes half your island paradise off the map? Your kid is gay and the place is homophobic? You have dietary restrictions or preferences requiring foods these folks have never seen? You've already got two cops with shotguns on every corner: is that what you want in your new home? Your dream island is paradise, except for the dumpster on the corner overflowing with foul-smelling garbage. Here's what we came up with. It's obviously not the definitive list, or the list for everyone, but it worked for us.

Climate
- Warm
- Breeze to mitigate heat and humidity
- Outside hurricane belt

Area, Amenities and Economics
- Ocean view
- Basic dependable utilities including Internet
- Ample water supply
- Clean
- Near nice beach
- Good medical care
- Availability of supplies
- Access for a boat
- Opportunity for business, investment
- Ability to work
- Smaller town
- Minimal traffic
- Relatively low crime rate
- Stable and growing economy
- Lower cost of living

- Easy to import car tax free (which would turn out not to be that important)
- Retiree benefits and incentives
- Tax advantages
- Clear title and ownership of property
- Stable currency and low inflation
- Accessible from the United States at moderate cost (we wanted our kids to be able to afford to visit)
- Some tourism
- Some infrastructure
- Home that looks interesting (and affordable) online

Government
- Stable government
- English widely accepted second language
- Legal system familiar
- Minimal corruption
- Respect for law but not "cop heavy"
- Residency options
- Dual citizenship option
- Family/friends visa options and ability to work

Culture
- Diverse, accepting, open, tolerant
- Friendly
- Stimulating environment – something to do other than "play golf"
- Opportunities to contribute
- No official religion or state church
- Optimistic and forward-looking attitude

OK, we didn't want much. But, hey, we were dreaming, and isn't that what dreams are about?

I created an Excel spread sheet, with columns for each location on my short list. Arbitrarily I created a ranking system using the information I had at the time based on my research and whether the location had the particular attributes we were seeking. I assigned points based on the ranking as follows:

5 points -- Definitely
4 points -- Yes
3 points -- Sorta, Kinda, Yeah BUT
2 points -- Depends
1 point -- Unknown
-2 points -- No

One important item had to do with the cost of housing. The criteria here was the cost of a house that I found listed for sale online that at least looked interesting to us.

5 points -- Under $100,000
4 points -- $101-200,000
3 points -- $201-300,000
2 points -- $301-400,000
1 point -- $401-500,000
-2 points -- Over $500,000

This may seem like a lot of sorting, charting and scoring, but picking up and relocating to a new country is a big decision. You want to put a lot of thought into your decision. My method was not perfect and were I doing it again I would definitely refine my rating system, but you get the idea.

This gave us an overall ranking by which to compare our five destinations. Using this system we ended up with:

171 -- Panama
145 -- Ventura
135 -- St John
124 -- St Croix
122 -- St Thomas
112 -- Costa Rica

Interestingly, for us Ventura, where we were living, ranked higher than any of the Virgin Islands or Costa Rica, so why would we change? But remember, not every item on the list was of equal importance to us.

So we said, "If we had 100 points to 'spend,' and only 100 points, how would we allocate that? What is really important to us?"

Remember what we ended up with?

> 30 points -- Lower cost of living
> 20 points -- Good medical care
> 15 points -- Warm
> 15 points -- Opportunity for investment, business, owner working
> 10 points -- Basic dependable utilities including Internet
> 5 points -- Availability of supplies

Now, seven years later, I would say that were we doing the same exercise today ... it would end up with pretty much the same results.

Taking a look at the overall ranking numbers and the weighted averages we had a better overall picture. Drum roll: here's what we ended up with

> **Overall 171 -- Weighed 475 -- Panama**
> Overall 145 -- Weighted 305 -- Ventura
> Overall 112 -- Weighted 305 -- Costa Rica
> Overall 122 -- Weighted 215 - St. Thomas
> Overall 124 -- Weighted 195 - St. Croix

So we in our case we already lived in a near paradise – if you took away the traffic, the crime, and the high cost of living. But when you weighed in what was important to us – lower cost of living being the most important since we needed to afford to retire – Panama won hands down. When you work through your own analysis you may just decide that where you are now is your paradise.

Now we knew where we wanted to end up. We'd found, at least on paper, our paradise, and its name was Panama.

9. Now go visit.

Once you've determined where you think you want to live, now go visit, not as a tourist, but as someone who is seriously thinking of relocating and calling the place home..

Say you're decided on Panama ... yes, it's a little squiggle of a country on the map, but when you are actually here it is pretty vast and there are lots of communities, and lots of places expats like to call home. Fortunately for you, today there are lots of resources available to assist you.

Once expat living became popular, and perhaps due to dissatisfaction with things in their home countries, lots of folks jumped on the relocation, expat, off shore bandwagon.

For U. S. citizens let's jump to the chase. As long as you are a U. S.. citizen you are not going to escape the IRS and paying taxes and you are not going to be able to legally hide your assets, so don't bother about all the off-shore hype and marketing. What we learned as young people is still true: the only certain things in life are death and taxes. You will pay.

There are dozens of outfits promoting retiring and living abroad, hiding assets, and making a killing everywhere from Panama to Shangri-la, and yes, Kokomo too. Many of these outfits offer enticing "opportunities" in real estate, growing .... take your pick ... trees, mangos, coffee, bananas, weed, you name it. Some offer investment seminars in fancy downtown hotels with paid "presenters" and carefully coached expats to report on how perfect everything is in .... wherever.

The good thing about these outfits is that they teach you to be cautious ... about what to believe and who to trust., essential if you are going to have a happy expat life. So you need to sort through the offerings and sort out the bad and focus on those who are honest, genuine and have satisfied clients who you can talk to and check out.

People tend to believe what they want to believe. If in a world where you can get one percent interest on a certificate of deposit,, someone is offering you a 15 percent guaranteed return on a cabbage farm ... warning bells should go off! Yet it is amazing how many people continue to be scammed.

I particularly like Jackie Lange's Panama Relocation Tours for several years. They are small groups, usually only about twenty people, led by Jackie who has a wealth of knowledge about living in Panama. They visit a number of the most popular places in Panama that expats call home and you get to meet and talk with real expats, one-to-one and get the real, unrehearsed story of expat life in Panama. It is a boots-on-the-ground tour of the real Panama. You'll have chance to evaluate the pros and cons of the various places expats choose. You'll look at some real estate examples, but it is not a real estate tour and nobody is selling anything. In the five years Jackie has been doing her tours, within a year of taking the tour, over 50 percent of the people actually end up moving to Panama, many of these to Boquete and folks I regularly see around town.

Ten years ago when we moved to Panama we didn't have this opportunity.

10. Take a test-drive.

You wouldn't, buy a car without taking a test-drive would you? Well, I might if I'd done enough research, but most folks wouldn't. I'd suggest taking three to six months and renting a fully furnished place wherever you have decided you want to live, coming down, renting a car, and actually trying it out. It's still not a guarantee ... there really are no guarantees in life except that thing about death and taxes! ... but you will have a far better chance of making a choice that works.

Now that I've lived in Boquete for over ten years, I understand that Boquete alone has over a dozen different microclimates and all are very different. Some of these are seasonal variations, all of which you are not going to experience in a few months, but you can talk to lots of people and learn a lot living here for several months.

We didn't do the test-drive. Like Caesar, we came, we saw, we conquered ... and we've loved it for over ten years! But we know what we like, and in our married life we have seen opportunities, both felt they were good investments and the time was right, and its usually worked out.

Now fast forward to the present day. You've seen the way we zeroed in on Panama. Now, having been here ten years, how well has it worked for us? The fact that we've happily lived in Panama ten years should tell you something.

Here's that original list with some notes as to how things worked out until now.

Climate

Warm – We can enjoy the year-round spring-like climate of Boquete and, if and when we want visit Boca Chica and get a boat to take us out to one of the islands in the Marine National Park where we can enjoy white sand, 80 degree water, and snorkeling for the day..

Breeze to mitigate heat and humidity – Although Boca Chica is hot almost every afternoon there is a nice sea breeze. Boquete, although humid, may reach 25 degrees Celsius [78 degrees Fahrenheit] during the day and drops to around 16 degrees Celsius [61 degrees Fahrenheit] at night. So we really do have the best of both worlds. The "breezes" where we live can get pretty strong January to March, something like Chinook winds in Colorado or Santa Ana winds in California.

Outside hurricane belt – check.

Area, Amenities and Economics

Ocean view – Actually, from my farm on a clear day I can see the Pacific islands, including Boca Chica, and the Bay of

Chiriqui, far, far in the distance.

Basic dependable utilities including Internet – check. We do get power outages, often related to afternoon electrical storms during the rainy season. Usually power is restored in a few minutes, or, once in a while, a few hours. Internet is better in some areas than others, but workable ... usually.

Ample water supply - In the areas where we live we get more than enough rain, but the problem in some areas of Panama is that the infrastructure to deliver the water is inadequate. Many people in Boquete have storage tanks in case the water in town goes out for a while. We have both town water and our own well, and we have storage tanks.

Clean – On the whole Panama is pretty clean, although there still is the mentality of tossing trash and letting someone else deal with it. This usually isn't evident along the roads during the rainy season since things grow so fast, but during the dry season all the accumulation of cans and tires needs to be cleaned, and usually is picked up. Garbage collection can be a problem in some smaller cities, particularly if the town truck is broken.

Near nice beach – In Chiriqui the nicest beaches, the white-sand picture post card beaches are mostly on the islands accessible by boat. The nearest long beaches to Boquete are Las Olas [outside of David and about an hour from Boquete] and Las Lajas [about two hours from Boquete]. Some people have two homes, one In Panama City or Boquete and another at the beach, others may have a boat. Many of the large all-inclusive resorts around Coronado offer special rates to locals off season.

Good medical care – For the most part, yes. A little later I'll talk in more detail about medical care.

Availability of supplies – What we need is readily available, as are most of the things we want.

Access for a boat – It seemed important at the time, but I've pretty much outgrown my need for a boat since I'm off working on cruise ships four to six months a year where someone else worries about all the hassles of owning and operating a boat! But there is an anchorage and a boat yard in Boca Chica and quite a few folks in Boquete have boats.

Opportunity for business, investment – We've taken advantage of investing in real estate. Although it remains a better investment than real estate would have been in the States, the jury is out on what the long-term return will be. There are certainly opportunities for business in Panama although we've chosen not to take advantage of them: I am retired.

Ability to work – I work on ships, and it really is work. We have friends work online. Some folks work under the radar making and selling artisan objects, mostly to other expats. Panama does have "friendly nation" visas now that do allow you to work. The *Pensionado* visa which I have does not allow you to work in Panama. There are several other visas, which I'll talk about in the chapter on "Legalities," that do allow you to work in Panama.

Smaller town – Boquete was originally that ideal small town and still is, although it is becoming larger. Nikki enjoys going to the local market and bumping into *gringos*[8] and Panamanians she knows.

Minimal traffic – Despite the fact that SUVs have replaced horses in Boquete and at times parking can be a bit of a hassle, Chiriqui still has minimal traffic. .

Relatively low crime rate – check. We use common sense, obey the law, know our neighbors, and haven't had problems. Of course my daughter attributes this to the fact that, "Dad, you don't have any electronics worth stealing."

Stable and growing economy – yes! Growing faster than I would ever have expected. Panama has experienced 6-10 percent GDP growth for the past five years, while other countries limped along a 1-3 percent.

Lower cost of living – Although a booming economy, falling U. S. dollar, and high cost of oil have combined to create inflation in Panama, prices have zoomed upward in the United States as well. Although it costs more in actual dollars, we are living better for less in Panama.

Easy to import car tax free – I don't know about "easy." Certainly it can be done, but whether or not it makes sense depends on the make and model of the car, etc. Generally it is easier to get replacement parts for a car you purchased in Panama. And Toyota seems to be the top-selling brand in Panama and the easiest for replacement parts. There's even a Toyota-only junk yard in David.

Retiree benefits and incentives – The *Pensionado* visa does offer some benefits and incentives, although I think these are overrated, as I mentioned earlier.

Tax advantages – Panama does not tax income generated outside Panama.[9] If you are a U. S. citizen you are taxed on everything everywhere. However, if your permanent residence is outside the United States, you do get a break on *earned* income, but not on passive income which would be income from investments and pensions. But if you are a U. S. citizen, you still end up having to pay Social Security taxes on that earned self-employment income even if you are collecting Social Security.

Clear title and ownership of property – check. Actually this has become a little easier since we've been in Panama, and we'll talk more about real estate later.

Stable currency and low inflation – Since Panama uses the U. S. dollar as its currency, although it's called the "Balboa," the currency here is as stable as the U. S. dollar, which many would argue isn't that stable. Although it is still viewed as one of the world's more secure currencies, devaluation of the

U. S. dollar has created inflation in the United States and in Panama as well.

Accessible from the United States at moderate cost (we wanted our kids to be able to afford to visit) – Accessible from North America, yes, but not necessarily at moderate cost. Panama is becoming the airline "Hub of the Americas" so there are more flights from more places in the world to satisfy demand, but demand is high, so airline fares aren't cheap.

Some tourism – Tourism is booming in Panama and growing rapidly in Chiriqui and Boquete, which is a good thing.

Some infrastructure – Panama's infrastructure keeps improving with improvements like a four-lane highway between Boquete and David, improvements at David airport, and the new airport at Rio Hato. In Panama City everything is being done at once: expanded Canal, Metro, city bus lines, new highways and interchanges, which, for the moment, results in a lot of confusion.

Home that looks interesting (and affordable) online – We found a number of interesting places at prices which, when compared to Ventura, were very attractive. We made a mistake here by comparing prices in Boquete to Ventura, California. Yes, we got a whole lot more in Boquete than we could have gotten in Ventura, but, honestly, we paid too much. We should have done more comparison to prices in Panama, than California. As a result when we sold our first home, in Valle Escondido, we broke even rather than making a great profit.

Government

Stable government – check, although without an entrenched civil service, all the players change when the government changes.

English widely accepted second language – Depends. Many Panamanians speak some English but are hesitant to try it out, afraid they will make fools of themselves. But when they hear you murdering their language, making a fool out of yourself, it's amazing how much English they know, even from just watching English movies and TV. In Boquete the locals are all trying to learn English and many of the expats are struggling with Spanish. Right now there are tremendous opportunities for Panamanians who speak American-style English without the heavy second-language Spanish accent.

People who've had the advantage of attending private schools are more likely to speak English. The government has decided that English should be taught in public schools starting in grade school, but the problem is that many teachers do not know English and the government hasn't given them the time or resources to learn.

Legal system familiar – not. Panama's legal system is based on old Spanish and Colombian legal systems and not on English common law, so it is very unfamiliar to many expats who come from countries where the legal system is based on English common law and case precedent. We will talk a lot more about this in the chapter on "Legalities"

Minimal corruption – Everyone talks about transparency and eliminating corruption, but that usually means eliminating other people's corruption, not their own. Although Panama is slowly making progress, talk to a member of any political party and they will detail the sins of the other political parties, but never their own. Right now the current party in power is aggressively pursuing and exposing the sins of the former party in power.

Respect for law but not "cop heavy" – When we first moved to Boquete if you needed one of the dozen or so national police stationed in Chiriqui you either went to the station to pick them up or promised to pay their cab fare. Now, much like in the United States, there are a lot of cops. Training has improved as has professionalism, although it still has a way to go. There is money for equipment. Many *gringos* in the past complained that there wasn't enough police protection. Now the same *gringos* are outraged in Boquete when they receive a traffic ticket for parking on the wrong side of the street or are stopped by a Transito with a radar gun that actually works.

Residency options – There are far more residency options available now than when we first came.

Dual citizenship option – There are a number of options that enable you to get a Panamanian passport and citizenship. Additionally once you've lived here five years and have a clean police record you can apply for citizenship. This has become much easier.

Family/friends visa options and ability to work – Again, much easier than when we first came, especially if you are from one of the many "friendly nations."

Culture

Diverse, accepting, open, tolerant – All are very characteristic of Panama and Panamanians.

Friendly – check.

Stimulating environment – something to do other than "play golf"- check. Life here is what you want to make it. There are those who just want to play bridge or golf and hang out with other gringos. There are those who want to get involved in a variety of community service clubs and projects. Some folks just want to sit back and relax and others want to jump into business ventures, or keep working online.

Opportunities to contribute – There are many opportunities to contribute and share as long as you don't come in with the attitude that you know all the answers and want to change everything.

No official religion or state church – There is no separation of church and state. The Roman Catholic Church is the official religion, whatever that means. Everyone in Panama is free to exercise whatever religious beliefs they have or not to have any religious beliefs. But nobody is going to make a federal case out of trying to remove God from public life.

Optimistic and forward-looking attitude – check. This is more important than you might think at first glance because it defines in many ways national character. Nations clearly on the rise are more interesting and stimulating than nations where power, influence and importance are on the wane.

Interestingly, and significant if you are thinking about relocating, in 2014 for the second year in a row, Panama has won the Global Well-Being Award as measured by the Gallup-Healthways Global Well-Being Index based on seven years of research and more than 2 million interviews.

Data was collected from 145 countries and areas and more than 146,000 interviews looking at five areas of life:

- Purpose: Did people like what they did each day and feel motivated to achieve their goals?
- Social: Did people enjoy supportive relationships and having love in their lives?
- Financial: Could people manage their economic lives to reduce stress and increase security?
- Community: Did people like where they lived and take pride in their community?
- Physical: Did people enjoy good health and enough energy to get things done daily?

So, welcome to the happiest country in the world!

Action Items and Points to Ponder

1. As of right now, what places would you include on an initial list of possibilities?

2. Think of the places on this list that you've already visited. As an exercise to start getting the hang of this, start thinking of what you remember of these places in terms of pros and

cons. You may have only looked at them as a tourist. Think of them now as potential places to call home. Any difference in how you'd rate them from that perspective?

3. What are you going to do this week to start your research (aside from finishing this book)? This one is easy: head to a good bookstore, get a cup of coffee and start browsing.

4. How you do your analysis is up to you.

Like me, you may want to do charts and weighted averages and even more. Give me credit: I didn't do an ROI [return on investment], but understand that when I was looking at things like government structure, economy, currency, inflation, stability and the like, I was definitely thinking investment and ROI. You may just want to make a chart with checkmarks: fine, whatever works for you. The important thing is that you figure out a way to compare and analyze that works for you.

Our first home was in Valle Escondido, Boquete, one of the first planned, gated, guarded communities appealing to expats and wealthy Panamanians.

Our first home was one of the first houses built in Valle Escondido. As the development built out it became more and more like any gated community anywhere in the world, which wasn't why we came to Panama.

4. Work Until You Drop

*T*hat's what I thought when I started out.

To understand why I intended to work until I dropped, you have to understand a little about me.

I graduated from college in 1964 and then from theological seminary in 1968. I entered the workplace with certain basic assumptions:

- I would change the world – for good;

- I would work one job all my life, in my case the church;

- People would appreciate my work and reward me;

- I would be loyal to the "company" and the company would be loyal to me;

- Social Security would be bankrupt by the time I retired;

- I would need, and want, to keep working until I died.

I guess I grew up in what seems today to be a pretty enchanted and unreal world. We lived in a little town in Somerset County, New Jersey, really just a crossroads then, called Neshanic. My father was pastor of a church founded before the Revolution. Every day I rode the school bus an hour to a regional high school in Somerville, but life centered on the church and our gang of high school kids who were active in various church youth organizations.

In later life I would "adopt" or be "adopted" by so-called "at-risk" teens. One of these guys, Mario, became a good friend and would lament my deprived adolescence: "No sex. No alcohol. No drugs. What kind of life was that?" Hmmm. Mario sometimes had a point.[10]

I was lucky enough to get a rare, four-year, full-ride college scholarship from the State of New Jersey which could be used at any school. I went off to my dad's alma mater, Gordon College in Massachusetts. In the meantime my dad accepted a call to a ministry in Grand Rapids, Michigan. It was then that I discovered, as the bumper sticker says, "Shit Happens," or as I prefer to think, "Things Change."

"Things change!"

New Jersey didn't look with favor on the idea of paying for my college education when my folks were no longer taxpayers, so they yanked my scholarship. I ended up living at home in Grand Rapids, which was the last place I wanted to live in the entire world.

There's nothing wrong with Grand Rapids which is really a very nice place. In junior high my dad had a church in Paterson, New Jersey and I went to Eastern Christian school where I was determined to try and prove myself the most bad-ass kid in the school. Many of my junior high teachers had gone to school in Grand Rapids and thought it was the New Jerusalem.

So I ended up in Grand Rapids living at home and going to college at Calvin College, living in the epicenter of the Reformed Jerusalem-Mecca. It turned out to be a really quality education that provided me with, in Calvin College terms, a "world and life view." In order to stay in school and pay my own way I had to work full-time as a night watchman. Between working all night and going to school all day I had very little time left to enjoy college. (Mario, the at-risk kid who lamented my sorry childhood without sex, drugs, or alcohol, also saw my college career as a time of more lost opportunities!)

I guess I went to seminary because I wanted to help change the world. One of the things I learned in seminary, that would later help me keep everything in perspective, was that God's people can be a pain in the butt to God. Look at the Biblical history: God calls and delivers his people and blesses them and what do they do? They turn on God. They wreak havoc and destruction and fight with each other and even with God. Eventually I would discover that since God's people can be a pain at times to God – well, why should I expect anything different?

But it was time to graduate from seminary and change the world. Both Kennedys had been shot when I was in college and seminary. The United States was bogged down in the first of what was to become an ongoing series of devastating modern wars, including the foolish so-called War on Drugs.

I was ready to change the world, but I needed a job to do that. I was talking with anyone who knew anything about getting a job, including the church's Field Secretary from New York, a kind of bishop in a church that doesn't have bishops. Somehow he got the impression I was interested in a big city church, and I guess if it were Marble Collegiate Church on Fifth Avenue, he would have been right. Instead I was invited to candidate (a dog and pony show to see if a church likes you) at The Protestant Dutch Reformed Church of Mott Haven. The name shouldn't throw you. Mott Haven was a tiny all-black church in a Puerto Rican neighborhood in the South Bronx. My church kids used to explain the fact that the "Protestant Dutch Reformed Church of Mott Haven" was mostly black by saying it was just "Dutch chocolate, the best kind."

I knew I wasn't interested, but was told by the seminary dean that I would go and act interested. We only had a few black churches in the RCA and in the interest of race relations I would go and candidate. Really! Race relations? If you had given me an hour I could probably have thought of one black person I knew vaguely.

I went to the Bronx, preached at Mott Haven, and had a great weekend in New York. The people at the church were gracious and welcoming, but I knew I wasn't interested. Then a few weeks later Martin Luther King, Jr. was assassinated. A few weeks after that I was invited to become the pastor at Mott Haven, and I accepted. I became the white pastor of an all-black church, in a predominantly Puerto Rican neighborhood, in the South Bronx, in the late sixties.

I suppose if you wanted to change the world the South Bronx was as good of a place as any to begin.

"Black" – forgive me if Afro American, "people of color," or some version thereof is your preference. Six years in the South Bronx with the Black Panthers and "black is beautiful" slogans, forever indoctrinated me.

The people at the church were patient, accepting, loving and amazingly tolerant of this white kid who knew nothing about being black, Puerto Rican, or living in the South Bronx. Together we turned the church inside out to serve the community. We started a day care, community center, drug rehabilitation program, and worked with other churches to build new housing. We worked with anyone and everyone who had an agenda to serve the people.

We tore down the old church sanctuary and built a multi-purpose community center. And when the cops and building inspectors came looking for payoffs, I sent them away with a fistful of contribution envelopes instead of cash, "knowing," as I would put it, "that they would want to contribute to the building fund." They'd see me coming to the 42nd Precinct to collect and they'd hide in the locker room. And the building inspector who'd tried to shake me down ended up being busted accepting a bribe - not from me! – while he was standing at the urinal in the Bronx County Court House.

In New York I came to know Norman Vincent Peale[11]. Peale was an amazing man who took a grandfatherly interest in me and my ministry. Later I would write a book about Peale called, *Norman Vincent Peale: The Man and His Ministry*. Peale was pastor of the famed Marble Collegiate Church. The Collegiate Church is actually a collection of churches that go all the way back to the settling of Nieuw Amsterdam and the arrival of the Reformed Church on Manhattan in 1624. What makes this interesting is that much of Manhattan, including the incredibly valuable land in places like Jay Street, Wall Street, and even parts of Rockefeller Center, belong to the Collegiate Corporation, parent of the Collegiate Church. Even more interesting – and this is the part that relates to "Work until You Drop" – the Collegiate ministers, like the Pope and the Supreme Court justices, are hired for life.

So, my long-term goal was to become a Collegiate Minister. I fancied myself someday occupying the prestigious Fifth Avenue pulpit at Marble Collegiate. Aside from the prestige, the real reward was in never having to retire. You could work as long as you wanted, and even if you chose to semi-retire, retain the Collegiate Minister position until death do you part.

Raising money for the ministry in Mott Haven across the Reformed Church had given me exposure in the RCA and I was developing a reputation of someone who could get things done and handle tough situations. I married; we lived in New York a while and then we accepted a call to a dying First Reformed Church in Milwaukee, Wisconsin. We renamed the church New Life Community Church and it grew, bought land on the edge of town, and started a new building. Now adding "church growth minister" to my vitae I went on to another difficult situation in Littleton, Colorado. The church was meeting in a shopping center and had a brief but tumultuous history. This church started growing. We added a counseling center, a day care, built a new multipurpose church center. I became known as the western field secretary's (remember, like a bishop only supposedly not) "fair-haired boy" and I became known as a pastor who could help churches turn themselves around.

After enduring winters in Michigan, New York, Wisconsin and Colorado (although Colorado winters were never that bad), I guess it was natural that I'd always wanted to live in Southern California. After all, I grew up with "California Dreamin'" and the sounds of the Beach Boys. The Reformed Church in Thousand Oaks, California had been started in a drive-in theater following the model of the well-known RCA television pastor Dr. Robert Schuller[12], but the church languished and never grew so they called me in.

I loved Ventura County and Thousand Oaks. We were fourteen miles from Ventura, nestled in the Santa Monica Mountains and it was the ideal community in which to raise our children. It was warm, the beach was nearby, and the schools were good. My wife Nikki had been a marriage and family therapist in Colorado. But in California the board that licensed palm readers and therapists (interesting juxtaposition) insisted that therapists coming in from out-of-state redo their training and supervision. Unwilling to reinvest all that time and money to protect California therapists from being overwhelmed with incoming competition, we began to look at other opportunities for Nikki.

When I graduated from seminary and moved to New York, I started spending my vacations serving as a volunteer chaplain on board the ships of Holland America Line. Later we started taking groups from our churches on cruises. Nikki and I both loved cruising and for years had talked about opening a travel agency. The timing seemed right and so we opened what at the time was a new concept, a cruise only travel agency called Just Cruising.

After investing all our money in the new cruise travel business, and struggling with the church for a year, I realized the Thousand Oaks church had a fatal flaw and would never grow. It had been started for all the wrong reasons and was being smothered by a few families who lovingly sought to control everything. The church board and I recommended to the field secretary (the bishop wannabe) that the church be closed and after a short time reopened in a new location with a new name and vision. Ventura County was rapidly growing and the new location we proposed offered a great opportunity to plant a church. The field secretary decided to accept the recommendation to close the church, but, much to my surprise, not to undertake any further efforts in Ventura County. Suddenly I was out of a job.

It was two months before Christmas, and I had no job. We had to be out of the parsonage the church had rented for us by New Year's Day and every penny we had had been sunk into a travel agency that had yet to earn anything.

One of my most memorable moments in the ministry happened as we faced that uncertain and tragic Christmas. I received a call from the Ventura County Sheriff's Department. They explained that they had a program to provide help for needy families at Christmas. I explained that the church had closed and so I didn't know of anyone to suggest. There was a pause and the gal from the Sheriff's Department said, "No, we were thinking of you. Is it all right if we send something over?"

I'll never forget the paddy wagon driving up and Santa jumping out of the back with toys for the girls and food. And some of the former church members dropped by anonymously and left bags of food on our front porch.

Once Again, "Things change!"

Both my wife and I were children of Reformed Church pastors and had grown up in the church with the idea that the church was a community where people cared for and took care of each other; it was fundamental to our understanding of the church. With the exception of the Sheriff's Department and a handful of former members, the denomination could have cared less.

Falling assumptions

My initial assumptions were falling like flies.

Turned out I wouldn't change the world.

Although I'd remain an ordained RCA minister, I wouldn't work just one job for life. Although I wanted the Reformed Church, it clearly didn't want me.

It helped to understand that if God's people were often a pain to God, there was no reason they shouldn't be a pain to me as well. What also helped me was an epiphany I had one afternoon while watching my kids play girls softball. I'm not a sports fan. The only reason I was sitting through an afternoon at a softball game was because my kids were playing. I just wanted my kids to play and have fun. But I'd noticed that softball was a very political thing for some parents. They could have cared less about the kids; it was all about organizational politics and control … the chance to be a big fish and a little pond. Suddenly I understood the church. It wasn't really transforming the world or serving people in need. Another assumption bit the dust.

So we had this fledgling "Just Cruising" travel agency with posters of beaches and palm trees. My wife sat at one desk and I sat at the other. A few people wandered in. Occasionally someone bought something. For us at least, working in the same tiny office while struggling for survival was not an endearing couple experience. We decided we'd both put out resumes and whoever got a job offer first would take it and the other would run the travel agency. My wife's skills were obviously more marketable. The best moment of that dismal Christmas came on Christmas Eve day: Nikki was offered a six-month job running a program for pregnant teenagers for Ventura County Public Health. Six months were all we needed. We splurged and bought a split of champagne and celebrated. Nikki went off to public health, a job she would continue for 18 years, and I stayed at the travel agency.

Eventually "Just Cruising" became successful. We had two offices, sold a ton of cruises, and became top producers for the major cruise lines. We never made a fortune, but there were wonderful fringe benefits! So I became a small businessman.

I watched Carnival Corporation grow from a bottom-of-the-barrel cruise line that all the other lines looked down on, to the foremost cruise line in the world. Watching the success of Carnival fascinated me and, at 53 years of age, I decided to get an MBA, with the thought of going to work for one of the cruise lines. The hardest part was the math. The last math class I'd had was in eleventh grade. I don't know why it never dawned on me that they called MBAs "bean counters" because it involved a lot of math. Math had changed. At one point my daughter Rebecca was trying to help me understand negative numbers and finally exasperated said, "Dad, just accept it and get on with it!"

We managed to sell off the travel agency just before the retail travel business shifted to the Internet. I finished my MBA about the time the Internet was just coming into its own. I had been serving part-time as an associate minister at a United Methodist Church in Westlake Village. One of the key laymen was CIO for a company called 24 Hour Fitness, a privately held chain of over 400 fitness centers that was rapidly expanding from the West coast into other areas of the United States as well as Asia and Europe. 24 Hour Fitness' Internet presence consisted of a single page that gave an 800 number to call for information. I became director of e-commerce for 24 Hour Fitness and jumped into the corporate world.

I worked mostly from my home in Ventura, flew to the corporate offices in the Bay Area for meetings, and spent about two days a week with the IT staff and developers in Carlsbad. Like everyone at 24 Hour Fitness, I worked long hours, but I loved it.

24HourFitness.com became one of the Internet's premier fitness resources. Along the way we gave away millions of free passes that got prospective customers into 24 Hour

Fitness centers. We were the first fitness company to begin selling memberships online. We spent five years writing and rewriting business plans for the ultimate online fitness application and during that time the dot com era came ... and went bust. I suppose we saved the company millions by never actually perfecting our business plan.

Since 9/11 changed the whole world, it should come as no surprise that it changed things for me as well. Like most companies 24 Hour Fitness was rocked by 9/11. We had been in a period of rapid expansion up to that point, and like everything else in the States, we battened down the hatches to survive. Positions were cut, including mine. And although I would continue to work as a consultant for 24 Hour Fitness and its Apex Fitness subsidiary, I knew that if I wanted to "work until I dropped" I would have to find yet another line of work.

Real estate appealed to me. I'd always enjoyed buying and selling our homes. I'd remodeled several homes and built three churches so I knew something about construction. I enjoyed watching the real estate market and watching our ocean-view home on the hillside in Ventura go up in value. Real estate seemed to be the kind of thing you could keep on doing at whatever level you desired for as long as you wished. The real estate market was good and I did very well. I was a top producer my first full year in the business. We loved Ventura. Life was good ... and I finally found something I could do for as long as I wanted. But make no mistake; real estate is demanding and a lot harder than it looks.

What do you want to do when you grow up?

Minister, travel agency owner, director of e-commerce, Realtor: I began to wonder what I wanted to do when I grew up. I discovered a little earlier than many of my contemporaries that people would no longer do one job their entire lives. People would migrate from job to job and have several careers in the course of their working lives and this is even truer for my children.

If there was a common thread that ran through these seemingly diverse careers it was selling, or as I prefer to think of it, communicating. Faith, a wonderful cruise vacation, health and fitness, a beautiful home; all were dreams to be communicated and sold.

Social Security: still ailing, but still kicking. Scratch yet another assumption. Social Security hadn't gone broke and would in all likelihood survive me, although I'm not sure it will be around for my children. But because it was still there, it allowed me to consider retiring.

I've worked hard all my life. I enjoy working hard, whether it's mental work, or renovating a house or gardening. And I still work hard and enjoy working hard. It fits my Protestant Calvinist work ethic. Maybe it was turning 60. Maybe I was slowing down or running out of steam. Maybe it was a post 9/11 reaction. Maybe it was watching what the stress of schizoid California government was doing to my wife's health.

A successful drop out

I didn't drop out in the sixties but I thought that maybe I should reconsider the idea now that I was 60. Maybe I should chill out and enjoy life.

Whatever it was, for the first time I began to question if I really wanted to work until I dropped. The world wasn't going to change, or at least I wasn't going to change it.

Your experience and assumptions obviously have been different, but it's important that you identify them and how they have changed. Things change, assumptions change and people change.

Action Items and Points to Ponder

1. What careers have you had? What were the common threads?

2. What were the assumptions when you began your employment and how have they changed?

3. "Things change" in life. What things have changed in your life?

4. What were/are your retirement plans? The saying "if you fail to plan, you plan to fail" applies in this area of life as well. Plans can and will change, but you need to start with some kind of a plan.

With baby howler monkey at wildlife rescue center.

Cottage in Cerro Punta

5. Change Is Good

*T*he Greek philosopher Heraclites observed that, "We are living in a world of constant change." Yet many of us, consciously or unconsciously, resist change, particularly when the change threatens familiar patterns in life.

Yet change happens. We look in the mirror and note how we've changed. We age. We move from one stage of life to another. Sometimes the events in life change us.

Sometimes we have a choice to change, and sometimes not.

Retirement looms as a major change in life. Will we be able to adapt? What will we do? How will we survive without the daily nine-to-five routine of work?

Pretty much how you look at change determines how flexible you are and how successful you can be at managing change in your life. The operative word here is managing. You have a choice to be the passive victim of change, or to manage change as it comes along. You can fight change, or you can embrace it. Change can be threatening or invigorating: the choice is really yours!

You can GO through the changes in your life or you can GROW through them.

Face it: most of us are going to live to be 90. If you're thinking about retirement, you're probably at the age where you've already beat some of the odds. For most people life divides somewhat neatly into three segments:

Youth – Preparation. Roughly the first 30 years. Yes, I know that many of us who grew up in the 60s thought that life damn near ended at thirty – remember, not trusting anyone over thirty? But we know now that we were really just kids when we were in our twenties trying to figure out which end was up.

Responsibility – Roughly the second 30 years. I was tempted to call it "slavery," but that really would be a bit harsh. Thirty years of "getting ahead," building a "career," raising kids and pets, paying a mortgage, accumulating "stuff," and, hopefully, putting something away for retirement.

Your time – Roughly the last 30 years. Now you could call this the traditional "retirement" period, or, in my mind worse yet, "maturity," but I prefer to think of it as your time.

You've paid your dues, you've worked your ass off, you've raised your kids and now it is time to enjoy life!

It's all a matter of how you choose to look at it. In many ways this last thirty years of "your time" should be the time of your life. Sometimes we get this incredibly negative attitude, usually starting around forty or fifty, that "it's all downhill from here." Bull! It's only downhill if that's what you choose. Just think of all you packed into the first thirty years – and you really didn't know which end was up! Or the second thirty years. Even while a slave to a job and career, look what you were able to accomplish. Now, with all of that experience, just think what you can do with the next thirty years!

Like most people, as "kids" Nikki and I looked at growing old and decided it wasn't for us. We didn't want to grow old. Old, first defined as thirty, gradually got pushed to forty-five, then fifty-five, then sixty-five . . .

Nikki was commiserating with her mom about growing old and said, rather flippantly, "I don't want to grow old and decrepit. If I do, I'm just going to walk in front of a bus."

Nikki's mom said, "Oh, no, Nikki!" And Nikki glowed with her mother's care and concern until her mom said, "Don't step in front of a bus, step in front of a train, it's much more effective."

You have a choice to embrace change and grow through it or just endure. Growth is characteristic of all living things. Bob Dylan sang, "He not busy being born is busy dying."

When you retire, by choice or force, you leave behind a part of you. It may seem like a big part, but in the grand scheme of things it is just a part, nothing more, nothing less. That part is gone and it will never be the same. There is a loss and a natural grieving process over the loss of something that was very important in your life. You are forever changed. And in this fact lies both the crux of the problem and the opportunity. As with many changes in life, you can go through it or you can grow through it: the choice is yours!

I've always liked this poem by Gordon and Gladis DePree which, for me at least, captured the essence of growth.

> Growing
> is seldom a graceful process
> it is shoots and half-formed leaves,
> big teeth and bony knees.
> Growing is the process of something
> becoming larger, taller,
> more mature.
> And although growing
> is not always a graceful process,
> poised and polished and finished,
> it is preferable to its alternative . . .
> For when a plant or animal or person
> or mind or spirit
> stops growing,
> it begins the process of dying. [13]

You are passing from one stage of life to another. Gail Sheehy in her book *Passages* uses the illustration of a lobster, which sheds its hard protective shell in order to grow as an example of the challenge of growth in the "passages" of our lives. During the period after the shedding of the shell, the lobster is exposed and vulnerable as a new covering grows to replace the one that was lost. Sheehy says, "With each passage from one stage of human growth to the next, we too, must shed a protective structure. We are left exposed and vulnerable – but also yeasty and embryonic again, capable of stretching in ways we hadn't known before."[14]

I like that – "yeasty and embryonic again, capable of stretching in ways we hadn't known before." When the kids were at home, when you had to be at work every day, when you had to struggle to make the mortgage, you didn't have the opportunities that you have now!

Sheehy observes that in each passage of life, in each change, "Some magic must be given up, some cherished illusion of safety and comfortably familiar sense of self must be cast off, to allow for the greater expansion of our own distinctiveness."

She writes, ". . . we must be willing to change chairs if we want to grow. There is no permanent compatibility between a chair and a person. And there is no one right chair. What is right at one stage may be restricting at another or too soft. During the passage from one stage to another, we will be between two chairs. Wobbling no doubt, but developing ... Times of crisis, or disruption or constructive change, are not only predictable but desirable. They mean growth." [15]

So this is your time! Your time to grow!

When Nikki and I moved to Panama we both lost twenty pounds while eating better. Our blood pressures dropped to more acceptable levels. We started walking. Nikki left a high-stress job managing programs for the Ventura County Public Health department. I tell her that the best thing she ever did for her health was to leave the health department.

Nikki faced such a round of pressure and deadlines and

meetings getting ready to phase out of her responsibilities that she said when she came to Panama she didn't want to see anyone for three months. That only lasted a few weeks. Now she luxuriates in having three or four books in the process of being read, has worked hard to become a really good coffee farmer, and is active in several local community groups. I decided to start lecturing on luxury cruise ships and now spend half the year cruising around the world. I'm not ready to sit in the rocking chair, listen to the rain and watch the coffee grow, although, I confess, at times I do enjoy it.

When we first moved to Boquete we were, as the movie folks said back in LA, "on hiatus," not sure exactly what we would end up doing, but "yeasty and embryonic again, capable of stretching in ways we hadn't known before." We knew we were in a growth mode, just not sure where it was going to lead. For some people that is too challenging and they need a road map with detailed directions and mileage a la MapQuest.

We were challenged by feeling open and free to explore possibilities we hadn't had time to think of before because we were too busy with family and careers.

At first I thought I might stay in real estate, or open a business, but eventually I decided to enjoy the freedom of not being "locked in" or doing the things I've always done. We've developed our little coffee farm, found a beach *casita* to fix up, and I've rediscovered my love of cruising and the sea. Now I lecture on cruise ships, allowing us to travel and meet people from all over the world. Life is good!

For me to switch from just going on ships occasionally, for a week or two at a time, to sailing on a contract for three to five months at a time was a big jump. One of the major cruise lines had offered me a six-month contract. I probably wouldn't have done it, except for the fact that my wife and kids said I would never last, so I had to prove them wrong. At the time I was reading a novel by Phillip Friedman and these words jumped off the page: "He was poised on the unforeseen cusp of his life. He could either leap into the unknown or slide back down to where he had been stagnating, where he would continue to stagnate, sustaining himself on illusions of renewal."[16]

I leaped and I love it!

Follow the string

I've always had a philosophy that you should "follow the string." I've taught this to my kids as they were growing up. You simply "follow the string" and see where it leads. If you don't, you'll never know what might have been. And if you follow the string and no longer like where it's leading, you simply stop following. That philosophy has led us as a family to many interesting discoveries, discoveries that would not have occurred had we not taken the first steps of following the string to see where it leads. And we're still following the string.

I will admit that there can be limiting factors. If you haven't been climbing mountains all your life it's unlikely, though not impossible, that in this stage of your life you'll scale Denali. This is where your gene pool, attention to your health, and fitness all these years pay off. If you have serious health problems, they may be a limiting factor. As you get older the availability of good medical care becomes an issue, which was a consideration in our move to Panama.

It's interesting in our society how we watch our grandchildren and are happy to see them growing because they are developing the way they should. We see their aging as growing and think it is great: people are supposed to grow. But when you first saw gray hair, or faced a physical challenge or limitation brought on by aging, how did you look at growing older? Did you feel good because you were getting older? Were you pleased that you were doing what people are supposed to do? Why are we so inconsistent? At one period of life we look on aging as something good and positive, and at another period of time the same process precipitates a crisis.

Would you really want to go back and relive your youth? I wouldn't! I thought I enjoyed it, Mario's observations about my pitiful youth lacking in sex, alcohol and drugs notwithstanding, but I wouldn't go back even if I could. Each period of life has its own unique opportunities for experience and growth. Having grown through one period of life, I value and treasure it, but I'm anxious to go on and grow through the next period.

Douglas MacArthur said, "Nobody grows old by merely living a number of years. People grow old by deserting their ideals. Tears may wrinkle the skin, but to give up interest wrinkles the soul." He was right. More people die from hardening of the mind than from hardening of the arteries. The mind hardens when you give up on dreams and become rigid and inflexible. People who have a negative outlook on aging resist it and resent it. They see the changes in themselves but instead of accepting them they reject them. But the changes continue and they become bitter. Unable to accept the changes in themselves, they can't accept change in others or in society. They become very bitter and angry old people. Unless there is some radical surgery of negative ideas, these attitudes will kill them.

God made us and He made us to grow older. He designed the various stages of life, each with its own rewards and opportunities.

Part of living life abundantly as God intended, is for us to seize each stage and live it positively, fully and with enthusiasm!

Earlier I mentioned Dr. Norman Vincent Peale. I remember getting into a hotel elevator in Milwaukee with Dr. Peale. He had just finished a rip-roaring speech to 9,000 prominent and successful sales people. He was in his late seventies and it was late at night, but he was still filled with vigor and enthusiasm. I asked him in amazement, "Dr. Peale, how do you keep going? How are you able to keep flying all over the country making three or four speeches a week, sometimes two in a day, and preaching in New York on Sunday?"

Dr. Peale cleared his throat and in his gravelly voice said, "Well, I'll tell you one thing: I don't eat the cold, rubbery chicken they serve at these gatherings. I go in, give my speech and I get out!"

I've always suspected there was more to it than that. Peale says, "Successful old-age is built on earlier years lived right." He said in old-age you'll be the same kind of person you were when you were younger, only more so. If you were positive and enthusiastic at thirty, you'll be that way at eighty. If you were a grouch and negative at thirty, just imagine what you'll be like at eighty.

Whatever your age, it's not too early or too late to start loving life and approaching it positively and with enthusiasm.

Growing is a great adventure!

There is evidence that openness to new adventures can actually decrease stress and help you live longer. According to Dr. Norman Anderson, coauthor of *Emotional Longevity: What Really Determines How Long You Live*, "People who successfully try new things develop a high sense of self-efficacy – 'a can do attitude' – which can lead to better health." Some studies have shown that this adventurous, positive attitude overrode other life-extenders like low blood pressure, low cholesterol, not smoking, low body fat and even regular exercise.

While there is no way to prevent Alzheimer's disease, there is evidence that continuing to learn and use and exercise your brain, can reduce the risk of developing dementia. What better way to exercise your brain and memory than learning a new language?

Just a few words of caution here . . .

Sometimes people who are bored with their lives, or their relationships, or themselves, think that just changing location is the answer to their problems. When all you do is change location, generally you take all the underlying problems with you. You need to be basically happy with you before you think about changing location.

Take care of your business first: if you've got issues, deal with them. It's a lot easier to do it where you are, than to try and find a psychiatrist, counselor, or whatever, in a new country. If it's not working at home, just moving to a new country isn't going to "fix" things, in fact, it probably will make things worse.

Working for a cruise line means on the way to the ship you sit in the back of the plane and take the cheapest and most circuitous route the cruise line can find. At one point, after spending hours on planes and in airports, I was being driven from the airport to the ship. I don't even remember where in the world it was, but I do remember seeing a big billboard along the road to the port that said ...

"Amazing things happen when you say yes to life, with no strings attached!"

How true! Try it.

Action Items and Points to Ponder

1. In what ways has your life become predictable and boring?

2. If you could change three things about your life, what would they be?

3.Would these changes be "growing" changes, or just "reacting" changes to get away from your current situation?

4. In what ways is your life already changing?

5. If you could do anything, and nothing was impossible, what would you do?

Panama Relocation Tour exploring rain forest at El Valle.

Horse parade in Boquete.

6. Running the Numbers

Most of us avoid numbers. **Few of us know exactly where we spend our money, or exactly how much we will have for retirement.** We like to think we know, but deal in generalities, and don't really know exactly.

If you're going to think about escaping, now, or in the future, you have to "run the numbers." You have to know exactly how you spend your money now, how much money you can depend on in retirement, and what life is going to cost.

When we began this process, we quickly realized how little we knew. Money came in, money went out, and generally at the end of the year, it was all gone. Sometimes more went out than came in, so, like most Americans, we depended on credit cards to tide us over. Our household income generally ran between $150.000-200.000. You'd think we would have had lots of money. We thought so too. When I did my taxes I could never quite understand: if we made this much, why wasn't there anything left? I'd see folks who I knew made a lot less than we did, and they had pickups loaded down with adult toys. We didn't have any toys. They ate out all the time. We seldom ate out. I'm still not sure exactly what I did wrong. We were convinced that we could never afford to retire. But then we never really ran the numbers, so we didn't know for sure.

There is no way around it. You have to run the numbers. And you have to start by analyzing your current spending. You need to know exactly what's coming in, and exactly how it is being spent.

Craig Hay has been my friend since we were in high school. In New York we shared an apartment. In Littleton we lived down the street from each other and our wives and kids were best friends. Craig has been my accountant and more than anyone else, he knows how "numerically challenged" I am. He would look at my tax scratching and just shake his head. And when I got my MBA and officially became a "bean counter" he really shook his head. But no matter how much it violates your sense of who you are, you need to run the numbers.

When we actually recorded and looked at our spending in Ventura, it broke down like this:

36% Taxes
29% Housing
10% Children, gifts, donations
8% Transportation
8% Food and clothing
6% Enjoyment
3% Medical

The single biggest percentage of our money was going to pay off Uncle Sam and his various cronies. And, frankly, I didn't like what they were doing with my money.

The second biggest chunk was going for housing. Most Californians spend a much larger percentage of their income on housing than typical Americans. It used to be a kind of forced investment and in our case our major, and at times our only, investment. One of our goals was not to have a mortgage when we retired, so we had a fifteen year loan which required larger payments.

So what will it cost when you retire? A lot of the conventional wisdom is that with inflation factored in, to retire comfortably you will need 50 to 70 percent of your current income, and I think it's more like 70 percent. In our case using $150,000 for example, that would mean we would need retirement income of about $105,000 a year.
Every year the Social Security Administration mails contributors an estimate of what your Social Security

payments would be if you retire at various ages. In my case, if I retired at roughly 62.5 I would get around $15,200 a year. There's a big gap between $15,200 and $105,000! If I waited until 66 to start collecting, I would get Social Security payments of about $22,000 – still a big gap! To fill that gap with investments, at a 5 percent annual return, we would need about $1.7 million, which we definitely did not have. And history has proved that my assumption of five percent annual return was far too optimistic.[17]

Unless you run the numbers you have no idea .

So we kept looking at the numbers. We hadn't factored in various Individual Retirement Accounts [IRAs]. We didn't have a lot of IRAs, but these weren't really going to kick in until later in life. I had a small Reformed Church pension, but over the years it had been mismanaged by ministers, with much of it sucked up in fees. I knew that it wouldn't amount to much, if and when I was old enough to get at it. I think the strategy was that you were supposed to go to your eternal reward first. Unlike most pension funds, this one seemed designed to make sure that the principal never increased.

I was a Realtor in Ventura County and watched the value of real estate soar back in the good old days when you wrote out offers on the hood of your car for more than the asking price praying that the seller would accept your offer over the others. So, what if we were to "cash out?" I'd been worrying about the value of everyone else's home: what about mine? Well, it turned out we had about $400,000 to $500,000 equity in our home though we'd owned it for less than six years.

Meanwhile, the value of my Reformed Church pension was roughly the same as it was six years previously. The equity in our home made the idea of cashing out, selling our house and retiring early more interesting.

Although I'd never been a gambler, I had the sense to know that there comes a time when you need to cash in your chips and get out of the casino.

I began to ask some questions.

What if we didn't have a mortgage to worry about?

What if we weren't paying 36 percent of our income in taxes?

What if we could find a place that we both liked, that fit our "dream" specifications and still had a lower cost of living?

Could it be possible?

We started looking in earnest at my wife's retirement possibilities. She'd been with the county eighteen years. She was fully vested and could retire whenever she wanted, she just had never thought about retiring. California lives in a state of perpetual budget crisis, but the last one Nikki endured was kind of the straw that broke the camel's back. Nikki was dedicated to her programs working with teen mothers, teen dads, their babies, and "at-risk" kids with real needs … about 2,000 kids at any one time. To the state her programs were just another budget line item, to be retained or eliminated based on political benefit, not the needs of kids.

My Excel spreadsheets and budget analysis started in earnest. We started making the lists and analyzing them. When we finally settled on Panama as our first choice, we began collecting everything we could find, talking to anyone who would listen, scouring the web, seeking out information about costs in Panama.

When thinking about a budget for retirement, you need to budget for you, not some imaginary or hypothetical person.

If you eat out every night, don't expect to change once you retire. If you require first class accommodations, don't plan on living in a thatched roof hut. Make a budget that reflects your lifestyle and the lifestyle you want in retirement.

By the time we actually moved to Panama we had a pretty

good budget worked out, based on our understanding of how we spent money and our understanding of the cost of items in Panama. We knew health care and health insurance would be a killer (Isn't that a telling line!) and we budgeted accordingly.

The only area we were really off on was the cost of food. Our actual food cost is about twice what we budgeted, and most of that difference is in the cost of prepared food items, like Cheerios, Diet Coke, paper goods, and the like. Strictly food, we'd have probably been very close.

Here's a quick comparison:

Item	California	Panama
Housing and utilities	29%	17%
Enjoyment	6%	12%
Food and clothing	8%	18%
Medical	3%	20%
Transportation	8%	8%
Taxes	36%	20%
Children, gifts and donations	10%	5%

The comparison should not be interpreted to mean that everything is cheaper in Panama. A lot depends on you and how you choose to live. We were able to pay off our mortgage in California and still have enough money to pay cash for a very nice home in Boquete. We're not paying a mortgage, but we do have a 3.5 acre farm to maintain. Because I work on cruise ships we don't spend as much on the travel aspect of "enjoyment" as others might.

For our first few years in Panama I was a stickler for recording everything we spent because I needed to know if this was working and if it would continue to work. When we drew all this up I didn't know that I would continue working part-time with the cruise lines, so that has made things a little easier.

I've done spread sheets showing how much money we will make until we have both reached 98 years of age as we start drawing down various pensions and IRAs. If – and let's accept it, life is always an IF! – if all goes according to plan, we will live comfortably in our retirement and hopefully leave some money to provide for the education of our grandchildren.

As a *Pensionado* I cannot work for anyone in Panama. I can, however, consult or have my own business and, in my case, work on cruise ships. Since our permanent residence is outside of the United States my wife and I can each make up to $100,800 [2015] *earned* income without paying United States taxes on that amount. Until you reach "full retirement age" your Social Security check is penalized if you earn over the Social Security limits. Unfortunately if you have self-employment income you still have to pay Social Security on the money you make while at the same time you're collecting Social Security.

While Panama taxes expats for income earned within Panama, it does not tax you on income earned outside Panama, like Social Security, pensions and the money I earn internationally on ships. Even though I am a full-time resident of Panama, worked on the high seas for a Bermuda company, owned by a Panama company, I have to pay Social Security on what I earn from ships!

Some expats do earn money on things such as apartment rentals[18] when they are not in residence in Panama, "snow birds" for example, and the Panama tax consequence of this needs to be discussed with a Panamanian accountant. If you are going to enter into any kind of business in Panama you will need a Panamanian attorney and accountant on your team.

These are big decisions, decisions that you don't want to make blindly. They are decisions which could be very costly if they are the wrong decisions. Don't hesitate to seek out professional help as it will save you money in the long run. People sometimes ask, "Won't all the *gringos* moving to Boquete drive up the cost of living?" That's exactly the kind of question you need to be asking. The answer is, yes, and no.

The cost of land had already been driven up, some would say "through the roof," by the time we got here, particularly in Boquete. The town is changing. Old buildings are being replaced. There is now a four-lane highway between Boquete and David. We even have Mail Boxes Etc. -- can Kentucky Fried Chicken be far behind? In some ways it reminds me of the transformation we saw when had a cabin outside Breckenridge, Colorado.

Is it good for investment? Absolutely. Is something valuable also lost along the way? Absolutely. But, as noted previously, we are living in a world of constant change. I guess it is natural that everyone, when they find their paradise, wants to close the door, but it doesn't work that way nor should it work that way.

As Panama moves forward and enjoys one of the few booming economies in the world, the cost of living is going up, not just in Boquete, but all over the country. In Boquete simultaneously almost two economies are developing. For example: Romero is the *gringo* store of choice, and the choice for more affluent Panamanians and it looks and feels somewhat familiar, well a little! Mandarin is the store of choice for many locals, and Bruna is generally the Indigenous choice. Both Bruna and Mandarin often have lower prices for the same goods. You can have breakfast (eggs, local fry bread, a corn tortilla, juice and coffee) at Central Park Cafe for $5. (The same breakfast at Central Park when we came ten years ago was $2.50). Or you can have the same breakfast at one of the *gringo* restaurants for $9.50 but it has a flower on the plate. It's your choice.

There is no question that the economic growth in Panama, driven mostly by expansion in Panama City, the Canal Expansion and other major projects, is driving up the cost of living. Because Panama uses the U. S. dollar, the value of the dollar takes a hit here just as in the States when the U. S. Treasury decides to print more dollars to solve every problem. When the dollar drops against world currencies, inflation is inevitable. If the cost of oil goes up in the world, the cost of diesel goes up here as well. If the price of oil drops we benefit the same as everyone else. The haircut that used to cost $2 now costs $3. A maid that used to run $8 a day is now $18 - $25. A gardener used to get $8 a day, and now gets $15 - $20.

Yes, costs have gone up in Panama but they have elsewhere as well. When I go back to the States, I'm shocked by the cost of everything. So although costs have increased in Panama, compared to Southern California at least, Panama is still a whole lot cheaper.

It's not just about the cost of living; it's also about the quality of life. For us the quality of life is better in Panama for less money.

Over the ten years we've lived in Panama, I've noticed a number of interesting changes that, for me, are indications of the growth of the economy in Panama and the fact that prosperity is indeed trickling down.

- Ordinary Panamanians are adding rooms, porches and improvements to their homes. We see this in our little hamlet above Alto Boquete. The home improvement stores in David, like Do It Center and Novey, are doing a thriving business.

- People now paint the entire outside of their house, not just the front side as they used to do in the past because that was all they could afford.

- Graffiti is increasing: it's not that easy to steal spray paint in Panama, so you have to have money to buy paint to be a graffiti "artist." And, with more money, unfortunately, you see more young people taking up smoking.

- Gyms, real U. S.-style gyms, are opening and thriving. Gym memberships here cost money just like in the States. People have time and money for Zumba and spin classes. You see more and more people jogging because they have the time and opportunity to worry about their health.

- Giant malls are swamped with people and Panama has even introduced "Black Friday." Although Panama doesn't have a U. S. Thanksgiving holiday, but what would be the day after U. S. Thanksgiving is now being touted in Panama as "Black Friday," the day when retail stores, hopefully, start turning a profit for the year.

- With a cell phone penetration of 1.9 phones per person, almost everyone has a cell phone. Blackberry is still popular in Panama and more and more people have smart phones.

- With all the infrastructure improvements, taxes are going up, and being collected.

- The cost of tickets for speeding and other driving infractions, like using your cell phone while driving, has gone through the roof.

- Cycling, complete with $8,000 racing bikes, and thousand dollar skin-tight Spandex outfits, has become wildly popular.

- Pretty much everyone who is working has a newer car. The only "old" cars are driven by old farmers in the country and budget-conscious *gringo* expats.

- When we came to Panama there were no directional signs, no stop signs, *nada,* and frequently in Panama City manhole were missing. The manhole covers had been stolen leaving a gaping hole in the sidewalk or street and the signs had been stolen and sold as scrap metal. Today there are signs everywhere and with a few exceptions, manhole covers are in place in Panama City. It's only the ones that are missing that will *get* you.

- There are more people with braces, more decorations and lights at Christmas, more, more, more as Panama gets caught up in consumerism.

- When we first came here the big treat was a single scoop ice cream cone at Anna Sweets for 25 cents. The same cone now costs 80 cents, and the big treat is real Italian gelato for $1.25 a scoop, about the same price as in Venice! The biggest patrons are Panamanians who plunk down $16 for a liter [a little over two pints] of gelato!

So now with a booming economy in Panama, and many would-be retirees having lost equity in investments due to the world financial crisis, is moving to Panama still an option?

For many people I would emphatically answer, "Yes!" You may have to scale back your expectations. Maybe you won't go the "dream house" route, which frankly many folks end up regretting. But the cost of living in Panama is STILL a whole lot less than it is in *many* places in the States, although not all places, and **the quality of life is better** in many ways.

Let me give you a few examples of "affordable" living in Boquete, even if your home equity has mostly disappeared.

I built a nice 900 square foot *casita* or little house for my brother: two bedrooms, comfortable, cute and nice, including the cost of land for $50,000.

When I go to David I drive by a guy's home made of two 12 meter [40 foot] containers [about $4,500 each delivered to Boquete], nicely painted with windows and doors, both covered along with the center section. The space in between is an open living area, which makes a lot of sense in a place like Boquete. It's creative, comfortable and funky and I'll bet he has less than $35,000 in the project, including land and the fancy Chinese front door.

Another friend of ours bought a small coffee *finca*, took what had been run-down Indian housing and turned it into the cutest little cottage you can imagine. This gal is super creative and she basically renovated the place using scrap construction, hard work and a ton of imagination and creativity.

Or you can just rent a decent place in Boquete for $700 to $2,500 a month, depending on your wants. You don't need a million dollars or to have cashed in your chips before the crash in order to take advantage of moving to paradise.

Action Items and Points to Ponder

1. So what do you know, REALLY (and be honest!) about your current spending? Everything, including both partners' "cookie jar" accounts.

2. If you don't know, and most people don't, what are you going to do about it this week? Don't cut back anywhere, just record what you're spending so you have something with which to work.

3. What do you anticipate to be your Social Security payments?

4. Using the 70 percent rule, what would you need in investments to retire now?

5. What sources of income would you have after retirement, and how much could you anticipate from each?

6. Looking at your current costs of living, if you removed certain categories (like mortgage expenses), or reduced some (like taxes), how much would you need for retirement?

7. This is probably the most significant question in this book, not just in term of finding "paradise" but in terms of your general happiness in life: What is *really* important to you?

If we ever retired, this was our idea of what retirement would be like and what we could afford. On the set of Dr. Quinn, Medicine Woman[19] at the original Dr. Quinn cabin.

But it all ended up well in Panama, not that we spend that much time sitting in the rocking chairs sipping pina coladas!

7. Visit a Leather Bar

O<small>K</small>, **I debated changing this title, but it really does say what I want to say, so stay with me!**

I know that this title may make some folks nervous, but nobody is going to change your sexual orientation. I just want to make a point about cultural differences. Your ability to recognize, accept, and adapt to cultural differences is a key factor in whether or not you will come to love Panama, or any other paradise.

So chill out!

I remember the first time a good friend "came out" to me and told me he was gay. And he wanted to take me to a gay bar, a very macho, gay leather bar. Fortunately I could come up with jeans and a white T-shirt so we got in, even though I didn't have a leather outfit with the seat of the pants missing.

If you live in or near a big city, the bar will probably have a name like The Corral, Spike, or Eagle. It won't look like much from the outside and is probably on a back street. It may be hard to find and may not even have a sign. There may be bikes out front, although this is not a biker bar. It may or may not have a rainbow flag. I suggest you leave your Hawaiian shirt and surfer shorts at home. Levis and a white or gray T-shirt (used, not new, best avoid any logos). A black leather vest would work nicely, if you happen to have one tucked away. Leather boots if you've got them: Doc Martens are best. No fragrances. Walk in, belly up to the bar, order a beer and soak up the ambiance.

If you can't find a leather bar, try any old gay bar. Looser dress code and fragrances work here. Order whatever you like, preferably a martini, or at least a drink with an umbrella in it, and soak up the ambiance. At least the dancing will be good.

If leather or gay bars are your thing, then you'll want to find a very conservative, fundamentalist church. Dress code here is white shirt, tie, and jacket. Replace the red AIDS-awareness pin with a national flag pin. Tuck a Bible conspicuously under your arm and soak up the ambiance. Nothing against conservative fundamentalists, since some of my best friends are "fundies." And some of my best friends are gay, and some are theologically conservative and also gay, and I believe God loves them all. The point I'm trying to make is that you need to experience a culture radically different from the one to which you are accustomed. The point isn't for you to convert or change your lifestyle.

The point is to enter into and observe a culture that is different than your own.

Face it: if you are even considering relocating to another country, the culture, the customs, the language, the food, the mores, the laws – it's all going to be different. Some people do different well. Others are threatened by anything that's different.

This is a key point, key to your ultimate success and happiness in a new home. Do you find differences in culture and people fascinating, something you can't wait to experience and explore, or does it threaten who you are and what you believe? What is your level of tolerance?

Do you appreciate the broadness and color of the Kingdom of God, or do you just assume everyone should be like you?

Now in our first experiment you visited a leather bar, a gay bar, or a church with a totally different "flavor" than you are used to, and at least tried to fit in. You kind of dressed to look the part. Now imagine doing the same thing, dressing and acting the way you normally dress and act. You walk into the leather bar in your Hawaiian shirt, surfer shorts and Havaiana sandals, or show up in church in your wildest Saturday-night-party-your-ass-off outfit. Imagine how you feel sticking out as a definite minority.

You can do the same thing in a lot of other ways. I am not a car racing fan. When I worked with 24 Hour Fitness someone in marketing got the brilliant idea for us to sponsor a race car. And so we found a car with the number "24" in what was then the Winston Cup. So we had our 24 Hour Fitness car and team. Talk about expensive! Car racing really is the sport of kings! Not only did you need a car, you needed a huge van with 24 Hour Fitness painted all over it to cart the car around, and you needed a spare car, and another van, and a portable shop with extra engines. The list and expenses went on and on and on.

A bunch of us from corporate got to go see our first race with VIP passes, a chance to see the race from the perspective of our pit crew, and lots of gifts with NASCAR and our 24 Hour Fitness logo, which started to give me a clue as to why this was so expensive. I had never been to a car race before, and I was awe-struck. There were thousands and thousands of people interested in NASCAR racing and lined up to buy $500 leather NASCAR jackets, NASCAR underwear, you name it, they sold it. There was the even the Viagra car booth, I guess selling blue pills with the NASCAR logo probably guaranteed faster performance so one could hurry back to the couch, the beer, and the remote. Here was this incredible subculture of which I was completely ignorant and with which I had no experience.

Thrilling as it was to watch the cars go round, and round, and round, and round, and round some more … I suppose everyone was hoping for a spectacular crash … my marketing acumen was shrewd enough to look around at the decidedly overweight and out-of-shape crowd and know that while these folks could certainly benefit from 24 Hour Fitness, they were not a very promising market. Eventually after we'd spent a ton of money on racing, our marketing geniuses realized the same thing and we got out of racing.

NASCAR is one of those niche subcultures where, if you're not a NASCAR fan, you can feel very much like a minority.

I had a similar situation recently when I stayed in a hotel which happened to be hosting a major Goth convention. The parking lot was jammed with souped-up, restored hearses, and old military trucks decorated with skeletons and blood, and zombie-like creatures roaming the halls. The second floor conference rooms were an "adult" area – heaven only knows! But this was obviously a very expensive hobby, taken quite seriously by a thousand folks who probably in their regular life were IRS agents, meat cutters (sorry!), and orthodontists, and likely a few clergy thrown in.

Those of us who are white in America often have very little minority experience.

As I told you, my first church was an all-black congregation in the South Bronx of New York City in the late sixties, at the height of the Black Panther "Power to The People" era. There I was, this white boy from Michigan who knew nothing about being black or being in the city, dropped into the South Bronx. I found out very quickly what it meant to be a minority! For a while it seemed like everywhere I turned there was a black fist in my white face, not literally, but certainly figuratively.

The head of my Usher Board was a lady by the name of Mary Ida Vandross[20]. Now the Usher Board is probably the most important organization and power in a black congregation. Mary Ida took pity on this single white boy and used to invite me over for Sunday afternoon dinners. I learned to love soul food. I mean that woman could cook.

Mary Ida had a teenage son who used to always be fooling around with music, singing, dancing, and doing awesome things with his voice. His name was Luther Vandross. She had another son with serious drug problems who was in and out of jail. I hadn't been in the Bronx very long when Anthony got out of Riker's Island jail and ended up staying in the church's parish house while he got his life together. One night Anthony sat down with me and had a heart-to-heart talk. He said, "D, you have all these degrees, but you don't know shit about the street. You're not going to live long unless you start to learn. There are people out there who don't have any college degrees, but in terms of street-smarts they have master's degrees and PhDs. I feel sorry for you, so I'm going to teach you and we're going to meet some of these people."

I'm alive today because of Anthony Vandross.[21] He took me around the Bronx and Harlem and into bars and clubs. He'd say, "See that guy over there, he controls all the drugs in Harlem" and on and on. It took me a while, but I caught on.

Preaching was another matter. I came out of seminary trained in expository preaching. Take a Biblical passage, discuss the Hebrew and Greek words and their meaning and the theological significance. It wasn't what they were looking for in a black church. They tried, and prayed a lot, and were very patient, and I tried. When I preached people would be yelling out, "Help him Jesus! Help him Jesus!"

One Sunday morning when I was finally getting the hang of preaching with a little more freedom and zing, Ms. Foreman got the Spirit. And she started jumping up and down, and crying, and shouting, "Thank you Jesus! Thank you Jesus! Praise you Jesus!" And I was so startled, I stopped!

After the service, Jack Evans, my Senior Elder, took me aside, put his arm around my shoulder and said, "Boy," – I used to hate it when they called me "boy" – "Boy, let me tell you something about women. When they start shouting and moaning, whatever it is you're doing, don't stop."

Well, I learned a lot about being a minority. And I learned that the way we did things in Grand Rapids, Michigan, or in the white world, wasn't necessarily the only way or even the best way. I learned to appreciate being black. After a while people weren't black, white, or Puerto Rican. It was Jeanine, Bats, Tito, Octavio, Eddie, Henry, Mary and Victor. Today I'd have to stop and think to remember if they were black, or brown, or white. They were just family and friends.

If you like where you live, if you're convinced it is the absolute best, the be all and end all, why even think about moving?

If you believe you have the best medical care, the fastest freeways, the greatest entertainment, a just justice system, the best shopping, and know what's best for the rest of the world, just stay where you are and keep exporting McDonald's, Subway and Kentucky Fried Chicken to the rest of the world. Pay your taxes and vote for the same folks the same way and enjoy the same results. Why change?

A friend of ours in Boquete was born in Panama, educated in the United States and Europe and makes doors, cabinets and furniture. She knows wood. Wood is tricky in Panama. You don't go to Home Depot or Lowe's or someplace else and buy kiln-dried wood. You find someone who has trees to sell, size up the tree, buy it, chop it down when the moon is right, store it until it has properly dried and then make something out of it. A louvered door isn't made by some machine in North Carolina out of kiln-dried pine. It is hand crafted, piece by piece, out of *cedro*, teak or some other termite resistant wood. Michelle Brewer and her guys are artists in wood. It may take a while, but when it's finished it will be beautiful and worth the wait. The building boom in Boquete makes finding good woodworkers one of the most difficult things in building a home, and the wait can be frustrating.

Michelle was in her office at the shop and as she describes it, "This *gringo* came swaggering into the office. Military buzz cut, looking like a retired LAPD cop." Michelle is blonde, speaks three or four languages fluently, including English. He assumed she was a *gringa* and he started unloading about being "sick and tired of these stupid, fucking Panamanians who can't do anything right." He was looking for woodworkers who could do things the "right" way, his American way. Michelle, this very gracious, gentle woman who's attended all the right schools in the United States and Europe said, "Well I'm a fucking Panamanian and this fucking Panamanian is throwing you out." And she threw him out of her shop.

The same guy went down the road to another, U. S. expat woodworker and started the same routine. Without knowing Michelle had just thrown him out, he said, "Sir, I'm a guest in this country and my workers are all Panamanians, so you can get out of my shop and don't come back."

Who did this ugly American think he was? And why was he in Panama anyway?

Another sweet-looking lady in her 70s told a real estate agent she'd look at any property in Boquete, "Just as long as it isn't next door to any people talking Mexican." Did she realize she was in Panama, not Mexico? If she wanted only to hear English, why was she even considering living in Panama?

Don't go to another country wanting to change it or Americanize it or make it the way things were "back home."

If you want LA, stay in LA! The reason why you even consider another country or another culture is because you appreciate the difference!

I confess that I struggle with this every time I drive to David and start shopping and get the lousy customer service that characterizes much retail business in Panama, or when I have a workman or service person scheduled to come to my house at, say, noon on Tuesday, and they don't show, don't call, but finally end up showing up Friday evening at dinner time.

People always ask me what the "toughest" thing is about living in Panama. It's not that we don't have Home Depot or

Costco, although that IS tough, but it's the cultural differences that sneak up and grab you, sometimes when least expected.

Two examples . . .

First, *gringo* time and Panamanian time: totally different. Since time dominates the lives of most North Americans and Europeans, I guess this shouldn't be surprising, but it keeps "getting" me. If you are invited to a Panamanian's house for a party at 8:00 p.m., and you show up at 8:00 p.m., the hostess will still be in the shower. Nine p.m. or better 9:30 p.m. is the culturally appropriate time to show up for an 8:00 p.m. party.

Second, Panamanians like to please. It's a way of life, an expression of good manners, and so they tell you what they think you want to hear, which is not always what you need to hear. North Americans just want to hear it the way it is, straightforward and direct. Given my cultural mindset, it's easy to conclude that people are lying to me because they are not telling me what I consider to be "the truth," when in the reality of their culture they are just being polite.

When I asked some other expats to read and proof this book before publication, one gal who has lived her longer than I have, added at this point, "In my humble opinion many Panamanians are passive-aggressive. They smile and say yes, but they are thinking 'no'. Service people and contractors keep you on the hook, promising they will finish a job when they have no intention of finishing it. They ARE lying to you. I am not as charitable in accepting this as you are. I just stop dealing with the ones who do this."

That may be more of an indictment of service people and contractors in general, more than it is of Panamanians. But, it does express the frustration of living where the culture is different. The differences can be both a bane and a blessing.

Living abroad gives you the exciting opportunity to experience a totally new world, usually including a new culture, a different language, and different ways of doing things: new foods, new friends, and new experiences. The reward is to embrace the differences and learn from them. You may think that your particular "American way" is better, but you may just discover that others sometimes know more and have better ways than what you'd assumed was the "best" way.

Return with me, if you will, to the dugout canoe, cruising up the river to visit my Embera friends. Understand that this was a surprise visit. They didn't know I was coming. Erito's wife had no idea he was bringing home a *gringo* for dinner and to spend the night. As far as I was concerned, I was just visiting a friend.

Naturally the village, which consists of around 10 family groups, about 20 individual families, and around 125 people, found this visit interesting.

It turns out that Erito was kind of the mayor of the village. Erito's wife, the village preschool teacher, is very protective of traditional Embera culture. Still nursing her baby, she was obviously embarrassed to be found by this *gringo* wearing a bra. She quickly slipped out of the bra to be culturally appropriately dressed for guests. She graciously whipped up a delicious dinner of fried, freshly speared tilapia right out of the river, plantains, fry bread, and thick, sweet coffee for this surprise Anglo guest.

Embera homes are built on stilts about six feet off the ground. The floors are strips of palms, the roofs are thatched, and the sides are all open. A log with notches provides stairs to the home from the jungle floor. After dinner we settled down. Erito, his wife, and two children were on one mat and I was on the other. Fires flickered from other homes in the village. And we talked. Talking was interesting because I knew only "*un pocito*" Spanish. Until the United States turnover of the Canal, the U. S. Army Jungle Survival School had hired Embera to teach astronauts and pilots jungle survival. Several of Erito's people had worked for the US Army so he knew a few English words. Somehow, as we had when I first met

Erito, we managed to talk into the night for hours. We discussed 9/11 and its impact on the United States and the world. We discussed Christianity. A movie company had filmed a movie about Nate Saint and missionaries who had been killed in the fifties by Indians in Ecuador, with the Embera playing the part of the Ecuadorian Indians.[22] We talked Southern California freeways. The concept of twelve and fourteen-lane highways was mind-boggling sitting in the jungle, listening to tree frogs, and the village disc jockey providing entertainment. At about 9:00 p.m. the genre of the music changed to North American love songs, presumably to encourage tribal expansion.

By midnight the entire village was asleep ... everyone but me. And the music was still playing. I was wrapped up in a sheet I had borrowed from the hotel to keep centipedes from crawling up my arms. About 4:00 a.m. the damn music stopped and I thought, "Finally! I can get some sleep!" And at 4:30 a.m. the roosters started crowing!

In addition to acting as mayor, Erito is also the village doctor. We discussed the whole range of illnesses and treatments. The Embera have plants for diarrhea, arthritis, heart problems, rashes, depression, even plants for venomous snake bites.

Have sexual problems? There are plants that act as aphrodisiacs. Cheaper than Viagra.

Childbirth: "Well, there are women who understand that kind of thing." If the child is breeched? "We take them down river to a town with road access and then get a cab or ambulance to the hospital."

Broken leg? It is set, bound with plants and sticks and allowed to heal. Someone slices their arm with a machete? A plant helps stop the bleeding, the comb of a rooster is cut off and placed in the gaping wound, sutures are provided by a bug that has a jaw that clamps shut like a surgical clip, and the entire thing is bound up tightly with plants. The next day Erito showed me some of his handiwork. An ER doctor with the finest stitching technique couldn't have produced a less obvious scar.

Erito's treatment: First, Erito talks about the problem with the person. A lot of illnesses are "spiritual": a person is out-of-sorts with their spouse, or someone else in the village, and the physical symptoms are just manifestations of another kind of problem. The next step in the line of treatment are various plants for various illnesses topically applied. Then come teas and brews made from local plants. If none of these treatments work, Erito has no problem transporting the person to the hospital in Panama City. There is no anti-medical attitude. It's just that it is cheaper, and often more efficient to use the remedies God has provided in the jungle.

The next day Erito and his grandfather, the senior medicine man, took me on a hike through the jungle, stopping to point out various plants and explain their use in treatment. Not surprisingly representatives of major drug companies have made this same trek.

I have a lecture I do on ships about the importance of rainforests. Consider ...

- The U. S. National Cancer Institute has identified 3,000 plants that are active against cancer cells and 70 percent of these plants are found in the rainforest?

- Most medicine men and shamans remaining in the rainforests today are seventy years old or more?

- When a medicine man dies without passing his arts on to the next generation, the tribe and the world lose thousands of years of irreplaceable knowledge about medicinal plants?[23]

My point here is simply that often we just assume we are the be-all and end-all and that because we're so modern, scientific and technological we know it all and that our ways are the best and the only way. Folks, it just isn't so.

There is a vast world of people, and cultures, and knowledge just waiting to be explored. If we open ourselves, drop our ethnocentricities, have a humble attitude and listen, there is much that we can learn. That's what entering into a new culture is all about. If you can buy that, you're ready to think about actually making the move. If not, you're better to stay put.

An interesting postscript to this story: After we'd moved to Panama, since I'd visited Erito in his home, I invited Erito and Zuleika to visit us in our home in Boquete. Much to my surprise they accepted and we enjoyed five days together in Boquete. They had never been across the Bridge of the Americas before or even visited Western Panama, much less Boquete. Since my Spanish is very limited, thinking and communicating in Spanish for five days left my brain feeling like mush, but we had a wonderful time. It was a thrill to show these people their country.

The first time they stayed with us, I laid out the ground rule. I said, "How we live is different. It's not better, it's just different." Erito smiled because he knew. He knew that he has a whole lot less hassle and problems with his house than I do with mine!

Erito and Zuleika and some of the other Embera have since visited us in Boquete several times. It's been fun! I served pancakes one morning and they were all eating them like *tortillas* until I explained the pancake syrup routine. Fernando complained about how cold our shower water was until I explained *both* handles. They told us how cold they were at night and we kept giving them more blankets. Finally my wife asked them to show her how they were sleeping. Then she explained you need to get *under* the blankets. Sleeping under blankets isn't necessary in the steamy Chagres jungle.

Action Items and Points to Ponder

1. Make a list of friends or acquaintances that are different than you. The difference may be lifestyle, race, economic background, culture, sexual orientation, hobbies and interests, style, generation, whatever. Make it as complete and varied as possible. Then think of the things that you like and find interesting about the differences. Finally, list the ways in which you find the differences threatening. You may want to explore this further with your friends.

2. Make a list of at least four different cultural venues in your community that you could visit as a cross-cultural experience. It may be a church that's different than yours, a NASCAR race (only if you're not a fan), a gallery exhibition opening (again, only if that's not your normal thing), a different ethic area of your city, a restaurant of an ethnic variety of food that's totally different, or hang out with your grandkids and their friends and attempt to appreciate their music or electronics knowledge.

3. OK, now that you have the list, which one ARE you going to visit THIS week?

4. Go to Barnes & Noble or your local bookseller and browse through magazines designed to appeal to a different cultural or interest group than your own.

5. If you have tucked away a language course you've never used, or a Berlitz survival language handbook, or an old college language text, regardless of the language, pick it up and leaf through it. You may be surprised how much you remember. If you really wanted to communicate, and didn't give a rip what anyone thought, this language stuff might be easier than you think. The next time you see a Spanish-speaking person try a few simple greetings in Spanish. Communication as a for-credit course is a bore, but when seen as a game it becomes challenging and fun.

8. How Stable Is It?

*L*et's face it, before you go running off to live in another country, you need to know something about the history and the stability of its government.

You don't want to move to "paradise" only to find yourself in the midst of endless demonstrations, a coup d'état, or left holding a fistful of devalued money.

Panama is one of those countries which owes its very existence to the long-term U. S. world view that it has a Divine mandate, although the "Divine" is more and more tucked in the closet as a matter of political correctness, to manipulate the world for its own interests.

Although archeological evidence shows that people have been living in Panama for at least 11,000 years, the current Panamanian history begins in the nineteenth century when Panama gained independence from Spain. All across Latin America under the brilliant leadership of Simon Bolivar, the Great Liberator, Spanish colonies were fighting for independence. The move toward independence was brewing in Panama as well.

Fearing Spanish troops from Puerto Rico would be shipped in to quell their rebellion, and admiring Bolivar, Panama became part of Simon Bolivar's vision for a union of Latin American nations called Gran Colombia. Unfortunately Gran Colombia dissolved in power struggles and Panama found itself as a "department" of Colombia.

By the turn of the century Panama was more than ready to be done with Colombia. By 1889 the French attempt at a canal had failed, but the United States was very interested in the canal concept and sought to buy out the French franchise through a treaty with Colombia. Colombia said, "No way, Jose!" So the United States encouraged the existing anti-Colombian sentiment in Panama and supported the declaration of Panamanian independence issued by a revolutionary junta in 1903.

Conveniently the United States immediately recognized the status of the Republic of Panama, and when Colombia sent troops to quell the rebellion, the United States just happened to have warships sitting off Panama to repel the Colombians.

Fifteen days later the United States negotiated a treaty with the Frenchman Philippe Bunau-Varilla giving it "sovereign rights in perpetuity over the Canal Zone" and broad rights of intervention into the affairs of the newly created Republic. No Panamanian ever signed the treaty and it was ratified despite Panamanian complaints.

The Canal was built by the United States and opened in 1914. If you are interested in the Canal, or ever contemplating a cruise through the Panama Canal, be sure to get my book, *Panama Canal Day: An Illustrated Guide to Cruising The Panama Canal.*

Lest those of us accustomed to U. S. manipulation of international affairs just assume Panama was solely created at the convenience of Washington, R. M. Koster and Guillermo Sanchez point out, "Panama was always a separate national entity [and] was never organically integrated into Colombia. The chief reason was that Panama achieved independence from Spain on her own. The authors of this independence, perhaps frightened by their own audacity, then began to fear a Spanish re-conquest of the Isthmus ... Panama was both small and thinly populated, with no troops and few weapons. That is when the idea came up for Panama to join with a larger nation ... [Colombia] then governed by Simon Bolívar in a confederation called Gran Colombia. Bolivar was almost a mythological figure, almost a divinity. His prestige drew

Panama into a union with Colombia. In no one's mind in Panama, however, was this union intended to be permanent. When the danger of Spanish re-conquest was over, Panama would return to independence."[24]

"By the time Bunau-Varilla, Cromwell, and Teddy Roosevelt came on the scene, a revolutionary conspiracy was already in progress. But those directing it were realists. They knew Panama's weakness and the strength of Colombia's veteran army. They seized the moment when a coincidence of interests presented the best chance for independence. Here it is that Panama's national aspirations became bound up with the irresistible expansionism of the United States, the political ambitions of Theodore Roosevelt, and the turbulent intriguing of Bunau-Varilla.

"But the principal separatist impulse came from within Panama ... [Other countries achieved their independence with help from other nations] and Panama's founding fathers were no less brave, generous, far-seeing, or fallible than those of any other country."[25]

Colombia did not recognize the Republic of Panama until 1921 when the United States paid Colombia $21 million in "compensation" to buy a kind of Colombian recognition of legitimacy for Panama. The United States would continue to intervene in Panama's political affairs until 1936 when the United States agreed to limit the use of its troops to the Canal Zone and the annual rent on the Canal was increased.

The absence of U. S. troops led to an increasing role for the Panamanian military. Some three decades later, by 1968 the Guardia Nacional had become powerful enough to depose the elected president and take control of the country. The Guardia's General Omar Torrijos emerged as the new leader and military strongman. Torrijos undertook a program of land reform and public works and modernized Panama City, while incurring a huge debt.

It was Torrijos, much to the delight of Panamanians, who negotiated the 1977 Canal Treaty, signed by Jimmy Carter, that would eventually turn the Canal over to Panama at the end of 1999.

The CIA was concerned over the role General Torrijos was playing in Latin America. Torrijos, although not the feared Communist and socialist reformer Fidel Castro, was seeking similar populist reforms in Panama and Latin America. Torrijos' image and friendliness with Cuba and Castro was cause for concern, so the CIA nurtured a CIA operative already on the payroll and inside the Torrijos government. His name was Manuel Noriega.

Noriega, a member of Torrijos' party, became head of the secret police. When the enormously popular Omar Torrijos was killed in a plane crash in 1981, Noriega leveraged his position to down all opposition and take control.

The cause of the crash that killed Torrijos was never determined, although conspiracy theories involving Noriega and/or the CIA abound. Most likely the plane crash was caused by the violent weather that frequently builds up in the mountains of Panama.

Panamanians don't like to talk much about "the dictatorship" just like most Americans from the United States don't like to talk about Spiro Agnew, the Nixon presidency and Watergate or the McCarthy era witch hunts. The dictatorship in Panama was a dark period when anyone who criticized Noriega was likely to be beaten or disappear. His thugs, ironically called the "Dignity Battalion" had free reign. Many families who could afford it sent their sons and daughters abroad to study and/or work.

Relations between Noriega and his former CIA spy-masters went from bad to worse. Noriega murdered opponents, rigged elections, and committed the cardinal sin of disrupting the States ill-advised and long-failed "War on Drugs" by becoming involved with drug trafficking. Never mind that the CIA was running its own dirty drug trafficking operations.

Noriega raped and pillaged Panama economically and in the process shipped millions of dollars to his accounts in Europe. Feeling invincible, the dictator taunted his former CIA spy master, now U. S. President, George H. W. Bush.

Bush, when running for President, attempted to pass off his relationship with Noriega claiming the last seven U. S. administrations had paid Noriega. Retired Navy Admiral Stansfield Turner, who took over the CIA from George Bush in 1977, said, "Bush is in the government during the Ford administration and Noriega is on the payroll. Bush is out of the government during the Carter years and Noriega is off the CIA payroll. Bush comes back and so does Noriega. Those are the facts, and you have to figure out for yourself what they mean."[26]

The United States instituted sanctions against Panama which, along with Noriega's greed and corruption, left Panama in economic shambles.

The United States had agreed in the Torrijos-Carter Treaties to turn over the Canal to Panama just before the Millennium. Factions in the United States, including Bush's Texas Republican Party, were urging the United States to abrogate the Torrijos-Carter Treaties. Panamanians were ready for change and fully expected that eventually the United States would negotiate Noriega's early retirement, but also feared the United States would renege on the Canal turnover. There were huge vested interests in maintaining U. S. control over the Canal and the Canal Zone. While most U. S. citizens assumed things were well in Panama and the Canal Zone, relations were increasingly strained. Things exploded when an unarmed U. S. Marine in civilian clothes was killed by Panamanian soldiers after running a roadblock checkpoint outside the Canal Zone.

Instead of the negotiation Panamanians expected, the United States launched a massive invasion of Panama in an operation ironically named "Just Cause." A few days before Christmas 1989, the tiny Isthmus of Panama was invaded by 26,000 U. S. troops attacking with tanks and sophisticated aircraft so secret that it had never been used before. At least six times as many civilians as Panamanian military personnel died in the U. S. invasion, according to Physicians for Human Rights.

The exact numbers are still being argued, but Physicians for Human Rights estimated 300 civilians and 50 military personnel were killed, another 3,000 injured and 15,000 left homeless. It is said that in this nation of 3.7 million people, where most people are related, almost everyone has a family member or knows someone who was killed or injured by the U. S. invasion. Most Americans from the United States like to think that Panama, like the rest of the countries the United States invades, should be grateful for the intervention. Although most Panamanians ape North American styles and trends and genuinely like North Americans, and although they were happy to be rid of Noriega, the violence with which it was accomplished remains a sore spot.

Many Panamanians lost everything as a result of the invasion. After the invasion Panama was in chaos; incredibly the United States had no plan. The old police force was in hiding and so there was no law. People's homes were bombed out and they had no shelter, food, or water. The United States had "liberated" Panama only to bring incredible hardship, chaos, and anarchy in the streets. There was wide-spread looting. Many small businesses were destroyed. Larger businesses, unable to collect accounts payable, went bankrupt. (Incredibly the United States showed the same lack of foresight and planning when it invaded Iraq.)

For twenty years Noriega languished in prison in Miami. After a lengthy legal fight, in April 2010 Noriega was extradited to France. TV cameras caught glimpses of a frail, old man being escorted onto an Air France jet. While in the U. S. Federal Prison, because he was considered a war criminal, Noriega continued in prison to be addressed as "general" even though Panama no longer had a military. He was given all the prison perks of a POW general including general's uniforms, private quarters, exercise machines, the works. When he went to prison in France he was treated as just another criminal without the perks or rank of a make-believe "general."

In December 2011 Noriega was extradited from France to Panama and currently resides in El Renacer Prison (*renacer* interestingly meaning "rebirth") which is located right beside the Panama Canal just south of where the Chagres River flows into the Canal. It is a simple, nondescript Panamanian prison and Noriega has a simple cell with some accommodation made due to his poor health and to protect his security. Some of his friends and family would like to see him under house arrest due to his age and infirmity, but that is unlikely since he faces additional very serious charges and sentences already handed down for multiple murders, kidnapping, and corruption. Sometimes, for whatever reason, I've noticed the pilot on a cruise ship transiting the Canal, will order the ship's horn to be sounded as we sail by the prison. In 2015 Noriega made an apology in a TV interview which may have been genuine or just an attempt to secure house arrest instead of prison.

Panama has now successfully elected five Presidents since Noriega and the U. S. invasion, changing parties with each election, possibly as a result of their fear of another Noriega taking over too much control. Two former Panamanian Presidents were educated in the States. Martin Torrijos, the illegitimate son of former military strongman Omar Torrijos, was partially raised in the States, managed a McDonald's, and graduated from Texas A&M. Ricardo Martinelli, businessman who owns the largest chain of supermarkets in the country, a major TV station, and a host of other businesses, has a business degree from the University of Arkansas as well as an MBA from the INCAE Business School[27]. Martinelli's heavy handed, business, "get it done" style, worried some Panamanians, but no one can deny that during his tenure there were major improvements throughout Panama: new hospitals, the Canal project with is still underway, new roads in Panama City and throughout the country, and a Metro for Panama City!

Panama's current President Juan Carlos Varela is a businessman as well. U. S. educated with an engineering degree from George Institute of Technology, Varela's family owns the largest distillery in Panama, and produces my favorite Abuelo dark rum. Varela served as Martinelli's Vice President in an alliance government that fell apart and went on to oppose Martinelli's hand-picked candidate and won a surprising victory.

All of the Presidents of the Republic who've been in office while we've been in Panama -- Mireya Moscoso, Martin Torrijos, and Ricardo Martinelli – have promised to end corruption, but the opposition parties all claim they acted differently. When Martinelli took office he famously declared, "In my administration you can put your foot in your mouth, but not your hand in the till." Opposing parties claim that what Martinelli meant to say, was … "only I can put my hand in the till." Maybe that's just the way things are in Panama.

Martinelli's last Presidential act was to issue immunity and pardon to himself and his cronies before fleeing the country on this private jet. The current president, Varela, seems intent on rooting out what may be bill billions of dollars of corruption and ill-gotten wealth taken by the previous administration. Almost everyone who had any fiscal responsibility seems to be under investigation and the corruption apparently extended into the judiciary. Two members of Panama's Supreme Court are now sitting in jail. Varela has promised that by the end of 2015 the investigations will be over and the country will once again focus on moving forward. And what happens when the next party comes to power after Varela? Anybody's guess!

Democracy is not easy, nor is transparency and Panama struggles along, but because it is such a small country it may be easier to root out corruption than in a country like the U. S.

In Panama, largely as a result of the "dictatorship," the President is not eligible for immediate reelection. Without an entrenched civil service, when a new party comes to power it pretty much cleans house across the country replacing government employees with their political supporters. A friend in Immigration told me after an election when a different party came to power, "Of course I'll be looking for a job. The only person who may not lose his job is the janitor."

Safety and efficiency have improved in the operation of the Canal and it is making more money even as the world financial woes have caused the number of transits to decrease and the new locks that will handle more and larger vessels go into operation in 2016.

As a result of the lessons learned in "the dictatorship," Panama, like Costa Rica, has abolished the military. Of course Panama can afford not to have an army since according to the Torrijos-Carter Treaties, the Canal must remain open and neutral for all nations in both peacetime and wartime. While the first treaty returned the Canal and the former U. S. Canal Zone to Panama, the second treaty gave the United States the responsibility to protect the neutrality of the Canal which ipso facto means Panama can look to the United States for protection.

There are no remaining U. S. military bases in Panama although the U. S. military does quietly assist Panama with protecting borders and fighting drug traffic. Divisions of the National Police at the border look and act very much like an army, and the nautical police look and act very much like the U. S. Coast Guard. At least officially, they are not "military," but part of the National Police.

The relationship between Panama and the United States strikes me somewhat as the relationship between an older and younger brother. The younger brother obviously wants to strike out on his own and not be ordered about, but if you get in a jam, it's nice to know you have back up from your older brother. This gives Panama a stability that goes beyond its borders and own political system.

A word about red tape: Panama has no more red tape than the States, and maybe less. Government workers and bureaucracies are pretty much the same the world over except Panama uses a lot more rubber stamps. Everything with the government takes time, exacerbated when there is a change of political parties.

Action Items and Points to Ponder

1. What DO you know about the history and political stability of the new places you are considering?

2. What SHOULD you know about the history and political stability of the new places you are considering?

9. Getting Off the Hamster Wheel

$\mathcal{N}$ot only had I never planned to retire, I'd never even thought of retiring early.

Retirement means different things to different people. For me it has never meant sitting in a rocking chair. Forget shuffle board. Retirement to me never meant not working.

I guess for me retirement means not *having* to work.

Retirement means not being locked in or tied down and having the freedom to do what you want, when you want.

When I sold real estate in Ventura I sold a lot of "coaches" – never call them "mobile homes" – and "manufactured homes" in "senior parks" or, as the boomers preferred, "over 55 parks." I noticed an interesting phenomenon. The people who left the "55 parks," were mostly in their 80s. As one elderly lady told me in Lemonwood Senior Park, "This is God's waiting room." People left either to be cared for by children, to move to an assisted living center, or by hearse. So I was selling homes owned by older people, complete with sculptured shag carpeting, and tangerine and avocado kitchens. A lot of young people I knew in their 20s would have killed for this retro look.

The people who were buying in the "over 55 parks" were for the most part younger people, who were just counting the days until they turned 55 and could get in. They'd buy the older units and renovate them or pull them out and put in a modern, manufactured home.

These younger newcomers weren't interested in the indoor shuffleboard courts. They were making the move because they could "cash out" of their traditional homes, buy something for cash, and ditch the mortgage. The parks and "coaches" had virtually no maintenance. In an adult community they didn't have the noise and hassle of kids, skateboards, teenagers, and cars with cacophonous boom boxes. They could invest some of their equity for retirement income, and the remainder went into the home and travel. Most of the parks had parking areas where they could keep their mobile homes and when they went on the road or traveled abroad, there was high security primarily provided by lots of close, and even nosy, neighbors.

Interestingly, when we made the decision to move to Panama, the cost of a new manufactured home in Lemonwood Senior Park in Ventura was just about the same as the cost of a new 279 square meter [3,000 square foot] home overlooking a golf course in Boquete, Panama! Plus the monthly "space rent" in Lemonwood was over $650 a month, forever! The homeowner dues in Valle Escondido were less than $100 per month, including water. I now know making that comparison is the reason why I paid too much for our first home in Panama.

I loved life in Ventura. It was the stuff of dreams and movies. We lived on the hillside overlooking Ventura, the Marina and the beach. I could watch the sun rise over the Santa Monica Mountains and see the ocean waves breaking onto the beach. Had I been a surfer, I would have immediately known if the surf was up. It was ten minutes drive down the hill to a beautiful beach. I could walk down the hill to the old downtown of Ventura, filled with trendy restaurants, a movie theater and two live venues, antique shops, and tons of funky, trending upscale charm. It was Santa Barbara without the tourists, with better beaches, fewer transients, and without the attitude.

Our home was perfect for the two of us. We bought it from the old man who had built it in the fifties and it still had sculptured shag carpeting over virgin hardwood floors. The house had minus seventy curb appeal when we bought it, but it had a killer view. We had a pool, huge avocado trees (I do miss the endless supply of guacamole!), orange, lemon, peach, and apple trees. We had great neighbors. I could sit in my spa and during the day see the famed arch on Anacapa Island, and at night see the lighthouse light. We had tons of birds, could hear the foghorn at the harbor, and even on rare occasions the sounds of seals barking out in the ocean. Selling real estate was a job I enjoyed and I was good at it.

Life was good! Who would want to give this up?

But life was also very expensive.

Increasingly I felt like a hamster running on the cage wheel, constantly running, and getting nowhere!

Following 9/11, life in the States seemed to be getting increasingly oppressive, not necessarily from the threat of terrorism, but from the talk of terrorism which seemed not only good politics for a President seeking reelection, but providing opportunity for more and more governmental intrusion and the chipping away of rights which, once lost, would never be regained. All this was cleverly wrapped up in slogans like the "War on Terrorism," protecting "The Homeland," and the "Patriot Act."

I'm not sure the traffic became worse, but I became increasingly frustrated by the hassle and waste of time sitting on the Freeway at a dead stop.

I was also getting increasingly fed up with gang culture in the Oxnard/Ventura area, the crime and the drugs that lurked beneath the tinsel-town-like, Santa-Barbara-wantabe surface. I was tired of kids shooting kids, and cops shooting kids. I was tired of excessive and oppressive policing, the injustice of the so-called "justice system," the hypocrisy of the "War on Drugs," and the California prison industry.

You say, "Gee, what do you want? You bitch about the gangs and crime, and then about cops, the justice system and prisons. Why do you think we have cops, the justice system and prisons? It's to deal with the gangs and crime, stupid."

Unfortunately that's what a lot of people think in North America. The truth is it's the same problem: the drug lords, the gangs, the justice system and the prisons are all sucking at the same teat. All of these institutions have a common interest, keeping the "War on Drugs" going so they can reap the huge profits and keep their jobs.

As long as the citizens live in fear of the drug lords, and the cops, keep telling kids to "Just Say 'No'" while "Just Saying 'Yes'" to every request for more police, more courts, more prisons, the system can continue. Using drugs is stupid: you can kill yourself and others using drugs. Abusing alcohol is very legal, and very chic AND you can kill yourself and others abusing alcohol. Smoking cigarettes is not only legal, it is also subsidized by the taxpayer AND you can kill yourself and others smoking cigarettes.

Dah! But I realize most of the country doesn't get it.

When I was an associate pastor in Westlake Village and the senior pastor was away, I received a prayer request dropped in the offering plate: "Please pray for our son, Brandon Hein, who is facing life in prison without possibility of parole for a crime he didn't commit." In a nutshell Brandon, just eighteen at the time, was with a group of five other boys who went to buy marijuana from a boy who sold it out of his backyard "fort" in Agoura Hills, California. A fight broke out with the boy who was selling drugs, his friend and so-called "bodyguard," and one of the boys who went to buy marijuana. Fists flew. When it was over one of the boys with whom Brandon went to the "fort" had stabbed the drug dealer and his "bodyguard" friend. One of the stab wounds to the "bodyguard" friend went directly to the heart and he died.

The combination of teenage testosterone, alcohol, drugs,

bravado and stupidity is not unusual, but on this day it ended tragically for everyone involved. The boy who died also happened to be the son of an LAPD officer. Although the boy who actually did the stabbing confessed, under California's felony murder rule[28] all of the boys were charged with felony murder and received sentences of life without possibility of parole, including Brandon, whose only "crime" aside from using alcohol and buying pot was to be at the wrong place at the wrong time.

That prayer request came over 20 years ago, while Brandon was still at LA Central Jail, not yet "State Property #K24820." When no one else could get a face-to-face visit, I went to see him, exercising my clergy privileges. Because he was "LWOP" (life without possibility of parole) and a "high power" prisoner (i.e. convicted of murder) he was brought in chains and shackles, and shackled to the floor and table. Brandon has always looked younger than his years, and that day he looked all of sixteen. At first I was skeptical, but the more I studied the case, the more I became absolutely convinced that this is one of the worst miscarriages of justice in United States history and an embarrassment and affront to all the honest, law-abiding Californians who believe in justice.

It has been over *20 years* and Brandon still sits in prison.[29] The case has made its way through the appeals process without remedy. Former California Governor Arnold Schwarzenegger did see fit to take the first step toward justice and remove the "without possibility of parole" from the sentence, but in the end pardoned the son of a political crony, a guy who really did kill somebody.

Hopefully the present Governor will have the moral courage to right this wrong and give Brandon a complete pardon.

No one has ever said that Brandon killed anyone, that he had a knife, or that he knew anybody had a knife, or even knew that anyone had been stabbed until after the fact. Yet he remains in prison. There have been articles in newspapers, magazines like *Rolling Stone*, segments on *"60 Minutes II,"* two documentaries, even a play by Charles Grodin. His case is known and provoked outrage around the world, yet Brandon still sits in prison.

While we lived in California, I visited with Brandon through his many senseless moves from one maximum security prison to another. All looked like you worst nightmare and were located in depressing California towns where the prison was the main industry. I am amazed at Brandon's maturity, his ability to adapt and survive, and his enduring belief that somehow, someway God has a purpose for all of this hell. He can sit calmly and talk with other Level IV prisoners, many of whom really have done some very bad things, or he can sit down for a *"60 Minutes II"* interview with Dan Rather, equally poised and calm. He is also a fantastic artist with some of his best artwork being on the only canvas he had available, his body. One day, if this nightmare ever ends, we have promised to relax on the beach in Panama.

More than anything else, Brandon's case[30] has caused me to question the fundamental principles of liberty and justice upon which we claim the United States is founded.

My great, great, way-back-great grandfather came to America from Bavaria on a ship called the MINERVA, landing in Philadelphia in 1767. He married the girl he had fallen in love with on the crossing and they settled in Pennsylvania on the banks of the Conococheague River. When the Revolutionary War broke out he joined the Lancaster County Militia and became known as the "Drummer Boy of the Conococheague."

I have no doubt about the principles of liberty and justice upon which the United States was founded. I just question the ways in which those principles are or are not being applied. I confess, I had similar questions in the South Bronx in the late sixties. I didn't drop out then, but, damn it, I'm dropping out now.

I haven't "left" the United States, it has left me.

Except for a brief stint as an Independent in New York, which allowed such a thing, I was always a Republican. My maternal grandmother was a big shot in the local Republican party and very proud of her collection of elephants. On my paternal grandmother's side, President Herbert Hoover is a distant relative. I even liked Reagan, although his economic theories have come home to roost with a vengeance. During the Bush era I was appalled at the ways in which Republican principles were twisted and the government was allowed to intrude more and more in individual lives and freedoms. I will always remain a United States citizen and I'll keep voting, irrationally dreaming that my one vote counts, but until the country recaptures its vision and renews its commitment to the freedoms and principles that made it great I will happily spend much of my time outside the U. S., thinking of myself more as a citizen of the world.

9/11 forever changed both the United States and the world.

It is ironic that the terrorists, by creating a climate in which liberties are gradually being chipped away by something ironically called "The Patriot Act," have achieved something more devastating to the United States than the terrorists could ever have dreamed.

The result of 9/11 has been the U. S. government taking away basic freedoms and liberties of U. S. citizens, destroying key elements and freedoms of U. S. American life. Ironically it doesn't make any difference whether it is a Republican or a Democrat in office. The U. S. government monitors your movements, your money, your telephone conversations and Internet use, has armies of folks standing by to keep you in line (and not just at the airports), and the unmanned drones it sends to other countries to kill suspected terrorists, are also watching you. All this in what at one time was the "home of the brave and the land of the free." We have become a nation living in fear, being convinced that we need to give up freedom to continue to be free. It is fear that breeds dictatorships and a climate that passively accepts the erosion of liberty. FDR was spot on when he said, "The only thing we have to fear is fear itself."

The borders are being squeezed closed and it's only a matter of time until U. S. citizens are required to carry national identity cards, something most of the world already requires, but that, until now, most U. S. citizens have not been required to carry. No longer can a U. S. citizen move freely between our closest neighbors, Canada and Mexico. In the climate of fear created post 9/11, it is just another step to close down the borders to *outgoing* as well as incoming traffic. In other words, you will need to ask your government for permission to leave the United States. Already Uncle Sam says, "We know that you think it's your money and while we know that you earned it and paid taxes on it, we don't think you should be able to take all of it out of the country."

You say, "But it's my money!"

Uncle Sam says, "Correction, pilgrim, it's *our* money."

Not surprisingly more U. S. Americans than ever before are "escaping" while the borders remain open.

All of these factors began to coalesce, and I began to think, "Now is the time for a change." Both my wife and I were still in relatively good health, so why push it? Why not relax and enjoy life without the unnecessary pressure? It's not about how much you make, it's about how much you keep.

We knew we'd make much less in retirement, but in Panama at the end of the day we'd end up keeping just as much, and with a better lifestyle. The little benefit advantage I would gain by working until "full retirement age," which for me was sixty-five years and ten months, would be more than offset by being able to enjoy life together and preserving our health.

Panama was ripe for investment and we were still young enough, adventurous enough, and flexible enough to opt for a new challenge.

Before moving to Panama in 2004 I looked into my crystal ball. As a Realtor I saw what was going on, and while I loved writing offers on the hood of my car, I realized that there comes a time when you need to cash in your chips and get out of the casino. I saw the United States lurching away from traditional freedoms and foresaw the time when U. S. citizens would no longer allowed to freely leave the country, taking with them their possessions and money.

At least for the moment, although you can no longer take *all* your assets ... the money you earned, that you saved, and that you already paid taxes on ... with you, you can still physically leave the United States.

Interestingly, more and more U. S. citizens are looking to relocate abroad and for the first time people are openly discussing the option of relinquishing their citizenship. Personally, I'm not ready for such a drastic step, hoping, maybe against hope that the country eventually will get back on track. And I'm pragmatic enough to know that a U. S. Passport is still the most convenient passport for international travel. Significantly though, traffic is spiking to web pages with information about giving up U. S. citizenship, or, getting second and third passports. If that sounds tempting, before you give up a U. S. passport, I'd take a good, long and hard look at those passports and how readily they are accepted as you travel around the world.

It is perfectly legal for U. S. citizens to have dual citizenship and passports, but you need to be aware of the responsibilities and liabilities to *both* countries you are taking on with dual citizenship.

We've talked about obtaining a *Pensionado* visa for Panama, but there are also other visa options available to citizens of countries friendly to Panama and a few of these visas do offer the option of Panamanian citizenship. Additionally if you have lived in Panama for five years you can now apply for citizenship. I'll talk more about this in the chapter on "Legalities."

Lecturing on cruise ships I travel a lot and frequently need to depart, arrive or connect through the States. Returning to the United States after being away for a while is a strange and scary experience.

Compared to entering Panama, or most nations in the world, returning to the United States is like returning to a police state. You have to run a gauntlet of frequently rude uniformed officers and authorities to get in and out of the country. Coming back I almost had to take off my pants to get through security because the zipper on my fly was setting off the security scanner. How many men do you think have zippers on their pants? And how many airlines are hijacked by the zippers on men's pants? It has gotten ridiculous. And is the country any safer? Do you really feel any safer?

Unfortunately, the terrorists have already won.

With the help of our government we've created a climate of fear in which Americans in the United States are standing by watching rights which have endured over two hundred years being steadily whittled away. Yes, unemployment and under-employment are huge problems in the States, and I suppose TSA is keeping a lot of marginal workers off unemployment and welfare, so maybe this really has nothing to do with security. Who knows? But I'm always glad to escape back to Panama.

And let me say that I am NOT "anti-American!" I am SAR-certifiable[31] since my family has been in the United States since *before* the American Revolution. But I am fed up and I see nothing wrong with people who aren't commentators or talking heads on FOX or CNN also being concerned and critical about the way the country is heading. We do still have the freedom to think and speak – at least for the moment.

An interesting postscript to life in Boquete: when we moved to Panama many of the folks from the U. S. choosing to relocate, were coming in part because they were unhappy with the direction the country was taking under Bush-Cheney. Many of the folks now coming down are unhappy with the direction the United States is taking under Obama. I know it may be heresy to say, but maybe it is the *same* direction under *both* parties. Whatever the current political divide in the country you hail from, hopefully we can all get together in Panama, forget the politics from back home, drink Panama rum, celebrate our life in Paradise and sing "*kum ba ya*" together.

Action Items and Points to Ponder

1. What are your personal arguments for doing it NOW as opposed to later?

2. What are your personal arguments for waiting?

3. What are your own thoughts about the direction your country is taking and how much does this influence your interest in becoming an expat?

10. To Your Health

When folks ask about our life in Panama, one of the things they most frequently inquire about is health care. Whether you are living in North America or Europe, as you get older health care is a major concern.

During the ten years we have lived in Panama, on the whole, we have experienced good health care. In our case doctors and hospitals have been far less expensive than in the States, but drugs have been more expensive. There have been noticeable changes in health care in Panama, some good and some unfortunate, but, of course, that same assessment could be made about health care in many countries, including the United States.

Clean hands and a pure heart?

A few weeks ago I was in the women's rest room at one of two private hospitals in David, about thirty minutes from Boquete. Why the women's room? Well, I'm not sexist. In the waiting area for doctor's offices at the one hospital there are two tiny, one person restrooms, one has a female cut out on the door and the other a male cut out. The male restroom was occupied and I had to go. Frankly I don't see any difference except sometimes, although not in this instance, there will be a urinal in the men's bathroom and if there isn't a urinal the seat will probably be left up. Other than that ... I'm all for unisex bathrooms.

So inside the tiny women's bathroom on the back of the door, in Spanish, was a very detailed poster with explicit pictures, prepared by the national health department, and showing the universally recommended hand washing method designed to stop the transmission of norovirus. Wash thoroughly with soap and water, dry, then use paper towel to exit using the towel to avoid picking up germs from the door handle. Fair enough, except there was no soap or paper towels and not even a soap dispenser. By this time I was getting curious and the men's bathroom was free so I checked it out: no poster, no soap, no towels … and this is in the hospital!

Yesterday, this time at the other private hospital, the new bathroom in the office tower was clean, no poster, but it did have soap and towels, however the single waste basket (for used toilet tissue) was beside the toilet and there was no receptacle for paper towels near the door so you had to turn the door knob with your hand, potentially picking up the last person's illness. I explored a few more bathrooms in older areas of the hospital. They were very hit or miss with generally no soap, but with empty soap dispensers, and no towels.

None of these bathrooms had hot water. Hot water just isn't customary in much of Panama. Incredibly, in all these bathrooms there were light switches and usually signs requesting that you turn off the lights when you leave: what a fantastic way to spread norovirus!

This is Panama

OK, this is Panama! And there are often disconnects in Panama, as evidenced by the hand washing poster but no soap or paper towels. This is Panama. And that is exactly my point, it IS Panama.

So why all this time running around hospitals? My brother, who was living in one of the only two assisted living homes we could find (non-medical as we couldn't find any medical assisted living homes in Chiriqui), had been losing weight dramatically and we were running around to doctors scattered between the two hospitals getting a myriad of tests. This stretched out over months because it is difficult to get hold of doctors, tough to make an appointment if you don't speak the language, and when you do get an appointment it's not really an appointment but a day when you go and sit three or more hours hoping to see the doctor. My brother's "insurance" with the local David hospital allowed only one test per month, so with MRIs, various oscopies, ultrasounds, yada, yada, this has stretched on for four months. When we returned to the original doctor who ordered all these tests, his opinion was, "Interesting, but it doesn't show anything."

By way of comparison

My wife went back to Seattle to help out my daughter whose maternity leave had expired and needed to go back to teaching for two months, in order to remain with her job in the same school. Rather than have our new, infant grandson put in day care, Nikki went back to Seattle to help out.

Nikki, having just turned that magic age where one is eligible for Medicare in the United States, and having a history of heart disease, thought it prudent to take Part B of Medicare and sign up for an Advantage insurance supplement. She did a lot of research and ended up with a plan affiliated with Virginia Mason Medical Center in Seattle.

As a new patient they wanted to do a number of introductory examinations including, given Nikki's history, a cardiology exam. Amazingly in one week she was able to get an appointment with a cardiologist at Virginia Mason. Now in fairness, Virginia Mason happens to be one of the top hospitals in the Pacific Northwest and the Virginia Mason Heart Clinic is ranked as one of the top in the United States. At this point things started moving very rapidly. It turned out that Nikki had major blockage and needed treatment.

You're not in Panama any more

There were some major challenges and complications, but, as the Panamanians all say, *"Gracia a Dios,"* she is doing fine. But all this has demonstrated to me amazing differences between a top U. S., first-world medical center, and the hospital care available in Chiriqui.

Virginia Mason Medical Center is amazing. It is "Team Medicine" with everyone on board from the top cardiologist to the person maintaining the rest rooms. The staff is friendly, winsome, eager to help, obviously enjoying their jobs. Yes, I know it is the Pacific Northwest and there are different cultural attitudes, but ... staff are trained to make eye contact, to see people and not see through them, to greet people ... I could go on and on, but I have never experienced such a well-run organization with such well-trained people. And it is good medicine.

Everything is there: one-stop "Team Medicine." It's a big campus, but well-marked and easy to get around and if you get lost, as I did, or look lost, even a physician walking by in the hall will offer assistance, in my case actually walking me to the correct elevator. This was a physician, one who saw himself as part of the team, not just as a diagnostician or surgeon.

Nikki was allergic to aspirin and needed to be desensitized, which it turns out is a very tedious and risky process. The Allergy Clinic was two floors down. No running around town or waiting for weeks or months. Nuclear stress test? Next Monday. No problem.

And, they spoke our language, but they also have 24-hour interpretive service for non-English speaking patients, of which in Seattle there are many speaking many languages. I think we often tend to gloss over the importance of having a common language when dealing with sensitive and perhaps life-threatening medical issues. Sure it's Panama and we should speak Spanish, but if you're not fluent in Spanish just keep in mind that many of the medical folks with whom you will come into contact don't speak much, or any, English.

Yes, not all U. S. hospitals are Virginia Mason. Health care and hospital care in the United States is obscenely expensive. I agree that the system is largely broken. So everything in the United States is not necessarily "better." And things, although maybe cheaper, aren't perfect in Panama either. News flash: we don't live in a perfect world!

With eyes wide open . . .

When we promote Panama, as I do, and talk about the joys of living here, we also need to be realistic and honest. That's something I try to do and it's something that folks appreciate. It is easy to brush aside medical questions and concerns with easy answers caught up in the rosy glow of paradise. Medical care should be a concern for anyone considering moving to a foreign land and adopting an expat life style. It should be addressed with eyes wide open.

If you are going to live someplace, particularly as you get older, good medical care is important. Many Panamanian doctors are trained in the United States and many speak some English, although they may be hesitant about their English skills at first. One example: my brother's doctor is a young guy who told us on our first visit that he didn't speak English. But after listening to me murder Spanish we now communicate quite well in English with me sometimes lapsing into Spanish just for practice. Turns out he spends twelve weeks every year in Miami at a continuing education program focused on his specialty. We'd be lucky to have him as a doctor whether we were in the United States or Panama. But get him talking and he will tell you that the cutting edge research and treatment in his area of specialty is in the United States, not Panama.

There are four hospitals in David, thirty minutes drive from where we live. There are excellent, large hospitals and specialists in Panama City, about an hour's flying time from David. And Miami is just three hours flying time from Panama City. Granted medical practice in Panama is very different from the United States, but it is still cheaper in most cases than in the United States or most of the rest of the world, unless you live in a country that provides medical care.

Several of the well-known large hospitals in Panama City promote relationships with various U. S. medical institutions. Hospital Punta Pacifica has an affiliation with Johns Hopkins Medical International[32]. Paitilla Medical Center "maintains an academic agreement" with the Cleveland Clinic. Clinica

Hospital San Fernando has relationships with Tulane University, Miami Children's Hospital and the Baptist Health International Miami. Just be sure you understand what terms like "affiliation," "relationships," and "academic agreement" actually mean.

When we first visited Boquete my wife wanted to check out the doctor. So she went, without an appointment, to see a local doctor who at that time served many of the expats in Boquete. He had trained in the United States and spoke fluent English. My wife had to wait a little longer than usual because the doctor was out making a house call: our first clue as to just how different medical practice was in Panama.

He examined her and ran an EKG to check out how she was doing at the altitude in Boquete. She asked, "What happens if one of us has a heart attack?" The doctor said, "Well, you call me. I call the ambulance and ride with you to the hospital in David. We get you stabilized, and if it requires invasive surgery you'd fly to Panama City where the best cardiologist is located." He picked up his phone and said, "Let me see if I can get him on his cell." He chatted with the specialist for a while, handed the phone to Nikki and said, "Here, you talk to him." Unfortunately that doctor moved to Panama City and we've never found a doctor quite so good in Boquete, so now end up going to David.

Drugs and Pharmacies

We needed some prescriptions filled so we went to the pharmacy in town. It cost me $85 after my 20 percent *Pensionado* discount. I was grousing because if repeated regularly, this would break the budget, when my wife asked, "Well, how many prescriptions were there?" Five. "So, at home, five prescriptions with our co pay would have cost us $50. You paid $35 more for the full cost without any insurance." But overall we've found drugs to be more expensive in Panama.

Pharmacies in Panama are just retail drug outlets. Most of the people behind the counter may through the years have gained some understanding of the drugs they sell, but they are not registered pharmacists. Generally drugs don't require prescriptions: you only need to know what you need or have a box from the item, except for antibiotics and narcotic drugs which do require prescriptions.

Pills are sold ... by the pill. That's right, even 81 milligram aspirin are sold one pill at a time. That's because in a country where 75 percent of the households still have monthly incomes of $1,000 or less, people can often only afford one or two pills regardless of what the doctor prescribed.

In our experience drugs are not necessarily cheaper in Panama, even with the *Pensionado* discount. It took us a while to realize that just like in the States there are often generic versions of drugs available. But you have to ask and sometimes push for generic. Go to visit any doctor and you will end up waiting while a line of pharmaceutical sales "drug pushers" jumping the patient queue to visit with your doctor. If you have insurance in the United States that allows you to mail order a 90-day supply, you can have your drugs shipped to one of the mail forwarding companies in Miami and then shipped to Panama via an outfit like Mail Boxes Etc. The cost from Miami to Panama is about $8.50 per kilo [2.2 pounds]. It can take a few weeks but for most people this has been reliable and without customs hassles.

Medical Insurance

Medical insurance is, of course, an issue, and as might be expected the older you are the more expensive insurance becomes and the harder it is to get. The big challenge is naturally "pre-existing conditions. One local hospital provided a very attractive, rather inexpensive plan that provided partial coverage, primarily at their hospital and with their participating doctors. It didn't cover pre-existing conditions for the first two years, but it looked like a good deal and we've been enrolled for almost ten years believing that by now our pre-existing conditions would be covered. But over the years the coverage promised has been whittled away, the premium has increased, and the hospital offering the insurance has dramatically increased its charges, particularly for *gringos*. Yeah, I know ... but sometimes it just is what it is. But we thought, compared to the States, it remained a good deal. The deal must have been too good, or the actuaries didn't really consider that they were selling mostly to retired and aging folks. Now they have merged into another plan with a larger and more diverse risk pool, but without the same coverage originally promised, and it is a major hassle to get reimbursed. Of course, this kind of thing happens elsewhere as well.

There are various international companies that offer a wide variety of expat medical insurance policies, however, once you turn 70 many of these will no longer offer coverage.

When we came to Panama it was our intention to basically self-insure and use our U. S. Medicare as a fail-safe, last resort back-up plan. I didn't take the optional parts of Medicare because when I looked at the total costs of treatments in Panama and compared them to the out-of-pocket costs in the States, even with the optional Medicare coverage, it still worked out to be cheaper in Panama.

What we have noticed through the years is that the costs of medical services in Panama have been increasing, often dramatically. There are a number of reasons for this.

First the cost of everything has been increasing in Panama, just like in the States. Since Panama uses the U. S. dollar, as the dollar devalues, a dollar in Panama buys less just like in the United States. Plus, Panama imports most things besides food, so as the value of the U. S. dollar drops and the cost of oil increases, prices go up, including costs of medical supplies and equipment. And, doctors realize that with *gringos* they can charge more and, although technically illegal, they and hospitals often charge *gringos* more than Panamanians.

The cost of medical care in Panama is still less than in the United States.

What is lacking, at least in Chiriqui where we live, is emergency response. Ambulances are primarily used for transportation and we don't have an American-like 911 system or ambulances equipped with life-saving equipment and staffed by EMTs. For most of the ten years we've been here you get yourself to the hospital and good luck! There are two emergency rooms in Boquete, one in the national heath clinic designed to serve mostly the Indigenous and the Social Security clinic designed to serve workers who are covered by Social Security. Both emergency rooms are closed at night so you need to plan your emergencies accordingly. There are trade-offs living in Panama and although this is a big one, we feel that the overall quality of life and medical service in Panama offsets the lack of good emergency service.

A few years ago a company came in with a medevac helicopter that could fly, if needed, from Chiriqui to the major hospitals in Panama City. Like a lot of other expats we subscribed. The company had a new, fantastically equipped aircraft with a flying physician on board, but had problems complying with Panama's aviation requirements and closed almost before it started, but they did refund everyone's subscription fee. Remember that all-purpose phrase of explanation and acceptance, "This is Panama"?

Panama is developing a 911 response system with ambulances equipped to handle trauma, but this service is reserved for auto accidents and not general medical emergencies.

Fortunately we've had a couple, both Panamanian physicians, move to Boquete, buy and property equip an ambulance, so you can now call them and get a well-equipped ambulance staffed by two physicians. And we've developed our own system called *Alto al Crimen* ["crime stoppers"]. For a nominal fee you register, given them all of your pertinent information [disabilities, medications taken, etc.] *and* detailed directions to find your house. [In an emergency, when you need help, it's difficult to tell people how to find your home since we don't have addresses, especially if Spanish is not your native language!] Every member has a number, which is posted near the front of their property. When you need an ambulance, police, fire, whatever, you call the 24-hour Alto Crimen emergency number, give them your member number, and they contact the right service and give them directions to your home. And, here's the fantastic aspect of this service, the person who answers and dispatches help 24-hours a day is a quadriplegic who is fluent in both English and Spanish. The fees go to pay his full-time salary. Talk about a win-win solution! Part of the reward of living here is to find a need and fill it, as was the case with the folks who started Fundacion Alto al Crimen.

But it wasn't always that way ...

Mr. Toad's Wild Ride[33]

We had our own experience with an ambulance early on in Boquete. My wife, Nikki, had an allergic reaction to a medicine she had been taking and went into anaphylactic shock. She was totally unresponsive so a friend and I managed to drag her to the car and drove to the doctor's office in Boquete. The doctor was on vacation and the new medical school graduate who was covering for him put Nikki in a bed in the tiny bedroom attached to his treatment room, gave her an epinephrine shot, oxygen, started an IV, and said we needed to get her to the hospital in David. So she called the ambulance.

Now this was early on before Panama was awash in money from the Canal and a booming economy. Local governments and services had no money. If you needed the police you drove to the police station to get one or promised to pay their taxi cab fare. Fortunately at the time the one ambulance in town was actually running. With the ambulance folks on the phone, the doctor asked, "They want to know if you can pay for the gas?"

"Yes! I'll pay for the gas! Just tell them to get here!"

So the ambulance arrived. The bedroom was so tiny that there was no way to get the gurney inside so they struggled to get Nikki onto the gurney and into the ambulance. The driver and I got in the front and the other attendant in the back with Nikki. Problem number one: no way to hold the IV. So Nikki had to hold up her own IV all the way to David. Problem number two was far more serious. *Gringos* tend to be taller than a lot of locals so the back doors of the ambulance wouldn't close and Nikki's feet were hanging out.

This sounds hilarious now and is a great party story, but at the time it wasn't funny.

To keep the gurney from sliding out, with the doors flapping open, the attendant wedged himself between the inside of the ambulance with his legs pushing on the gurney to hold it in place as we went off down the hill to David.

Talk about "Mr. Toad's Wild Ride"! Our lights were flashing and the siren was going but of course nobody got out of the way on what was then a two-lane highway from Boquete to David. In Panama the more red lights that are flashing the more likely it is that it is a bus or brightly decorated truck, so nobody moves. And then it started to rain, not just gentle rain, but one of our famous tropical downpours, with back doors still flapping, and Nikki got soaked.

We made it and Nikki lived to tell her funny party story. And I gave them $30 for gas and $10 for beer.

My purpose is not to discourage anyone from the adventure of living in Panama. But it IS Panama, not the United States, Canada or Europe, and while Panama is making progress, we have a long way to go.

Part of the reward of living here is to find a need and fill it, as was the case with the folks who started Fundacion Alto al Crimen.

Don and Linda share their experience, their concern, and why the lack of emergency response in the area of Panama where they live might force them to return to the States ... "Linda and I have lived in Panama for two years. We loved Panama until a turning point came in our lives about two months ago. For three weeks in a row, we've had medical emergencies at 2:00 a.m. in the morning — twice for me and one time for Linda. I ended up with a heart stent and today, I feel better than at any time in the last ten years. I could sleep only five hours each night and that went on for over ten years. Today, I can sleep eight hours or more plus a daytime nap is always welcome.

"But for Linda, finding me on the floor with my eyes open, my mouth open but totally unresponsive, it was extremely difficult. She is now insisting on going back to the States where we can get 911 service and an ambulance ride with medical equipment and EMTs on board. It is hard to argue with her desire to return to the States.

"If we could solve the medical issues, we would remain in Panama. If we can't, it's back to the United States for us, although it has become a country of which we are no longer proud. Living where we do on the Coronado beach is like living in a state park, but we worry about the two hour trip to Panama City when we need emergency medical services. The trip would be longer if we were unfortunate enough to end up needing hospitalization during one of the many holiday week-ends when the road to Panama City is clogged with traffic. At those times, one could pass away on the Pan Am highway stuck in four lanes of traffic on a three lane highway."

But it's not just in Panama ... OldSalt1942 who frequently comments on my blogs, wrote ... "One of the problems with the health care system in the States, as I see it, is that the people have been fed the notion that somehow 'most expensive' is somehow a synonym for 'best.' Yes, it's true that the United States probably leads the world in medical innovation, but that's pretty much confined to large metropolitan areas like New York, LA and a few others.

"The reality is that if you live outside of those areas the health care services available to you aren't nearly as great as we've been led to believe. For example, let's say you've decided to take a trip to visit, say, Mt. Rushmore. You and your family have rented a car, or you're driving your RV towards the monument in rural South Dakota and your heart suddenly goes Arrrrrrrrgh! You know what? You're probably going to die right there in the country with the 'best health care in the world!' All those technological advances just aren't handy in much of our huge country."

Lisa wrote ... "Richard, I flipped an ATV in Boquete last June. I was wearing long pants and, though shaken up, didn't get to a clinic right away because the abrasion on my right quad didn't seem too serious. Two weeks later, however, I was in Bocas and my leg was very swollen and I became concerned. I went to the local hospital in Bocas and it was SCARY! It did not look like anything had been cleaned in years. Geckos roamed the walls in the treatment rooms. There was no paper on the examining table to protect me or other patients from the blood and other stuff that we might leave behind for the next patient to enjoy. Of course there was no hot water, soap, paper towels or hand dryer in the washroom. My husband said he never wanted to be an in patient there because he was convinced he would die there. However they did have shiny new flat-screen TV with excellent reception in the waiting room and the intake receptionist and nurse were glued to the *telenovela* that was playing at the time.

"To their credit, they did see me immediately. No wait, no 'who's your insurer?' and no triage. The rather bored doctor and irritated nurse told me I had an infected abscess and prescribed me medication, which I purchased in the hospital pharmacy after wandering around for about half an hour trying to find the pharmacy attendant, who was apparently on his lunch break. After I found him, he sent me back to the cashier, who was clear on the other side of the hospital, to pay for the medication first and then bring the receipt back to him. Then he dispensed the medication.

"I will say however, that the bill for the doctor's visit was only

$2. Yes, you heard right two dollars! The medication a two-week supply of antibiotics cost $8. The medication worked and my infection cleared up. The $2 charge did not include a good bedside manner from the doctor or nurse, but at this price, I wasn't expecting Marcus Welby or his Latino counterpart. I did have the free tourist insurance provided to tourists for the first thirty days supposedly good at any hospital, but this hospital claimed they weren't part of the 'network' that accepted it. But given the charge, I wasn't complaining.

"My husband did use the free tourist insurance[34] at the new San Fernando clinic in Coronado so his treatment for a rash was free, although he paid for the medication. In Coronado the doctor spoke excellent English, took his time to explain everything and was very pleasant and friendly. The clinic was spotless, too.

"When we were in Costa Rica a local explained to me that if you are an in patient at a hospital in Costa Rica, you are expected to bring your own towels, toilet paper, etc. for your use during your stay. However, in the States you may get those things but you are probably being charged $8 per roll of toilet paper and $20 for each towel you use.

"So which system is better? Lisa"

Dave in Reno wrote ... "The health care issue in Panama interests me because I have been managing a heart condition over the last eight years. Over this course of time I have done a lot of research about my specific health condition, as well as the U. S. health care industry as a whole (insurance, hospitals, and physician best practices). I've come to realize how corrupt the overall health care system is. The entire health care system appears to have modeled itself after a parasite. Most obvious is the routine hospital practice of overbilling (stealing) from patients.

"As a result of this immoral practice, and most everyone has a story about dealing with hospital bills, I am planning on taking advantage of the medical tourism industry. Why should I have to pay exorbitant bills to a hospital for routine monitoring tests (thousand of dollars) when I could get the same test in Panama at a fraction of this cost, plus be able to vacation in Panama?

"So a better strategy might be to take advantage of a medical tourism approach for low risk issues, while maintaining a connection to a reasonable hospital in the States for high risk issues."

Dave, that's exactly what we have decided. Based on my wife's experience with Virginia Mason Medical Center in Seattle and her supplemental Medicare insurance, I have decided to add Medicare Part B, pay the hefty penalty, and take out supplemental insurance similar to my wife's. We will return home to Seattle for major medical issues, but continue to be dependent on medical care in Panama for routine issues and emergency situations. In our case, since my daughter and grandchildren are in Seattle it is a logical home base for us in the United States and returning for health care is a good excuse to visit with our grandchildren.

Our plan in a medical emergency is to notify Alto Crimen, drag the other one to the car even if we have to wake up our workers and neighbors to help, and drive to the hospital in David which is now only a half an hour from our house with the new four-lane road. Thirty minutes driving to David is a sure thing, whereas waiting for an ambulance knowing that nothing happens quickly in Panama, might fritter away that "magic hour."

Is it ideal? Probably not, but it would take us almost the same amount of time to have driven down the hill from where we used to live in Ventura to the hospital and even longer to get an ambulance. We like the lifestyle in Panama and, for us at least, living in Panama is still a lot cheaper than Southern California, so we are willing to compromise on this very important detail and take some calculated risk.

Reports we get from friends as to the quality of medical care vary. We have heard some real disaster stories, but medical disasters happen everywhere. Although we'd like to think medicine is an exact science, it is not. Medical professionals are human and sometimes make mistakes. That can happen anywhere -- including Panama.

Our experience has been good. Nikki has had angioplasties and stents put in at Patilla Hospital in Panama City. Other than two nights in the hospital with cold water bed baths, no problem.

Our friend Jackie Lange of Panama Relocation Tours has had two major eye surgeries performed in Panama City. When she commented that she liked the top his assistant was wearing and hadn't seen anything like it in Boquete, her surgeon took her on a shopping tour of the best shops for women's clothing in Panama City that his wife liked, commenting, "I have the receipts to prove it."

One of the things we like about Panama is the different level of doctor patient relationships. The physician doesn't have to see ten patients an hour, nor is his medical judgment constantly being challenged by a twenty-year-old kid from the insurance company with a computer. Not every doctor will take you shopping, but ...

We have a friend, "Soup" Campbell, who lives out in the country above Volcan. Originally from the North Pole [That's right, North Pole, AK, outside of Fairbanks] Soup looks like a stereotypical Alaskan. The Campbell's came on a Panama Relocation Tour where I went along. The entire tour his wife sat in the back of the bus, arms crossed, frowning, unimpressed. When we drove into Volcan she lit up and said, "Soup, we're home!" Soup ended up having a stroke and received excellent emergency and recovery care.

Dental Care

It took me a couple of years after we came to Panama to find a really good dentist, but after a number of missteps finally found one in David. He's learned to speak enough English and his dental practice, office and equipment is more state-of-the-art than anything I experienced in the States. I have no dental insurance. The cost for a cleaning is $70. A crown is around $475. An extraction or root canal is only several hundred dollars. I've had four implants at a cost of $1,500 each. The price has increased to $1,600. I thought that was really expensive until I talked with a dentist from the Midwestern United States after a lecture on the ship. He told me that he charged $5,000 for an implant.

Medical greed?

Some stories do give us pause for concern and cause us to wonder if, as Panama moves more and more toward being a "first world" country, the medical community is getting just as greedy as elsewhere.

When we came to Panama, an emergency room visit was around $2.50 – today it's $10.50 ... and counting. Now I grant you $10.50 for an emergency room visit is still a bargain, but hospitals here are learning from the United States ... so that is now just a basic, entry fee. Then everything gets added on. And that is the price for Panamanians, not necessarily for *gringos*.

You can still get an EKG for around $20 and a cerebral MRI for about $600, but the costs of hospital stays and doctor visits are soaring. Panama uses the U. S. dollar which has become worth less and less. Oil prices have remained high and most medical equipment and supplies need to be imported. Plus Panama enjoys a booming economy. All of this is a recipe for inflation, so costs have gone up for hospitals and doctors just like every thing else.

There are a few doctors in Panama who may, like the U. S. doctors we love to stereotype, be making big bucks. However, most docs I meet who are abandoning medicine in the States to retire early to Panama are *not* making the big bucks, nor are they free to practice medicine. A Panamanian doctor leads a tough life with long days usually working a full-time job for the Panama government health system and also having a full-time private practice. The ones I see are doing well, but they don't appear to be driving the fancy cars and getting filthy rich.

But even taking inflationary pressures into account there also seems to be what appears to be a greed factor, particularly in regard to expat *gringos*. One lady encountered a doctor's receptionist honest enough to admit that there were Panamanian prices and *gringo* prices for services: illegal, but ... take the *Pensionado* discount. Ask and you will be told it is "included" or "factored in" but if you don't know what the regular fee is how would you know?

A friend checking her husband into a local hospital was told she had to make a $200 upfront deposit against hospital charges. When she pulled out her insurance card, with an insurance discount plan sponsored by the same hospital, suddenly the deposit requirement *increased* to $500. It's called "*Gringo Bingo*" and everyone plays that game.

I was scheduled to leave for a cruise contract for four months and so had a quick, regular check up. I was advised to see a cardiologist. With less than a week before I flew off to the ship, I went to see my wife's cardiologist. He wanted a stress test, an electrocardiogram and an ultrasound test. To get our local hospital insurance to pay or reimburse me I would have to get prior approval which, based on my experience, could take months. And since only one test was allowed a month ... Understanding my problem, the cardiologist said we could just forget the insurance and I could pay cash, the out-of-pocket difference to me being $50. And he kept his staff on duty to do the procedures on Saturday afternoon since I was scheduled to leave on Tuesday. Believe me ... even if you value your time at only a measly $5 an hour, I was way ahead of the game, given the time it would have taken me to jump through the insurance hoops and hope to get reimbursement.

My brother, who is my dependant, needed an endoscopy and we had it done by a good doctor whom I've used and respect. My brother had the procedure done and while he was recovering off in a corner, behind a thin curtain, a Chinese

Panamanian teenager was wheeled in for the identical same procedure by the same doctor. When I went to pay my brother's bill I asked for the *Pensionado* discount and was assured that it was "already included." However, laying right next to my brother's bill, on the counter, was the bill for the Chinese Panamanian teenager, everything identical … procedure, equipment, physician AND price … except the name, and the fact that he was Panamanian and my brother was a *gringo*, and my brother, by law, was entitled to a *Pensionado* discount. When I asked how that could be if they'd "already included" the *Pensionado* discount, the lady at the desk didn't want to discuss it. She called her supervisor who assured me that the *Pensionado* discount was already included and that what I saw, I didn't see. At the same time a security officer magically appeared.

Perhaps more disturbing is the thought that physicians may be using diagnosis to provide unnecessary services. The following stories didn't happen to me, but I know and respect the people involved who have shared these experiences. I won't name names because in Panama you run the risk of libel even if you state the truth. This is not the United States and the law is different.

Talk to enough people and you will hear stories that will make you both angry and scared. That's why you always want to talk to lots of people and get lots of opinions before you jump, particularly in regard to medical issues. Of course that's not always possible to do if there is an emergency

We have heard several accounts recently of people who have been told they needed surgery for one thing or another "immediately" and that their condition was "life-threatening" only to go to another doctor and discover that they didn't need *any* surgery.

Sam was feeling poorly, lacking energy so he went to a local doctor who ran a lot of tests including an MRI. His diagnosis was that he had a tumor on his heart, that it was life-threatening and that he needed immediate risky surgery at an estimated cost of $105,000 just for the surgeon to say nothing of hospital and recovery costs. After talking with his kids by phone he returned to the States for a second opinion at a major metropolitan medical center. There was no tumor. At best the doctor in Panama had misread the MRI. The person was fine: no surgery necessary. Of course: stuff happens. It happens in Panama as well as in the United States. No one is perfect and that includes doctors who, just like rest of us can make mistakes with life or death consequences.

Alicia, in her 50s, coming home from Costa Rica, didn't feel well and experienced chest pain. She feared she was having a heart attack so she stopped at a local hospital. They ran an EKG and said she was fine and should take aspirin. She went home and died of a massive heart attack. Now that can happen anywhere. Every time I've left a cardiologist's office or had a stress test and been told I was fine the doctor has added, "But that doesn't mean you won't go out of here and die of a heart attack." Stuff happens everywhere, including Panama.

Will needed an angioplasty and probable stent. He was told the cost of the stent was $1,500. As they were wheeling him into surgery he was told the cost of the stent was now $2,500. And when he got his bill the cost was $3,000. The surgeon was on vacation and another doc popped in to look at him on three occasions. "How are we feeling? Any pain?" These momentary visits were billed at $200 per visit! And – get this! – the hospital refused to remove the IV drip line when he was ready to leave until the bill was paid in full and the credit card approved! I know that's true because the same thing happened with my brother at the same hospital, only I was too dense to know why they were delaying taking out the IV.

A local *expat* who everyone knew had lots of money was dying. He'd put up a valiant fight, but it was his time to go. He was brain-dead but the hospital refused to allow the family to have the machines that were keeping him alive disconnected. Finally his widow put up such a fight at the indignity of not allowing her husband to die, that after a number of days the hospital finally allowed him to die. You've got to wonder about stuff like this.

And you've got to wonder about the overall quality of care. There are some excellent doctors in Panama and in Chiriqui. How do you know who they are? Ask around. Talk to a lot of people. Listen. People will tell you one-on-one what they can't in print or publicly. Ask other doctors. Sure, no doctor is going to bad mouth another, but ... as with most things in Panama where everyone is related to everyone ... watch the eyes. If the eyes go up or roll, you're being given a message regardless of the words.

Is health care in Panama cheaper than in the States? Yes, but increasingly, in my humble opinion, it is not the great bargain it was once.

Is the quality of care equal to that in the States, Canada or Europe? It depends. Depends on what you are comparing it to. It depends on the qualifications of your particular doctor ... which, by the way, is the same as in other parts of the world. And, unless you come from a country that has fantastic government health care, quality depends on what you can afford.

Unfortunately I think greed has infected some aspects of the medical system in Panama, just as it has elsewhere. Medical care in Panama is far from perfect just like it is far from perfect in the United States. My current take is that it's not a good idea to put all of your eggs in one medical basket. Miami is only three hours from Panama City. Granted it's a bit further to Seattle and Virginia Mason Medical Center, but it's still good to keep your options open.

A lady sent me a copy of a letter she sent to a local private hospital after her husband had been a patient, not that the hospital had asked or ever would ask for any feedback, but she just felt compelled to give it.

"I wanted to let you know about a couple of things that happened when my husband had his recent surgery. First, nobody came out to tell me what was going on during the surgery. A one to three hour procedure had not ended by five hours. I was frantic and nobody would help me find out what was happening. I did not know if he was dead or alive. I went to the nursing station several times from 8:30 p.m. to 10:30 p.m. and often nobody was there and the OR doors were still closed. You should not leave family members waiting unattended and uninformed.

"The second problem was after the surgery. My husband was so weak he could not stand or move on his own. The nurses did not seem to be trained to lift a patient safely from the chair to the bed. I would ask them to help me, and they just looked uncertain about what to do. On the day before he checked out, they put him in a chair and gave him a bath with cold water[35], even though hot water was available in the room. Then they left him in the chair. I had to go get them to ask them to help me put him back in the bed. When they did that, they dropped him into the bed. He was so angry about that, because it hurt him.

"The hospital does not seem to have any orderlies, strong men whose job it is to move and lift patients, from the bed to the gurney, from the bed to the chair, or wherever they need to be moved.

"Other than that, the staff was pleasant and caring, and the hospital food was tasty."

A postscript to this story: the gal's husband fell a few months later and had back pain that wouldn't go away, so they went back to the hospital and had an x-ray. The x-ray revealed that a one foot tube had accidentally been left in the patient from the earlier operation.

Our own experience with medical care in Panama has been adequate to very good.

Early on my kids were visiting us in Boquete and we had rented horses and were riding down along the Chiriqui River pretty far outside town. My son-in-law was having trouble controlling his horse so Nikki, who as a child spent summers on her grandfather's ranch in Montana riding out on roundups, changed horses with him. Unfortunately, the equipment was old and as Nikki pulled back on the reins to control this already unruly animal the bit snapped apart and she was left holding loose reins with no control. The horse bolted and in the process threw Nikki and she landed head first on the pavement.

Fortunately my daughter, Rebecca, is a "Woofer" (Wilderness Outdoor First Responder, pretty much like an EMT in wilderness settings, only a Woofer can't deliver babies but *can* pronounce people dead – not a happy thought at the time!) and automatically shifted from daughter to professional. Nikki was behind me when this happened and I could look back and see her lying still on the pavement and lots of blood. My other daughter, Noelle, said, "Dad, you're the only one who knows the way back to town. You have to leave Mom with us and go find a doctor." So I rode off not sure if Nikki was dead or alive, but I thought I saw her hand move before I left.

It was a long way back to town on a road nobody used. Fortunately one guy in a car had seen the empty horse running back toward town and knew there had to be a problem. I flagged him down, tied up my horse and jumped in his car and we drove to Dr. Leonidas Pretelt's clinic and surgery. Pretelt left his patients, we hopped into his brand new car and headed out to the accident site.

By the time we got to the accident site Nikki was conscious, stabilized and covered in blood. Pretelt loaded her into his brand new car with light grey fabric seats and we drove back to his clinic. For four hours he worked in his tiny clinic sewing up her head. Although we didn't know it, Dr. Pretelt was trained in emergency medicine and had done a residency in an ER trauma center in Miami – lots of head wounds.

He saw her weekly for 12 weeks. One day he saw her in the local supermarket and said, "Oh, Nikki, I'm so glad to see you. Are you all right! I had a dream about you last night and have been worried that something was wrong with the stitches."Prior to moving to Boquete Nikki worked for Ventura County Public Health. Every year the County shopped around for the cheapest medical plan it could find.

Before we left for Panama Nikki made a final appointment to pick up her records and the doctor who was seeing her asked, "And how are you doing with your diabetes and your diabetes medicine?"

Nikki said, "Oh, you must have the wrong chart because I don't have diabetes."

And the doctor replied, "Yes you do: you were diagnosed last year. Didn't anyone tell you?"

So much for good U. S. medical care.

So Dr. Pretelt, who still made house calls at the time, had a dream about Nikki. What doctor in the United States would even know your name, unless you had a social relationship, without first looking at your chart?

Unfortunately for us, Dr. Pretelt moved to Panama City.

By the way the total – total! – cost for emergency transportation, surgery, and twelve weeks of follow up care back then was $750. At the time we left California the ambulance ride alone would have been more than $750!

Nikki has heart disease and had a number of angioplasties and stents before we moved to Panama. Everything was fine for years, but then Nikki started to recognize familiar symptoms. We asked around, "Who's the best cardiologist in David?" Everyone agreed on a single name so we called and asked for an appointment and got one the very next evening. After all the hassles we always had in the States getting appointments with a specialist, this was amazing.

They ran tests and decided that Nikki needed an angioplasty and probably a stent. At the time local hospitals were not doing angioplasties so she was sent to Hospital Paitilla in Panama City and got the top heart guy in Panama to do her angioplasty and stent. The total cost was around $15,000 including an overnight hospital stay. Because at the time our local hospital could not do the procedure, our local hospital insurance paid half of the cost and we paid the other half.

Our total out-of-pocket was $7,500.

That was then, five years ago. Things have changed.

My brother, who lived in one of the two senior citizens' assisted living homes in the area, slipped one night, cracked his head, and needed to be taken to the hospital. There was no charge for the ambulance. He stayed in the hospital two nights. The total cost for emergency room, hospital room, and doctor was around $800. Prices had obviously gone up. The neurosurgeon who took care of him and sewed him up charged $280 and his follow up visits were $100 each, which, frankly I thought was excessive. But he did advise that my brother should discontinue taking 81 milligram aspirin, which almost every doctor prescribes for people 50 years of age and older. He claimed that combined with other common drugs it contributed to cerebral hemorrhages saying, "Half the people whose brains I operate on are taking aspirin." So we all stopped taking 81 milligram aspirin. Then a few weeks later this same doctor, who I really liked, died in his mid 50s of a massive heart attack. We all went back to our daily dose of 81 milligram aspirin.

So our personal experience with medical care in Panama hasn't been bad, but I know that it has not been the same for everyone, which is why you need to talk to a lot of expats and get a lot of opinions before making health care decisions.

Just yesterday, in the morning I talked with a lady who, largely because of a bad medical experience, was moving back to North America. In the afternoon I talked with a friend who just had her second eye operation in Panama City and was delighted with the surgeon and the outcome. So, it depends … just like it does "at home", wherever "home" is.

Action Items and Points to Ponder

1. What are your particular medical concerns?

2. What research are you doing on medical care in areas that interest you before your possible relocation? When visiting these areas are you talking to local doctors, hospitals,

pharmacies, and expats who are living there regarding their experiences?

3. What is your current medical insurance situation? What will it be when you retire? What are your pre-existing conditions that might create challenges getting insurance as an expat?

4. Are the medicines you require, or acceptable substitutes, available in Panama?

Moments before "the fall" and our own encounter with medical care in Panama.

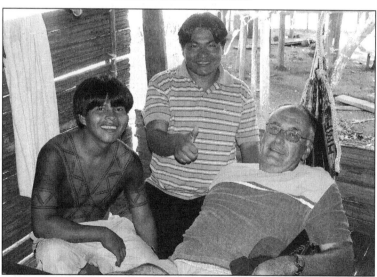

With Fernando and Erito in Fernando's home at Embera Puru village deep in the jungle of Chagres National Park.

11. Not in Kansas Anymore

One of the real problems people face is finding and buying real estate in the land they've chosen to call their new home. This is true anywhere, but particularly in Central America, and especially in Panama.

"Professional Real Estate"

The real estate market in North America, and particularly in the United States, is largely influenced by, and some would say controlled by professional real estate. Real estate in the United States is highly regulated compared to most places in the world. In California the real estate business is very regulated by the Department of Real Estate [DRE] and has a strong infrastructure of title companies, escrow services, inspection services, multiple listing services [MLS],[36] and local real estate associations.

If you want to become a real estate agent in California you first take a real estate course. This can be either in a classroom setting, online, or by home study. You then must pass a written exam administered periodically by the DRE. Then you are fingerprinted, you are checked for any police record, and given a provisional license. To get a regular license you must take additional courses. Licenses are renewed every four years and you must continue to take professional development courses mandated by the DRE. Most importantly, the DRE is always looking over your broker's shoulder, and your broker is always looking over your shoulder as an agent. Most, but not all, real estate agents in the States are Realtors and very particular about that trademark. This designation means the agent is a member of the National Association of Realtors and has subscribed to a very detailed Code of Ethics. Additionally Realtors are usually a member of their local Real Estate Board and the local Multiple Listing Service [MLS].

Once in a while a Realtor does get out of line. If it is a question of violating the Code of Ethics, usually the local Real Estate Board steps in and peer pressure alone leads to a change in behavior. If the infraction is a violation of California Real Estate Law the DRE steps in and puts the violator on probation or yanks their license. It is against the law in California to sell or represent the sale of any property other than your own if you are not licensed. This is why when you call a California broker in response to an ad in Sunday's paper, and just want a quick answer about a property, the receptionist cannot by law give you the answer, but must transfer you to a licensed real estate agent.

Professional real estate is set up with one goal in mind: to get the highest and best price for the seller. This is why the wise buyer will sign an exclusive buyer broker agreement which means that the real estate agent is working only for them, and not for the seller. All the brokers who list their properties on the MLS agree that they will share their commission with whatever broker actually brings the buyer. This gives properties the widest exposure in order to achieve the highest possible selling price in an open market. As I used to constantly tell my clients, "It doesn't make any difference whose name is on the sign. I can show you any property."

So most Americans come from a real estate environment that is:
- Highly regulated;
- Professional;
- Has a strong infrastructure of related services – finance, title, home inspection, escrow;
- Has a strong MLS system.

But come to Panama and "You're not in Kansas anymore!"

When you choose to purchase property in another country you are suddenly confronted with a real estate environment that is nothing like what you've always known.

There is little effective regulation. Panama has increasingly given lip service to regulation and does technically require real estate sales people to be licensed. Slowly, very slowly since this is Panama, things are changing, but you will still find everyone and his brother selling real estate – the dentist, the hairdresser, the taxi driver – everyone!

Even real estate companies. If a gringo wants to open a real estate office, and isn't fluent enough in Spanish to take the test for license, he just finds a Panamanian who will take the test and lend his or her name to the operation while continuing to enjoy the security and income of a "real" job.

There is almost no infrastructure of related services.

There is no MLS so every agent is only showing you properties on which he makes a commission, i.e. his listings and without an MLS there is no truly effective way to develop comparables. "Comps" show the exact price of comparable properties and when they sold.

Throw into this mix real estate laws that are very different from what you are used to, dealing with square meters and hectares instead of square feet and acres, and then add the fact that not all real estate in Panama is actually owned by title – well, you can understand why many Americans are confused and, sometimes, swindled.

When you don't know the "system" ... *Cuidado*[37]

Consider these events, all similar to actual events, any one of which would have caused the perpetrators to have, at the very least, their licenses yanked in California.

Affordable Ocean Front Lots!

The lots were small, but drop dead gorgeous. Bordered on one side by a not-bad-by-Panama standards road and sandy beaches with coconut palms on the other side, it was the stuff of dreams! With azure-blue waters and great fishing, you could pull your own boat right up on the beach and drift off to sleep with the sound of waves. And the price was fantastic!

Problem: Despite the signs, the flags, and the lot markers, the property between the road and the beach was actually owned by the Republic of Panama and by law wasn't for sale by anyone at any price.

Mountain Paradise!

"Spectacular views abound in this alpine paradise. American builder will construct your dream home for 20 percent less. Using a streamlined approach to building development, we can give you greater building quality for less money. We guarantee to have your home completed in eight months without the usual Panamanian delays. Top quality."

Problem: The builder required 80 percent of the cost of the construction up front. Although apparently well-intentioned the builder had never built in Panama before, got in over his head, and went belly up taking the dreams of several dozen unsuspecting families with him. Interestingly these people were mostly back in the States, assuming their homes were progressing as promised. They accepted at face value glowing emailed "progress reports" only to find they had nothing but cement slabs to show for the 80 percent they'd paid up front.

Caribbean Island Dreams

"Spectacular sun sets, coral reefs, turquoise-blue waters, Captain Kidd's Fancy has it all! Live on your own private island with only thirty others and enjoy your own marina and 8-hole golf course. Only ten beautiful sites remain. Hurry!"

Problem: Although the development was spectacular, and the homes already built were really nice, everyone was in for a big surprise, including Captain Kidd. The developer had purchased and sold "rights of possession" that were acquired from an American company. Unknown to the developer or the American company, a Panamanian family had acquired prior rights of possession twenty years earlier, and had maintained a tiny, rundown wooden house on one tiny point of the island where members of the family occasionally visited to relax and fish. Enter lots of lawyers, long litigation, and major uncertainty for everyone involved.

Pacific Sunsets

"Pacific island property, just meters away from a marine reserve with spectacular views, palm-fringed beaches, protected anchorage, and just off shore some of the most spectacular fishing in the Pacific; twenty hectares, $7 per square meter[38]."

Problem: The American expat knew paradise when he saw it, and began negotiations with the real estate sales person who had shown him the property. He was ready and anxious. The agent came back and said that there was a slight problem. It seemed another unknown buyer had come in at the last moment and snapped up ten of the twenty hectares and the seller had now raised the price on the remaining ten hectares to $14 per square meter. The price had doubled overnight. The prospective buyer walked away. In the meantime the seller, who knew nothing about "the last minute unknown buyer" and still had twenty hectares to sell, contacted the prospective buyer directly asking, "What happened?" When buyer and seller compared notes, it turned out that the real estate agent was carving off ten hectares for herself, as additional "commission," while the prospective buyer was to pay for the whole thing.

Understand that this does not apply to all real estate sales people in Panama.

There are real estate firms and sales people who are professional, dedicated, have great integrity, and who will bend over backwards to steer their clients through waters sometimes infested with sharks. There are Panamanian real estate firms who have been in business for many years and have a long and enviable history of servicing their clients. But there are also folks who've been kicked out of one country or another and who've left a trail of disillusioned and "taken" clients.

The point is: be careful. You are not operating under the same assumptions and rules to which you are accustomed. Take your time. Talk to people. Don't believe everything you hear, but if you talk to enough people, the same names will come up again and again, both in terms of recommendation and caution.

I think the "buyer broker" concept, where the agent is hired by you to work for you and to negotiate the best deal for you, makes a lot of sense, particularly in Panama. If your agent knows that he is going to be paid a certain percentage by you regardless of what you purchase, it opens the door for your agent to go out and beat the bushes and find the property that meets your needs at the price you want to pay.

Because Panamanian real estate is not as developed and organized as real estate in the States, many sellers question what, if anything, they are getting for their commission. So "for sale by owner" offerings are very common. Drive almost anywhere and you'll see tons of "*Se Vende*" signs with the owner's phone number. When owners are setting the prices without consultation they may be asking too little or, in some cases, far too much. "*Gringos* will pay anything," also known as "*gringo bingo*"[39], may be the key pricing consideration.

In North America with organized real estate, MLS, and local real estate boards, an agent with a few computer strokes can give you reliable "comps." This is critical when a market is changing. You can't depend on what people say they paid or what sellers say they got. Everyone wants to look good, so the actual prices tend to be adjusted accordingly. Again, this is an argument for hiring your own "Buyer Broker" who will work for you, scout the territory, and negotiate realistically on your behalf with "for sale by owner" sellers.

Don't think "for sale by owner" offerings are shark-free either. Sometimes sellers just don't actually own what they're trying to sell. Or they want to play games.

I was very interested in a property listed online for $399,000 for a nice coffee farm. I emailed back and forth with the owner in the States and went out to see the property several times. It was a nice property, attractively priced, and we were very interested only to discover that once he knew of our interest he jacked the price up to $600,000. I told him I was always interested in negotiating the asking price downward, not upward! Thanks, but no thanks!

It is fairly common with "for sale by owner" properties to find the seller jacking up the price at the last minute figuring that either *gringos* have tons of money, or are stupid, or are both! This has happened to us again and again!

Who owns what?

Traditionally there have been two types of property in Panama: titled property and rights of possession.

Titled Property

Titled property is similar to what we understand in North America, except for the fact that there are no comparable title companies to research the title and insure the title. In Panama your attorney will do a title search and confirm that the title or "*escritura*" is registered in the public registry. This includes verifying that there are no encumbrances on the property and that the property has been surveyed. And you should have the property surveyed by your own surveyor to verify the accuracy.

Rights of way are very tricky in Panama. Every piece of property must have access to the public, at least by a walking path and the access must remain public even if the ownership of the property changes hands. Once a right of way has been granted it must continue in perpetuity if it is regularly used, and regularly can be as infrequently as once a year. When property is subdivided the original owner must provide access from a public road and sometimes, over the years, these rights of way have not always been duly recorded and yet they still exist.

Sometimes developers in Panama will hang onto the title until your home is actually completed and you receive a certificate of occupancy. However, if the developer suddenly goes south after you've almost completed your home, but before you get your certificate of occupancy, you can either be out of luck or find yourself tied up in court for years.

Rights of Possession

Rights of possession is a type of ownership in Panama but does not constitute titled property.

To acquire rights of possession a Panamanian citizen files an application to the government including a survey and statements and agreements from the neighbors. He then has possessory rights. Hanging onto those rights requires that the possessor actually use the property and make improvements.

Improvements can be buildings, or something as simple as planting grass, palm trees, or fencing in the property. The possessor can then sell his rights of possession to you, after which you need to actually buy the property from the government. If you skip this important step, you have the right to use the property – sometimes referred to as "the right to pick fruit" – but you do not actually own it. Fortunately this is changing in Panama as the government seeks to have all property titled. Why? The government wants the tax money and can't collect taxes on rights of possession property.

Ways to Own Property

When you purchase property in Panama you can purchase it in the name of a real person (your own name), or in the name of a corporation, or in the name of a Private Interest

Foundation. Panama does not recognize joint ownership by husband and wife. If one dies, property is not automatically transferred to the other. Most expats choose to own property in the name of an S. A. corporation for various legal and confidentiality advantages. The owners of the corporation own the shares and the corporation owns the real property. In the past these S. A. corporations were bearer bond entities where whoever physically holds the bonds, owns the company. So if you or your spouse dies, the survivor has the bonds, so owns the property. This provided anonymity and protection from law suits and inquisitive governments. In order to get a trade agreement with the U. S. a few years ago Panama bent over and let the U. S. have its way with the traditional system. Banking in Panama is no longer private and truly anonymous bearer bond corporations are a pretty much a thing of the past.

Some people, in order to protect assets and easily transfer assets to heirs, create something called a Private Interest Foundation [PIF]. This is a relatively new entity in Panama, but one which has been used in other countries specializing in offshore corporate business. The Private Interest Foundation has no shares, and no owners, but there are beneficiaries. When the founder of the Foundation dies, in theory, the PIF and its assets pass automatically to the beneficiaries.

The United States, obviously wanting a slice of any foreign pie, now requires U. S. citizens to disclose these entities and any profits, insuring continued employment for accountants. Before you jump into a Private Interest Foundation you need to decide if it solves or creates problems. The IRS has now decided that a Panama Private Interest Foundation is the same as a Trust. So there is no way to escape the long arm of the IRS or the pile of onerous paperwork which, now that the proverbial camel has its nose in the tent, seems to increase yearly.[40]

Signing on the Dotted Line

Say you actually find a piece of property and you and the seller agree on a price, then what? This is where you're really not in Kansas ... or California any longer!

As a Realtor in California I used to chafe over the length and complexity of the California Association of Realtors residential purchase agreement. But it was a standard agreement that applied to the purchase of all real estate in California, and it prevented a lot of problems by clearly defining everything and anticipating problems in advance and indicating how these problems would be resolved should they occur. In Panama there are no "offer" and "acceptance" documents, no standard contract and no deposit or earnest money. Having reached agreement, the "intending" seller and "intending" buyer sign a "Promise-to-Sell" agreement and the intending buyer makes a down payment. The agreement is amazingly simple and doesn't anticipate problems, opening the door in my opinion, for misunderstandings and conflict. Once the contract is signed, the intending buyer makes a usually sizable down payment. The "Promise-to-Sell" agreement is then recorded in the Public Registry to prevent the seller from selling to someone else.

Since the official language of Panama is Spanish, to be enforceable all contracts should be translated into Spanish, although the courts have recently determined that if English or some other language was the language of both parties making the contract, that the contract is enforceable ... for whatever that means. In Panama it could mean years and years of legal wrangling costing you more in legal fees and time than any loss you might recover.

Say what?

There is no escrow. There is no neutral third party to hold the money in a trust account, to be sure the terms of the contract are fulfilled, and to parcel out the money at closing according to the contract. For this reason, real estate agents can often find themselves stiffed on their commission. Funds are sometimes held by the lawyer, assuming the parties are using the same lawyer or can agree on whose lawyer will hold the money. Sometimes a bank or even the real estate agent holds the money. If this sounds dicey, it is. It seems involves a lot of trust. Trust, when you're the new kid on the block and may not know who to trust. Trust, in a country where culturally people tell you what they think you want to hear which often is not necessarily what in North America we would call "the truth." We were lucky: our builder and his attorney not only were honorable and trustworthy, but they have also become our friends.

When the title is actually registered at the Public Registry the money changes hands. If you've bought property held by a corporation you'll also receive the shares for the corporation that owns the property.

Costs of setting up a corporation vary from attorney to attorney, but generally it runs around $1,000 to $1,500. Charges to maintain the corporation … pay nominal Panamanian directors, lawyer, accountant, annual corporate fee, file tax returns, etc. … run around $500 to $700 a year. You can do things like paying fees and filing returns yourself, particularly if you speak Spanish. If you're not fluent in Spanish it is easier and less hassle to pay professionals who know their way around the system to do the work for you.

Panama has several advantages over some of the other Central American countries retirees may consider. Foreigners can own property in Panama, which is not always the case in other countries, and in Panama you don't have to worry about squatters coming in, taking over, and claiming property rights if you are away.

Commissions

As a former Realtor, believe me, I understand the importance of commissions. When dealing with sellers in the States who were wavering between trying to sell on their own and using a real estate agent, I could explain the added value of using a Realtor and why professional real estate could bring the highest sale price with the least amount of risk and hassle for the seller. We liked to think the standard commission was six percent, but the reality was five percent. I took a listing and put the property on MLS making it available to all real estate agents knowing that, whoever actually brought the buyer, as the listing agent I would get half of the commission for promoting the property, putting it online, featuring it in the full page ads my broker had every Sunday in the newspaper, and always during business hours having agents in our office who could answer questions and show the property. Whoever brought a buyer would receive their half of the commission. Because the escrow company handled the money and the distribution of funds, the seller and buyer as well as all the agents involved were assured of payment.

In my opinion there are very few real estate agents in Panama who actively work to promote properties aggressively and effectively to prospective buyers. I've watched agents "show" a property without previewing it, with toilet seats left up, lights not turned on, no attempt to present the property at its best, and then just stand there mute without pointing out the special features or helping prospective buyers see themselves living in the home. Talk about a recipe for failure in real estate! Yet these same agents expect to be paid a commission from *both* sides of the transaction!

In Panama the person who brings the buyer, whether they have actually worked on selling the property and advertised it, assumes they should get the full five percent commission, both the "listing agent" and the "buyer's agent" portions of the pie! And, at least in Boquete, there are some sellers of real estate who, many believe greedily, are asking for seven percent. One agency in town tries to get visitors to "sign in" and then shows them a video of homes for sale, some of which aren't even listed by that agent. The agency then sends out emails to everyone whose home was on the video saying, "We *introduced* your property to . . ." hoping to be able to claim part of the commission without ever even having shown the property.

Panama has a value added tax called the "ITBS" [*El impuesto de traslado de bienes materiales y servicios*] of seven percent on everything but food. So if you buy a sack of cement, you pay an additional seven percent tax to the government. If you visit the doctor or dentist, add on seven percent to the government. And if you use a real estate agent and pay a commission *you* owe seven percent ITBS tax on the amount of the real estate commission!

Location! Location! Location!

Anywhere in the world, these are still the three most important words in real estate. To really understand the differences in location, you need to do your homework, ask around and spend some time in an area before you commit. Better yet, rent and live in an area for three to six months before buying.

Shopping Online

Funny thing, when the Boeing 707 made Trans-Atlantic travel comfortable and fast, people said the age of passenger ships was over, yet today the cruise industry is booming. When DVDs first came out, people said movie theaters were finished, yet today where there was once a ratty little theater you'll find a 20-screen movie theater with lines at the box office. When Amazon was launched, people predicted the death of bookstores, yet today local giant bookstores are vast emporiums of literature and community centers. When the Internet first started showing real estate listings, many brokers were wringing their hands, yet today the Internet is the single biggest marketing tool for real estate. Using the Internet you can dream about properties all over the world.

If you find a property that interests you and search diligently online you may find the same property listed on various sites with varying asking prices. The reason for this is because real estate in Panama isn't really that "professional," there isn't a lot of reason for sellers to give exclusive listings. Sellers of real estate in Panama aren't taking out TV ads, or full sections of the Sunday papers, or staffing their offices full-time with qualified real estate professionals. Pretty much they put your property online and sit like a spider in a web hoping to snag a buyer when they come to town. So for this reason a lot of sellers of real estate, licensed and unlicensed, will put properties online hoping to snag buyers and negotiate a commission whether they actually have an agreement to represent the seller or not. Even if they can't get a commission, hopefully for them the difference between what the seller is actually asking and what they can convince buyers to pay, will equal a profitable commission. And if they can land both the commission and the additional amount they are asking, so much the better, at least for them.

Like anything else, the web can be abused. Have you ever noticed how Realtors generally leave up the "For Sale" sign until the new owners are threatening to bring the sign to the broker's office and hit him over the head with it? Why? It's great and free advertising! I once took a listing for a home on the busiest street in Ventura, right by a freeway entrance. I thought to myself, this will take forever to sell, but what a great advertising opportunity. Fortunately for the seller, unfortunately for me, I sold it in two days.

Unfortunately, the same thing happens online. Either intentionally, or just because they don't know how to get the damn page down, properties remain "for sale" online long after they are sold. Aside from being very frustrating to Internet shoppers, this adds to the confusion.

There are sites where sellers can pay a monthly or flat fee to showcase their property for sale. Some of these are realistic sellers: others are people who've said, "Well, if we could get X dollars, sure, we'd sell." So they're not really looking to sell, unless some fool happens along who is willing to pay their dream price. Sometimes there are hotels, bed and breakfasts, and small businesses where the owner is tired of being an indentured servant, and would like to cash out, if they could get a price that really doesn't make sense if a prospective buyer runs the numbers.

Keep checking the same sites regularly. Notice how long some homes remain for sale. Because they drop off the listing site doesn't necessarily mean they've sold. The sellers may just have given up for the moment. It's amazing how some of the same properties keep cycling back onto the popular international real estate sites. Interestingly sometimes the price keeps inflating, as the seller keeps dreaming.

Many times the owner of a property really doesn't *need* to sell. Folks who have luxury homes in Panama often have enough resources to sit out the market and wait until the right buyer comes along, knowing that parking their money in Panamanian real estate often in the long run gives them a better return than investing elsewhere. Generally in Panama you don't find distressed properties with owners desperate to sell at any price.

Action Items and Points to Ponder

1. How is buying property going to be different from the experiences you've had where you now live?

2. Assuming by now you've identified some areas you might like to call home, start following the real estate market in those areas online. Do some comparisons.

12. Building in Paradise

*H*ere's a question similar to ones I hear frequently: "We are still in the States but thinking of building on our property in Panama. Do you have any recommendations, suggestions or tips?"

My best advice if you are considering building in Panama – don't!

I don't think that I am a novice to building. In my career as a pastor I built three churches, working with architects, builders, and city planning departments in New York City, Milwaukee, and Jefferson County, Colorado. We built a second home in Door County, Wisconsin. I partially remodeled two brownstones in New York, and remodeled our home in Ventura, moving bearing walls, building sheer walls, doing electric, plumbing, rough and finish carpentry. I've installed three kitchens. I'm not an expert, but I'm not a novice either.

All-in-all I am pleased with the home we built in spite of the worst efforts of some of the folks who should have been on my "team" but weren't. What was promised in one year took almost two years and never was finished by the builder whom I fired after he took 97 percent of my money and only did 70 percent of the work. I put together a crew and finished it myself.

I would never do this again in Panama nor would I recommend it to you. Panama is a great place to live and a wonderful place in which to retire. But building here is nuts!

My advice is to look around and find something already built.
Even if an existing place isn't perfect, with a little money, and
a lot less frustration, you can do some upgrades, some
redecorating and landscaping and make it into your dream
home. Trust me, the house you build, even if you are on site a
100 percent of the time, will not be perfect either. Most
building costs in Panama have doubled over the past ten
years, so often you do better buying an existing home
probably paying less than what it would cost to build the
same home today.

I had planned to build some other stuff in Panama, but after
the experience of building our home I've decided to abandon
those plans. There! My wife wanted it "in writing" so here it
is. "I may be stupid to do this in the first place, but I'm not
crazy enough to do it again!"

I love and admire good architecture. I like Frank Lloyd Wright
and Frank Gehry, even though their styles aren't my style. As
far as I'm concerned the art deco Chrysler Building in New
York is the closest thing to architectural perfection. I admired
Richard Neutra, who did the original buildings for the Crystal
Cathedral when it was Garden Grove Community Church,
and Phillip Johnson's Garden Grove Church when it was the
Crystal Cathedral[41]. The Getty by Richard Meier is close to my
definition of contemporary architectural perfection. But then I
also love the old gothic architecture of cathedrals in Europe,
and some modern church architecture, like the tiny chapel at
Seattle University.

I've hired architects and worked with them to design and
construct three church buildings. So I'm not a novice working
with architects. I have had very good architects and we have
worked well together. I know what an architect should do and
what to expect ... but not in Panama.

To my regret I have discovered that architects in Panama
generally draw a pretty picture, farm out the engineering, and
then let the builder figure out the details ... if it will work, and
how it should work. "Specs," which were generally a one to

three inch thick book in the States, are sketchy at best and are limited to notes on the plans.

The architect doesn't specify much of anything and the details are left to the builder.

So why do you need an architect in Panama? In my opinion, frankly, you don't. If I were doing it again, I might have a North American architect draw up plans and specs, then get a responsible, reputable Panamanian engineer with great references and impeccable attention to detail to draw up plans for Panama and get them approved.

Panama City is a sea of architectural extravagance, some of it really fantastic, some designed by local architects and some by firms from outside the country. I am sure there are good architects in Panama City. My frustrations were with local architects far from Panama City charging big city prices.

We started out on this project working with a friend and neighbor, Brad Abajian. Brad retired early as a successful professional Poker player. His dad was a contractor who did high-end custom homes in the Los Angeles area and Brad grew up in a contractor's world and so knew a lot about construction and design. We worked for months with Brad drawing up plan after plan using an inexpensive computer design program. Brad went over our ideas with us and made excellent suggestions, but the house was designed by us.

I wanted something with a Tuscan country feel that would somehow fit in a tropical, mountain coffee farm setting. We wanted a home that was light and airy and open. We wanted a home with an inside/outside feel since, after all, you come to Panama to enjoy life outside. I wanted our bedroom to be as close to sleeping outside as possible. And we wanted a patio that was an integral part of our home. Since it rains a lot in Boquete during the rainy season, we needed outside living areas that were protected from wind and rain.

So we take full credit for the design of our house. If you like it, credit us. In spite of the architect's best ... or worst ... efforts, it came out looking almost like we designed.

The "hot" architects for *gringos* in Boquete were mostly young men whose fathers had construction companies. We talked around and it came down to two guys we should talk with. I had seen a lot of both of their work. I liked the work and liked them.. We already knew pretty much what we wanted. The one guy told us that it would be at least two months before he could start on our project, and the other guy told us he would start right away. We chose the guy who could start right away. The reality was that he put us off for two months.

He charged us a design fee. I figured since he was an architect, and going to charge us a design fee no matter what, rather than show him what I had designed, I would describe what we wanted, and see what he came up with. He speaks English fluently and so I described what we wanted in a house, how we wanted it to flow and feel, our life style, how we wanted to use the house, and our budget.

A few months later he came back with a plan. It was immediately obvious that he hadn't listened to a word we had said. Parts of the unimaginative plan looked vaguely familiar from houses he'd designed that I had seen under construction. At first I thought it was someone else's house. It appeared as if he had cut and pasted together ... not very well, I might add ... parts of other houses he had designed. So much for design, and although he had done nothing we paid him for the design phase. I pulled out the computer and showed him the detailed plans we had designed with Brad that were VERY detailed including light circuits, cabinetry ... the works. I said, "Here, this is exactly what we want. We need you to take it and work on the roof lines and prepare working drawings. We're going ahead and ordering Burmese cherry cabinets from China, so we need to have you keep the exact dimensions."

So he prepared plans. We spent lots of time going over and over the plans, pointing out things he had omitted or changed, discussing the plans. Eventually we had listed all the changes we needed and he came up with the final set of plans. We reviewed those and pointed out a few glaring errors ... like dropping a skylight out of the kitchen that had been included previously ... changing our fireplace (North American style proportions) to a Panamanian style fireplace (totally out-of-proportion by our expectations). He promised corrections and we waited for our final, approved, stamped plans.

The architect spoke fluent English. The plans were in meters. At the time Panama was betwixt and between working in both systems with builders thinking in both meters and feet. He refused to do the plans in feet since it wasn't what he usually did. I admit that he was busy making plans for a wedding so he may have been distracted, but ... as the construction progressed we discovered major changes and errors, some of which we were able to correct, and some of which we've just had to live with.

Despite the hassles, we were able to create a home which still has 90 percent of what we wanted. It is a lovely home to live in and admired by all.

First rule of life in Panama: don't expect anything or anyone to "show up" as promised.

It may be your lawyer or doctor, gardener, maid, service provider, repair person or contractor -- it doesn't make any difference. Panamanians will promise up the wazoo but the "promise" is simply what they think you want to hear and in terms of future performance doesn't mean a thing. *If you can live with that you will do well in Panama; if not, you'd better stay put where you are.*

Based on our cultural background, building in Panama seems all backwards. When we came to Panama and moved into Valle Escondido we were the second or third house. Over a period of four years we watched the other houses being built. Our favorite Sunday afternoon activity in Valle Escondido was traipsing through homes under construction and critiquing everything. Based on our observations and feedback and suggestions from lots of people, we submitted our plans for bids to five different contractors.

Contractor A was an expat *gringo*. He was a young guy who asked a lot of the right questions -- questions about soil studies, topographical studies, the kind of thing I would have expected in the States. He had built a home in Valle Escondido that I liked and he spoke English.

Contractor B was one of the largest Panamanian contractors in Boquete and did both residential and commercial work. He spoke English, and we had admired his work. He built a large home for friends in Valle Escondido. He had a big outfit with lots of jobs running simultaneously. But based on our friends' experience the on-sight management was poor and the quality of some of the work left something to be desired. He did, however, have resources both in terms of money as well as access to good workers and subcontractors.

Contractor C's English was better than my Spanish and he had also built for a friend. We liked his quality, and we liked him. He'd built in other Latin American countries but had been building in Panama for about ten years, mostly low-end Panamanian housing projects. He had his own ironwork and window shops and seemed to have a pretty efficient operation. He had resources in terms of money and access to workers and subs. But he had established a cooperative relationship with an expat promoter who had a shaky reputation.

Contractor D spoke only Spanish and was definitely a small operator. He built a few homes a year, but was a local and had been building in Boquete for something like fifteen years. Frankly, we were skeptical until we saw a few of the houses he had built. We were impressed by the quality of his workmanship and frankly, by him. He had a small crew with whom he had worked for years, and since he was a small player had limited financial resources. We knew from friends that he had difficulty wrapping up projects, but that is pretty much a universal problem with Panamanian builders. (This was where the sirens and red lights should have gone off!)

Contractor E was a couple just starting out. Both were graduates of Texas A&M with impressive credentials. They had just completed a friend's house right on schedule and their work was better than any we had seen in Boquete. Her father was an established builder of larger projects in Panama giving them entre to workers and subs, but they lived in Panama City so would not be on the job on a daily basis. He was an electrical engineer and she was the contractor, but ... she had just discovered that she was pregnant with twins.

We gave all five a complete set of plans (well, as "complete" as plans are in Panama without specs), along with five pages of introductory explanation about us, and our expectations, and specific concerns and, if you will, demands.

Contractor A – Disappeared with our plans. Fortunately all I lost was a set of plans.

Contractor B – Came in with the high bid. He had a couple of other big projects getting underway. He had built our friend's house and knew our friend was not totally happy with his work, and I think the contractor was a little concerned that our friend would be helping us as an advisor, and I'm not sure he really wanted the job.

Contractor C – Came in with a bid right in the middle. He was definitely a major contender. He had the resources, his quality was good, but we were concerned about the business relationship he had with an expat promoter about whom we had some concerns. He assured us that he was severing the relationship, but it didn't appear that way.

Contractor D - was the low bidder, but the quality of his work made him a definite contender. He only spoke Spanish and I really only spoke English, so that was a concern. The fact that he was a small operator we viewed as both a blessing (more attention to our project with only one or two a year) and a curse (limited crew and resources).

Contractor E - Also came in with a bid right in the middle. Their background, fluency in our language and understanding of U. S. building standards, the quality of their work, and the enthusiastic recommendation of a friend made them definite contenders. We were concerned that they were new with only one, albeit very good, *gringo* house under their belt, and that they were in Panama City and she was pregnant.

So, which did we choose?

You know that if this were on HGTV that there would be a long commercial break at this point. Since I can't do that, I will hold you in suspense while I share some general observations about much of the building in Panama, at least in Chiriqui.

1) It looks disorganized ... and it is!

"Choreographed" is not a word that you would use to describe building in Panama, at least outside of Panama City.

It's a little like traffic flow in Panama City or David ... somehow, in the end, amazingly, everyone eventually gets where they are going, generally without major loss of life, but the process of getting there is a zoo! I know things are changing, especially in Panama City. You don't build a $6 billion addition to the Panama Canal without a closely choreographed team, which may be why the coordination and much of the work on the Canal project was contracted out to major players from around the world. And you don't build a magnificent structure like the F&F Tower (the high-rise that looks like CD cases piled up askew, also known as "Revolution Tower" and "Screw Tower") or the funky, but complex Bridge of Life Museum building without a lot of planning and coordination, but we're talking about building a residential house far from Panama City.

Panamanians in general seem to think lineally and certainly do in construction. The idea that you have multiple trades working simultaneously to reach a goal without stepping on each other or destroying each other's work seems totally foreign.

2) Labor is relatively cheap ... supplies aren't.

"Just in time" can be a very good concept, except in Panama where stuff is never "in time." And God forbid that anyone should order enough of anything, let alone some extra, no matter how inexpensive the items.

You always run short. So you have guys sitting around waiting for things like cement, sand, wire, nails or screws ... no matter how big the operation. Many Panamanians are used to living and thinking "on a shoe string." The concept that you might buy and store major chunks of the materials you need so the materials are on hand when needed is totally foreign. Buying what you need up front would make sense especially as construction supply costs are going through the roof. But generally that's not the way things are done. I now know that often money is being siphoned off each job to finish the job that precedes it. It's not just as simple as continually running to the construction supply store which doesn't always keep items in stock. They must order and you wait and wait. It could be simple ... and planned ... but it isn't.

You are not, repeat NOT, going to change that basic way of doing things in Panama.

3) OSHA[42] would go bonkers.

Some of the larger builders now issue hard hats to workers and require them to be worn. When we were building, chances were the hard hats wouldn't be worn but would be used as mixing buckets for tiny batches of cement with which to patch up walls. Crude, improvised ladders are made on the job ... and not a single one would get OSHA approval. Where in North America we would call in a crane to lift steel beams into position, outside of Panama City they are usually hoisted by hand with workers often standing on the top rung of rickety hand-made ladders holding the I-beam above their heads while someone welds it into place. Eight different saws, drills, etc., are routinely run off one jerry-rigged electrical line which sometimes gets changed to 220 volt without anyone telling everyone so heaven help you if you plug in your drill and don't know that for the moment it's 220 volts. Worse yet, we get one of the frequent afternoon downpours and you are standing on a wet surface using an electrical tool which is plugged into a jerry-rigged extension cord that isn't grounded.

My daily prayer while we were building was, "Lord, first, let us get through this day; second, may we get through this day without anyone getting hurt or killed; and, third, assuming we are allowed several requests, may I get through this day without killing the builder."

4) Estimates are guesstimates.

I suspect that jobs are estimated and quotes are put together based on a guesstimate of square foot costs without actually being costed out. Sometimes this works, but sometimes, especially when material costs are soaring, it doesn't work. So it is almost guaranteed the estimate and contract price will not be accurate, which is why builders take out their profit up front, but more on that later.

Construction times mean nothing; absolutely, positively, nothing. Safe bet: take whatever a contractor says and at least double it.

Panamanians like to please and they tend to tell you what they think you want to hear whether it is true or makes any sense or not.

5) Tools of the trade.

There are none.

Want to work construction in the States? You'd better come equipped, not only with skills, but also with tools. In Panama a really equipped worker *may* have his own tape measure, but that's it. All you need is two hands and a strong back. And the contractor isn't much better. All a contractor seems to need to be a contractor is a cement mixer ... generally one he is borrowing. If that doesn't work, a hoe will do. Panamanians are inventive and they are good at recycling and making tools as needed.

6) Promises, promises, promises.

OK, that's not unique to Panama. When we built a cottage in Door County, Wisconsin, some neighbors who had used the same builder, gave us some advice. Our builder was a great guy who had built and personally paid for the local church. He was a wonderful, caring Christian guy and we enjoyed working with him, but before we started our neighbors warned us, "He may be a Christian, but remember, he's a contractor first."

7) Prayer, booze and money . . .
Prayer, booze and money are the essential tools for anyone who is foolish enough to build in Panama.

The prayer is to pray for the safety of your workers and that the contractor actually delivers and finishes in this millennium.

The booze ... it's the key to patience and accepting that things aren't the way they were at home and that's why you moved to Panama in the first place.

The money ... well, particularly if you are building, Panamanians see all *gringo*s as multimillionaires with nothing but money and more money, so you'd better have an endless flow because you will need it.

Oh yes, we chose the builder behind Door D: wrong choice as you will see.

After I first published some of these thoughts on my blog, I received this well-written and thoughtful response comment on my blog from Charles Metz, which anyone who even thinks about building in Panama should read.

"My name is Charles Metz. We have met at Valle Escondido. You may recall that I am a custom home builder and developer living in Naples Florida. I have designed and supervised the construction of one house in Valle Escondido long distance which was also a bit of a disaster.

"No matter what quality of American plans you have, your plans must be submitted by and in the name of a Panamanian architect in order to get a permit. This is largely taken advantage of in Panama with the typical asking price being in the neighborhood of $15,000 to $20,000 by local architects who do nothing. Custom plans for a house in Boquete ended up costing more than for a house in Naples, Florida, which at the moment is one of the most expensive markets in the States.

"In addition once you turn your plans over to a Panamanian architect they are owned by him. If you ever decide to change anything or remodel you will need that architect's permission. I have heard of architects charging $10,000 just for their permission. So it is good to get something in the contract about this. If the architect is also the builder you will not be able to fire the builder halfway through the project since he controls the plans. You also will not be able to fire the contractor half way through the project and finish the job yourself since your original contractor must sign the paperwork for your occupancy permit, meaning you will have difficulty holding out the final 10 percent of the contract price as a penalty for shoddy or incorrect work. And forget taking anyone to court. The courts are not very dependable and *you are a stranger in a strange land.*

"It is important to remember that few of the local architects have had experience with the budgets that are used in the States to build custom homes. The few who have experience generally have designed for wealthy Panamanians with lifestyles and design expectations totally different than those expected by North Americans. Because of limited availability of trained craftsmen, local architects have learned to keep it simple. A large Panamanian house is generally a smaller Panamanian house with enlarged rooms.

"There is very little supervision on a Panamanian construction site. I don't care who the builder is. And if you want your house to look like your plan, you had better be on the site every day. The workers will do what they are used to doing unless told otherwise. And unless you are there they will not be told otherwise. There will likely be no plan at the jobsite and if there were the electrical engineer is probably the only one at the job who could read them anyway.

"For those thinking they can buy an American architectural plan on the web and build it in Panama think again. In Panama you are building a concrete block house for earthquakes not hurricanes, so your generic tropical plans will not work. The steel reinforcement bar designs are very different and specific. A house plan developed using California earthquake code won't work since the Panamanian system is very different.

"A Panamanian house is built more like a high-rise condo than like a single family house that North Americans have experienced. All floor systems are poured concrete. We are talking welded red steel here. And although the first house that I designed in Panama was of M2[43] and not block construction, I would not do that again.

"I have seen many 'experienced' Americans try to go to Panama and 'tell them how we do it back home.' Frankly, nobody cares how you do it back home and being the 'Ugly American' will likely cost you more money. It is amazing to me how easily the Panamanian people get insulted if they think you are being disrespectful. It is the Latin *macho* thing. So you need to have your contract very specific and then treat everyone with kid gloves. And unless you write your own contract it will be full of holes and opportunities for extra charges. It does not take long to learn that there are Panamanian prices and there are *gringo* prices.

"To those American builders who think you are going to go to Panama and take the business from the local builders to build for the *gringos,* please don't be so foolish. It is a closed and protected system. Not only do you not know what you are doing, you do not have the labor nor understand how to manage the labor. You do not know the true costs, the construction systems, or the local laws. The locals will blackball you in a minute. They are related and you are not. They know who to pay off and you do not. Heck, if you are like me you probably do not even know the language well.

"So what is a person to do if you want to build a home in Panama? I have a few thoughts.

"1 - Find those website plans that you like and buy them. Make sure they are designed for block construction and not wood frame. Buy the plans on disk in auto cad so they can be easily modified and if you have any changes to make have the original architect in the States make them. Keep in mind there are few flat lots in Panama and foundations are expensive as is site work for the grade. Make sure your plans work for your grade and will fit on your lot before you buy them.

"2 - Go find a Panamanian architect who is willing to redraw your plans in metric and in Spanish and for the local seismic construction code. All Panamanian architects are licensed over the entire country. So look in the larger cities rather than in the hot spots for development in the boonies.

"3 - Negotiate with the architect that you will 'own' the plans. Negotiate what he will charge for future revisions and what, if any, supervision of construction you expect from him. Keep in mind that your architect will have to visit your construction site and you will likely have to pay his expenses, so try to select someone within your region.

"4 – Find a bilingual Panamanian attorney to work for you in the creation of your requirements for a contract. Your contract will have to be both in English and in Spanish. English so you understand it and Spanish so that it will be a legal contract in Panama. Make sure your attorney has the power to legally 'authenticate' the translation: this is typically a specialty service from an authorized agency.

"5 - Establish an agreement with a local bank to make disbursements to your contractor based upon pre-agreed to phases of completion. They are not used to this but will do it for a fee. You will have to likely pay for each inspection by a bank person once your contractor requests a payment, but it will be worth it. The contractor will be less likely to try to jerk you around if the bank is involved. And at least you will have somebody speaking your contractor's language and who is paid to be on your side.

"6 - Now put your plans out for bid. Make sure your architect has detailed the specifications to your satisfaction. What you will find is that most of the contractors will no longer be interested in your project because you have taken away from them most of the tools to take advantage of you. But the ones remaining are the ones you want to talk to anyway.

"7 - If you are still inclined to 'do it yourself and save money', I suggest you at least contract with a local to build the shell of the house, what is locally referred to as 'in the gray' and then finish it yourself. Anyone can contract for laying of tile or painting, but keep in mind your 'in the gray contractor' will still have to submit the paperwork to get your occupancy permit, so get that agreed to upfront in writing.

"If you want to go to the next step, contract for construction management only. Go to your Panamanian bank and deposit enough funds to establish credit and then go to the building supply houses and establish your own builder account. You place the order for materials and you make the payments. This is a good strategy for several reasons. First, if you don't do this your builder will be getting a 10 to 15 percent discount and still will be marking up the materials to you at 20 to 30 percent over retail. And what did he do but make a phone call? Secondly, it is the only way you will know that all subs and materials have been paid for at the end of the job so you won't be stuck with the same kind of mechanic liens you are used to in the States.

"9 - Keep in mind that building only the shell is like building a log cabin. The log shell is a long way from the final cost of a house, so budget appropriately.

"10 – Finally, don't even think about doing it long distance: you have got to be on site. Period.

"Sound daunting? Sort of, but this is my recommendation after building one house in Panama and a few hundred over a thirty year period in the States.

"So let's see. We need a qualified architect willing to work under the terms outlined, we need a qualified attorney charging fair market fees, we need a banker willing to perform the service outlined, and we need a contractor willing to bid on the project under the terms outlined. And, it would not hurt to find some fresh out of university student willing to work by the hour as your translator.

"Wishing you continued success! Charles Metz"

There, Charles Metz just saved you hundreds of thousands of dollars, saved you from being ripped off, and, perhaps more importantly saved your marriage and saved you from a nervous breakdown.

I WISH, how I wish, I had his advice before we started building! Our experience wasn't as bad as some, but to give you an idea …

The "nice guy" builder we contracted with turned out to be not so nice after he took 97 percent of my money and only completed 70 percent of the job, after taking twice the amount of time he promised. Unfortunately he's pulled this same scam with other *gringos*. The lesson here: you can't talk to too many people! Unfortunately for us we only talked to one or two couples who were using him, and as it turned out later, they ended up having problems with him finishing without needing and demanding additional money.

Even more unfortunately, Panamanian contractors typically intentionally underbid the job. And this guy is still doing it! "Sue him!" Yeah, but he knows the scam so all of his assets are in his wife's name and even if they weren't it would take ten or fifteen years, and we, being outsiders to the system would probably lose anyway.

Like all these guys, he takes his profit at the beginning of the job, knowing in advance that there won't be anything left at the end. So I still see him driving around town in the new green Toyota truck for which I unknowingly paid.

But he was such a nice guy and played it so sincere and like most dumb *gringos* I bought it. I knew the cost of supplies was going up and he hadn't built any cost increases into the contract so frankly I expected to cough up some additional money at the end.

I wanted to help the guy out and that's why he ended up with ninety-seven percent of the contract money and I only ended up with seventy percent of the job being done ... a year late.

It all came to a head when he asked for an advance over and above the contract price to purchase a septic tank, and then after I gave him the money kept telling me it was on order, and there were no septic tanks in David. It was two months before I was to leave on a six-month cruise contract and the house was already a year late. I sent my wife to David to check out septic tanks and she came home with this huge septic tank strapped on our truck.

The next day, September 1st, I fired him on the spot. I then hired two of his workers who were now out of work. Of course they weren't his legal workers, just day workers, so now they were mine for two months. We moved into the partially completed house and roughed it while I worked with a team of three guys to complete the job. Two months later, the day I was leaving for the airport to work on the ship for six months, I was finishing up putting doors on the kitchen cabinets.

We were sitting in a restaurant just last week with some folks on a tour group when another expat, who'd been here for less than two years, started talking about this contractor who did such nice work. I asked the contractor's name ... and just about choked spitting out my wine when he said the name. The guy is still at it! Good first impression, not bad quality at least on the gray building (that's before any finishing), and I guess still living off naive *gringos*. So ... ask around! And then ask some more! Obviously the guy making the recommendation had just "heard" but had never tried to build anything with ... well, I can't tell you his name, but if you ask around, and ask expats who've been here a while and built, you'll find out.

Everything Charles says above, about firing your contractor and needing approvals is technically true, as is the fact that we shouldn't have been living in the house without a certificate of occupancy. I left for the ship leaving the responsibility for getting a certificate of occupancy in my wife's hands. It took her four months of trying to track down the contractor, the architect who had signed the plans, etc., etc. One of the big hassles was that the building department couldn't find the records or plans for our house. Not particularly unusual since back then nothing was really computerized and the building department was overwhelmed with plans and paperwork. Finally, it turned out that the builder had never bothered to pull a building permit! In spite of the fact that the fire department, of which the building department is a part, and the health department, and the electric company had all visited the house many times during construction and approved and signed off on everything ... there never was a building permit!

It took some doing on Nikki's part, but when it all came out
that there never was a building permit, meaning that both the
licenses of the builder and the architect who signed for him
were on the line, somehow the builder did come up with the
$2,000 for the permit and fine, the permit was issued
retroactively, and we got our occupancy permit.

Despite the architect, the builder and the "FUBAR"[44] process,
we ended up with a beautiful house.

Maybe because I was able to escape to the ship for six
months,, I never did have a nervous breakdown, but my wife
came close.

So my best advice, if you're considering building in Panama ...
don't! Find something already built and if necessary put some
money into it to remodel it to your specifications. It will still
be a hassle, but you will hang onto your sanity and a lot of
money.

Back then there wasn't an inventory of *gringo*-style expat
homes for resale, but now, as people have come and moved
on, there are lots of wonderful properties for sale. The bag of
cement that cost $5 when we built now costs $10! So with the
huge run up in the cost of building materials, often an existing
home, even if you have to remodel to your tastes, is a better
and cheaper option than building.

Ten years later ...

In the ten years we have been in Panama we have seen an
amazing improvement in the quality of building available.
Friends of ours who rented in Valle Escondido recently
completed building a beautiful home in Panamonte Estates.
He is 85 years old and a very accomplished retired architect
from Texas. I admire anyone with the courage to take on such
a project at that age, but he did. He found an excellent builder
in David who built a beautiful home to his very demanding
standards. Of course he was on the building site every day.
So it can be done!

There are now a number of very good builders in the Boquete area as well as elsewhere in Panama. How do you find them? Ask around. Don't take the recommendation of one or two people, but if you ask enough eventually the same names will come up again and again. And expect to pay! The cost of everything has gone up in Panama. Most building supplies have more than doubled in price since we built. Particularly close to Panama City there are more construction jobs available than there are qualified workers to fill them. The cost of living has gone up and wages have gone up as well.

Finally, whether you are fluent in Spanish or not, planning to build or just live in Panama and occasionally need maintenance help, a book well-worth getting is *Spanish for The Construction Trade* by William C. Harvey.

Action Items and Points to Ponder

1. The "big question" about building ... why? And the follow up, "Are you sure?"

2. The "rubber meets the road question" ... are you willing to physically be on site if you decide to build?

Our second home in Panama, the house we designed and built on our coffee farm, about fifteen minutes from "downtown" Boquete.

Going to the dogs: Nikki and I with (left to right) Baru, Spot and Monkey.

13. See Spot Travel

Since moving to Panama we have really gone to the dogs.

We were always cat people. When I dated my wife, she had this cat named Cassie who insisted on coming up to me and rubbing my leg. When I visited Nikki and she wasn't looking, I'd throw the cat across the apartment, but the cat never got the hint. When we got married Nikki made it clear that having a cat was a condition of the marriage so I learned to like cats. We had a very possessive and neurotic Siamese. When we had kids, both of our girls had a cat. Becky's cat was a fluffy white cat called Mia, and Noelle's was a black cat with white paws called, what else, Mittens. Each cat knew to whom it belonged and every night the cats were curled up on the right kid's bed.

Long after the girls were gone, we still had the cats. Mittens lived to be 21 years old which was quite remarkable since we'd lived in areas frequented by coyotes. Mia, who when Rebecca was home was, as far as I was concerned, "the cat from hell." As she got older, when the kids were gone and Mittens had died, Mia became very affectionate. She deteriorated to the point where we had to put her down when she was 22, a very sad day.

My wife had always looked forward to retirement threatening to write a book called "The Cats Are Dead And The Kids Are Gone." Everyone but the kids thought that was funny.

So when the kids were gone, the cats were dead, we no longer had to work, and were happily retired in Panama, why on earth would we start collecting animals? Beats me!

There are lots of strays in Panama. Part of the problem is that the Spanish *macho* cultural attitude means that you shouldn't take dogs' balls. This doesn't seem to apply to cattle since they are being rounded up and castrated all over Panama, but dogs and cats are different.

One of the things *gringos* introduced in Boquete was a spay/neuter clinics. A woman by the name of Ruby McKenzie saw a need … the problem of excessive numbers of stray cats and dogs … and found a way to meet that need by creating a group called Amigos de Animales de Boquete.

Originally we had a problem with small animals because most of the vets in Chiriqui were used to working with horses and cattle, not small animals. There was a vet in David the *gringos* used to call "Dr. Death" because he'd always over-anesthetize cats and dogs and they'd end up dying. We had a neighbor in Valle Escondido, Jeff Mullen, who had a very successful veterinary practice in the States. When he'd come down to Panama on vacation he'd be loaded down with tons of luggage containing veterinary equipment and supplies. He, along with some expat neighbors and volunteers, worked with Animales and started doing spay/neuter clinics enlisting local vets and vets from Costa Rica to help and, at the same time, learn additional techniques. At first almost all the animals belonged to expats. Today the clinics are held on a regular basis and 95 percent of the animals are owned by Panamanians. At each clinic they will do 100 to 150 animals.

When we lived in Valle Escondido in the early days before there were many houses, we always had feral cats having litters in our storm drain. Nikki got tired of this and since she was volunteering at the spay/neuter clinics, she trapped mamma cat and her kittens and had them spayed and neutered. To allow them time to recover she locked them in the guest bathroom. A day later they had managed to climb the tile walls, tear open the screen and escape. We thought we'd never see them again. Wrong!

They kept coming back and of course Nikki started feeding them. We still have three of the four cats on our farm. We still feed them, but mostly they feed off lizards, mice and rats which is good since it reduces the food supply for snakes.

I had a dog when I was in high school and somehow got the idea that now that I was retired with nothing to do that it would be nice to have a dog. Specifically I wanted a Dalmatian whose name would be Spot ["Mancha"]. Why Spot? Like a lot of folks my age I grew up on "Dick and Jane" reading books in school. "See Jane run. See Dick chase Jane." And since my name was Richard, and I used to be Dickie and then Dick before ... oh well, that's a long story of how words change in meaning[45]. So we went looking for Dalmatians and eventually we found Spot.

Dalmatians are high energy dogs so we took Spot to a dog training program. On the way home from doggy training school we stopped at the post office where a guy just happened to be selling Rottweiler puppies. If you've ever held a Rottweiler puppy you know that they are cuddlier than the softest plush toy. Maybe it was old age weakness, more likely a moment of temporary insanity, whatever, but we decided Spot needed a playmate and got our Rottie, Monkey ["Mono"]. And a few weeks later a woman on the other side of the Volcan Baru who'd promised me a Dalmatian months earlier, and who I thought had forgotten all about me and her promise, called ... and we got Baru, another Dalmatian named after the Volcano.

Although we didn't know it at the time, dog people tell us that two females who are not related and are about the same age create major problems. Spot should have been an only child. Alone she is the perfect dog, but together with the other dogs she is always fighting the Rottweiler for attention and dominance. Baru is the male and should be the Alpha dog, but he doesn't want to be bothered so just lets the bitches fight.

OK, three dogs and four cats. When we moved to the coffee farm in the teenaged son of our Indigenous worker wanted a dog. Nikki reluctantly said, "Fine, but any animal on our property has to be spayed or neutered." So they got a dog, a dog exactly like 90 percent of the street dogs in Panama, an unnamed breed locally called a "Caribe." He was just a puppy and all of my dogs welcomed him into the pack. Nikki then explained what spay/neuter meant to the Indigenous teenager.

"You can't take his balls!" the kid replied indignantly, maybe thinking we had the same thing in mind for him.

While the boy was at school Nikki hustled the dog off to the spay/neuter clinic where she was volunteering. She was actually working in the operating area assisting the vet when they brought Bobbi in for surgery. She asked, "Why do we have to castrate him? Can't we just do a vasectomy?" So they did. Bobbi kept his balls and the teenage kid never knew the difference. So it seemed that all's well that ends well except the Indigenous worker and his son left us and went back to live on the *comarca* leaving Bobbi behind.

Another mouth to feed. Bobbi is actually the sweetest dog. He spends much of his time wandering around town. He usually shows up to eat, but I suspect he works his magic around town with others as well. Frequently he will sleep in the house. Our dogs know they have to stay in the yard, but Bobbi is skinny enough to slip under the fence and our dogs don't seem to mind him coming and going.

There are lots of good dogs available in Panama. Our neighbor up the street raises beautiful pure-bred Mastiffs and another *gringa* nearby raises gorgeous Dobermans. None of our dogs are "papered," although all seem to have a father or mother who was a papered pure bred. Bobbi is a pure-bred Panamanian street dog and is happy just to be loved.

There are usually some amazing animals up for adoption that were pets of expats who had to leave for one reason or another and could not take their pet. And there are some strays which can actually turn out to be the best watchdogs as well as great pets.

Bringing your pet to Panama

If you want to bring your animal along here's how.

Shaun and Maureen Pilson rented our little *casita* while they were finding a home. They brought along their dog Digby who is a Belgian Malinios, a BIG dog and very affectionate. So I asked them to share their experience in bringing Digby to Panama from the United States. Procedures from other countries will differ somewhat. The procedure for bringing cats is quite similar although in most cases it is easier to bring your cat as carry on in the cabin with you.

So here's what Shaun and Maureen had to say about bringing a dog from the States.

"1 - Get a rabies vaccine more than 30 days prior to travel, and less than one year. If you get the rabies vaccine, say, 28 days before travel, your dog will be turned away from Panama.

"2 - Airlines want vaccinations 10 days or less before you travel. Panama says 14 days, but if you want your dog on the plane, abide by the airline 10 day restriction.

"3 - Your vet must be USDA[46] accredited.

"4 - You will have two trips to the vet, one for rabies and one for the vaccinations. The Panamanian Embassy website mentions a Hepatitis shot, which sent us into a panic, since we had not seen this mentioned elsewhere, but the hepatitis shot is mixed in with the other vaccinations already, so no worries. The vet must fill out a form APHIS[47] 7001 in *blue* ink. Our vet also signed an airline health certificate for us but in our case no certification was required. If your state has a USDA office, take this form and the rabies form to it, and get it stamped. This will cost around $38. If your state does not have a USDA office nearby, overnight it and include an overnight return label. Remember, you only have 10 days to get it all done.

"5 - Then, send these overnight, including a prepaid return label to the Panamanian Embassy with a $30 money order for each one along with a copy of the request for in-house quarantine. Instead of doing this, we took the forms down to our Secretary of State Apostille[48] office, and got it done then and there for $3 each form. (In our case, this was Phoenix, Arizona.)

"6 - Email the Quarantine form to Panamanian authorities [cam@minsa.gob.pa or dcontreras@minsa.gob.pa - phone 507-238-3855] or fax [507-212-9449] at least three days before arrival. We did it 10 days before. Just a short form, describing dog, and where he would be staying. You also need a Panamanian telephone number to put on the form. If you don't have a Panamanian cell phone you can use the number of your landlord or a friend.

"7 - Be very careful about the size of crate and the restrictions from the airlines. We traveled on United with their Petsafe program. They have very strict guidelines, because they get fined if they are found breaking the rules. United did not have weather restrictions I was told, but some airlines do, if the dog is going cargo.

"American Airlines said we could just take the dog to reservations, and if there was room on the plane, he could go. They were very cheap, but we would not risk the dog not getting on the plane. Copa told me they had stopped carrying animals. I heard Delta had a good record with animals. With a big dog, you must take him to cargo two to four hours before the flight.

"8 - When you arrive at Tocumen International Airport in Panama you first go through immigration, then head to baggage/customs. I suggest you have a bottle of water with you when you get your pet because it will be thirsty.

"We employed a service to meet us and take us to the vet's office and the Ministry of Agriculture [MINSA] office, and get the dog through customs. It was $85.

"Your dog will come in at the baggage area. You'll probably want to get two luggage trolleys, one for luggage and one for the dog crate. The offices are right at the left hand side of the customs area where baggage is screened mostly looking for drugs and wads of cash. I thought the vet would check out the dog, but I just ended up paying $16, then down to the next office to pay $130. If you have the money (CASH ONLY) and the paperwork, you will be fine. We arrived at around 7:30 p.m. and the office was still open perhaps because the service we had hired arranged something.

"We got a ride with the service we had hired right to Boquete in an old mini bus/van. It cost $475 for the dog, the crate, two of us, and luggage. It was a lot to pay, but it was from curb to curb. The driver spoke no English, so we gave him a map of exactly where we were going. You are definitely at a disadvantage if you do not speak Spanish, but they were happy to stop along the way to let the dog out. Carry the exact amount of money needed since no one ever has change.

"Petpassportstore.com - Offers all the forms and instructions for around $20 – Much of this you can find on your own if you search enough, but $20 will save you a lot of hassle and time.

"Veterinary Certificate Translation Service: Having the veterinary certificate translated into the language of the country you are visiting can make going through immigration much easier. The cost is $35 and takes two days. For more information send an email to Jerry@PetPassportStore.Com.

Airlines have special restrictions on flat nosed dogs. They want larger crates for better air circulation ... see United Petsafe. [United.com/web/en-us/content/travel/animals/petsafe.aspx]

"We really, really recommend the people to take a dry run to the cargo area, and meet the people there. In Phoenix, MapQuest sent us around and around; we would have been frantic at 4:00 a.m. trying to find it."

Shaun, Maureen and Digby were able to find the home of their dreams and purchase it within two months of landing in Panama. Their new home has a big fenced yard and they all, including the dog, love it.

One of the signs of the new prosperity in Panama is that more and more Panamanians have pets and like to spend money on their pets. Increasingly the pet department in stores is taking up more space. In Boquete we have specialists in dog training, providing security dogs, a dog grooming service and in Panama City even pet hotels. We have some really great vets in Boquete and David who know how to treat small animals and the cost is a fraction of what you'd expect to pay in the states.

One of our Dalmatians had a fatty tumor under his hip that needed to be surgically removed. Cost, including vet and medicine, $40. Our adopted street dog Bobbi showed up with a mouth and throat full of porcupine quills: we didn't even know there were porcupines in Panama but Bobbi found them. Evening call to the vet and he removed 75 quills from the dogs mouth and throat. Cost, including medicine, $45. Try that in the U. S., Canada, or Europe!

Action Items and Points to Ponder

1. Given the health and age of your animal, is bringing him to Panama the best thing? Might your dog or cat be better off remaining with a caring relative or friend?

2. If you come to Panama to "test drive" living here by renting and staying six months to a year before making the commitment to relocate – something I recommend! – does it make sense to bring your pet along?

3. What is your vet's advice?

4. There are wonderful cats and dogs that are always available for adoption.

14. Burn Rate

When I was involved in the early days of the Internet, one of the major concerns of start-up Internet companies that received initial money from angel investors was the rate at which the fledgling company burned through cash. The key was to develop your idea, execute and launch before you burned through all your start-up capital. Many companies with would-be "killer apps" burned through all their start-up money with nothing to show. A few made it only to crash and burn when the Internet bubble burst. One or two survived and are today household words.

The lesson here for retirees and would-be retirees is to know how much money you have and plan accordingly. You may find a way to make some additional cash, but don't count on it. Probably you will live longer than you expect so you will need more money, not less. And probably wherever you go you are going to have to deal with inflation and/or currency devaluation.

Everyone wants to be positive and optimistic, but you must also be realistic. Everything is probably going to cost more than you expect. The fact is that it is easier and a lot more fun to live within your means than worry constantly about money and fear that the money will run out before you do. There will be unexpected expenses: count on it.

Things change

It's fine to move to Panama, or elsewhere, because you figure that you can live for less, but things change. Economies change. Government policies change. The value of money changes. Health changes. The cost of living changes. And the value of your pension and/or Social Security may change as well. These are changes that you cannot control yet they can impact you, often in devastating ways. The key is to be prepared as much as possible.

Not to pop any bubbles, but . . .

- Don't rely on everything you read on the Internet. Since much material isn't dated it is easy to read and then depend on old and outdated information.

- If you are thinking of moving to Panama or any other place, visit that country and make a boots-on-the-ground assessment of actual costs. Visit pharmacies, hospitals and grocery stores. Talk to expats, the more the merrier. Get the real story. One of the mistakes people make is to go to real estate investment seminars which are held in fancy hotel ballrooms in big cities where paid presenters often blow smoke. That may be a fun and interesting introduction to a place, but it doesn't give you the information that you need to know.

- *Over estimate* your expenses and *under estimate* your resources. Unfortunately that's just the opposite of what most people do. Moving to paradise and having an "ideal" retirement is what most people want, so consciously or unconsciously they fudge the numbers to make it work. Your future happiness depends on being brutally honest on this point.

- Don't plan on any additional income. In Panama the *Pensionado* visa puts limits on your ability to work and make money. Yes, there are some ways around this, but don't count on it. Sure a few folks have figured ways to make money on the Internet and if it works for you, fine, but don't count on it. Maybe you make jewelry, or do woodwork, or bake bread and will be able to sell it at a local market, if so fine, but, again, don't count on it. If you need to work pass on the *Pensionado* visa and get a visa that allows you to live in Panama *and* get a work permit.

- Don't over estimate business opportunities. Yes, there are business opportunities, and it may work out, but don't count on it. In many countries, including Panama, the locals all know each other and are related and understand how business is done. Your *gringo* approach may fall flat. They have the connections: you do not. They know how to work the system: you do not. If you are smart enough to partner with a local, then you may have a fighting chance.

  When we first moved to Boquete, ten years ago, every *gringo* wanted and needed a well. But there were few well drillers in Chiriqui and those who were here were overbooked and used antiquated equipment. One *gringo* found a slightly used well drilling rig in the States that instead of pounding away for weeks, used hydraulic pressure. He went through the hassle of importing the machine and one his first wells was on my property. Instead of weeks it took a few days. But it wasn't long before the locals made him an offer he couldn't refuse and bought his equipment.

  Back then all cement mixing in Chiriqui was either done by hand or using the kind of small mixer you see for sale at home improvement stores. The result was cement that was often improperly mixed. In Chiriqui we didn't have the big cement mixer trucks like we had back in the States. So another expat brought in a cement mixer truck and set up business. The companies that control cement in Panama got wind of this and just refused to sell him cement.

- Don't count on the *gringo* or expat market. In most places, including places like Boquete that are popular with expats, the expat market is a lot more limited than people imagine and it is a very fickle market. Small businesses have a high failure rate everywhere, but in Panama, unless you have an incredible business plan that is thoroughly researched and very conservative, you *will* fail. Restaurants and cafes come and go faster than tropical showers. Running a little bed and breakfast may sound like fun, but it is indentured servitude twenty-four hours a day with, in most cases, little or no reward. Sure, you'll hire someone to manage it ... and the business will be run into the ground in six months ... or less!

Please, don't get me wrong. I'm all for thinking positively and dreaming dreams and dreams *do* come true. But if you are going to have a happy time in paradise, wherever that paradise may be, you need to be realistic.

Don Winner[49] is a former U. S. Army intelligence officer who served in Panama and has settled here. He runs an Internet site called Panama-Guide.com aimed at providing news and information to English-speaking expats. It used to be free, but now he charges a subscription fee. One of the interesting online projects Winner came up with was to ask people, mostly English-speaking expats, what was their monthly cost-of-living. He gave guidelines for people to calculate their costs and then printed the results. It was fascinating! You had a family of four living on a sailboat anchored in a tiny harbor off a little Panamanian fishing village getting by on *under* $500 a month and you had a single guy, living in Panama City who, in his words, "burned through" $10,000 a month, admittedly "a lot of it on wine and women."

Can you live on $600 a month?

The idea that you can live in Panama on $600 a month goes back to the time when in order to get a *Pensionado* visa in Panama you had to demonstrate a pension of $500 a month per person, or $600 per couple. That figure is now $1,000 per month and an additional $250 per month per dependent.

To put that into perspective, I saw a government statistic [2013] that 75 percent of Panamanian households have monthly incomes of $1,000 or less. The Panamanian *Pensionado* program wasn't started for *gringos* and expats but for Panamanian retirees, many of whom are living on pensions of *$100 a month.*

So, yes, you can certainly live on $500 a month and many

Panamanian *Pensionados* struggle to get by on far less, but they live as Panamanians do eating local food, using government health services, and living in tiny *casitas*. What might one of those *casitas* be like? Probably it is unfinished cement block, a single room, with tin roof and nothing to insulate the sound of rain beating on the roof. The *casita* has no glass windows, which actually is a good thing making these houses *less* likely to have mold problems than if they had windows. Usually there is some kind of running water, some kind of cooking arrangement either a two-burner hot-plate type stove run off a small tank of propane or an inside or outside wood fire called a *fogón*. There may be electric service with a few light bulbs and most likely a TV, sometimes an old one, but sometimes also a flat screen TV, and a basic toilet, possibly outside depending on the area.

So, yes, $600 is doable, but it is not what most expats moving to Panama are expecting.

I do know an expat couple who lived here on around $700 a month. They came to Boquete early on before land prices had run up and used their savings to buy a nice lot and build a simple, but comfortable, home. They had some skills and talents they were able to market so made a little money to supplement their meager pension incomes. Like many people who first came to Panama stationed in the military or with the U. S. Panama Canal and realized they had discovered paradise, these folks came back to Panama to retire. As U. S. government retirees they had some insurance benefits ordinary U. S. citizens don't enjoy. But these folks were always living on the edge, month-to-month and when their health deteriorated and the combined effects of a booming economy in Panama and devaluation of the U. S. dollar hit things went downhill, and eventually they were forced to move, back to the States.

Did they regret the experience? No way! The guy said, "This was paradise! This is the best place we've ever lived or ever will live! Sure, we hate to leave, but we are grateful for having been here."

If you live on $600 a month in the States, you can probably, with some adjustment in lifestyle, do the same in Panama.

The difference between Altoona, Pennsylvania and Ventura, California is a lot more than 2,614 miles.

Costs within the United States, Canada or Europe, vary widely. I was born in Altoona and my parents eventually retired there. When my dad died we sold his beautiful home in a prime area of Altoona, just off the Altoona campus of Penn State University for $180,000, Had that identical home been located in Ventura, where I was selling real estate at the time, it would have been snapped up at $580,000.

You can still live better for less in Panama than in many areas of the United States, Canada and Europe. But how much less depends on the cost of living in your area. When we moved from Southern California to Panama I figured that we lived better in Panama for about a third of what it cost us in California. Today with inflation in both places and devaluation of the U. S. dollar, I would say that we still live better in Panama but only for about forty percent of what it would cost us in California or even Washington.

Obviously the rate at which you burn through cash is going to depend on your expectations and life style. But if you want to be happy, and avoid lying awake *every* night and wondering ... you'd better be honest with yourself about the resources you have and the rate at which you will burn through those resources.

Action Items and Points to Ponder

1. Realistically and honestly, what do you *expect* and how does that relate to what you *need*?

2. Do you have a firm understanding of your resources and the dependability of those resources?

3. How are you going to come up with a realistic expectation of your cost of living in Panama or whatever other paradise you choose?

Casco Viejo, or the old colonial city, has been lovingly restored.[50]

Looking from Casco Viejo across the Bay of Panama toward the modern city. Today there are three Panama Cities: Old Panama, Casco Viejo and the new modern city. [51]

15. Exit Strategy

One of the aspects of business I had never really thought about, until I did my MBA, was the importance of having an exit strategy. Whether you are developing a new business, acquiring a new company, building a plant, or whatever, you need to have and factor in the cost of an exit strategy. How are you going to dispose of assets you no longer need? Who is going to clean up the mess you leave behind? What if your manufacturing facility has contaminated the ground with what may later be called hazardous waste: how do you clean that up and at what cost? Getting into business is one thing, but getting out is quite another.

So ... you're retiring. You're coming to Panama or some other paradise, but eventually you are going to make an exit, one way or another.

Not for us

We will talk later about some of the reasons why people leave paradise, but for now you should already have decided that Panama is not for everyone; however, it may be perfect for you, as it is for us.

There are people who relocate to Panama with all good intentions only to find out that for whatever reasons, this is not for them. One of the ways to avoid that situation is to carefully do your due diligence and take a "test-drive" actually spending some time living in Panama before making the move.

There is a sense in which the same advice about changing jobs applies to changing countries: don't burn your bridges. If you've told the Feds to take their tax policy and pound sand, you might find yourself going home and ending up spending your retirement years in a free Federal retirement center with all expenses paid. And I'm told, not based on any personal experience, that some of the U. S. "country club" detention centers, where they put the people who've stolen millions, not just a few bucks here and there, aren't all that bad.

If you've precipitously decided to give up your U. S. citizenship and now want to go home, you might find that it is a whole lot more difficult to get a visa to enter the United States, or travel the world, with your new Dominica or St. Kitts/Nevis passport.

If you thought it took a while to sell your home in the United States during the economic downturn, wait until you try to sell your home in Dominica or St. Kitts. Even Panama: it's not that homes don't sell here or that they don't sell for a lot of money, but that it takes time. You likely come from an area where a lot of home sales are the result of job transfers and relocations where people have to buy or sell. It's different in an international community where people don't *have* to move. When you go to sell in Panama you will get close to what you're asking, and maybe more than you thought, but it will take a while, particularly with high-end properties. Extricating yourself takes time, which is why, again, I suggest you rent first and do a trial run before selling everything and moving permanently.

When you have truly discovered paradise ...

Generally those of us who retire in Panama come expecting to enjoy the last third of our life and make it a great adventure. We don't come expecting to die, or even leave, but to live. Life is what it is about!

Our expectation is to live longer and healthier than our parents. Those whose parents are still living know that someday they will be in the same situation, but it is easy to brush all that aside. *Other* people get older, but in our heart of hearts we are still young and vital. Did you ever wonder why the celebrities you knew in your youth all look so old, while you, of course, are still young, vital, 30 ... OK, maybe 40-something ... at least in your imagination? The fact is, like it or not, we are all getting older. And sometimes it isn't pretty.

Time flies! It especially flies when you are having fun and living the adventure. Eventually, in spite of whatever face lifts, nips and tucks you indulge in, which by the way may be a whole lot cheaper in Panama than elsewhere, eventually your age catches up with you.

So how do you realistically prepare for that as an expat living far from your original home and family?

I've never understood why people relocate to Panama to retire and buy or build multi-story mansions. It seems a lot more sensible have a single story home without steps and with .9 meter [36 inch] wide doors. The more you can plan and anticipate the better. And why "downsize" only to build the home of your dreams that is three times larger than what you left behind?

OK, you've managed to pull most of your money out of your home country and invest it in Panama. Now what? When you shuffle off this mortal coil, how do you get that money back home to your kids and heirs? What if you decide that you need to go back home and into assisted living? How easy is it going to be to disengage in Panama, sell off your assets here, and move what, if anything, is left back home? And let's say you are lucky enough to take home *more* than you brought down – unlikely, but it happens. What tax consequences do you face at home?

Staying put in Panama

We live on the road to the cemetery. That's the name of the street, "the road to the cemetery." Since we don't have addresses, our "address" is a certain light pole on the road to the cemetery. When we built our home and moved in my wife said, "This is it! We're not building again and I'm not moving again. My next move is out the door in a pine box and down the road to the cemetery."

What if your kids don't want you, or you don't want your kids, or you never had kids? What if the country you left is no longer the country you knew and loved? What happens if you are incapacitated? What if you need end-of-life care?

We faced this problem with my younger brother. Ed has had many physical and psychological challenges throughout his life. To his credit he earned his way through college by working as a night watchman. In his early 20s, just three credits from getting his degree, he was driving home from work and drove his car head-on into a tree. He survived, but was never quite the same. Subsequent investigation showed that, unbeknownst to anyone, Ed suffered from epilepsy and the accident was caused not by falling asleep but by a seizure. So New York State pulled his driver's license and unable to find work in a tiny upstate town when he couldn't drive, Ed lived with my parents. Additionally all his life he suffered from a condition we now know as Asperger Syndrome, a type of autism. Ed ended up mowing lawns, doing odd jobs, and living with my parents. By the time both of my parents had died, Ed had also developed diabetes. He tried living alone in Pennsylvania where my parents had lived in retirement and thankfully we have some wonderful cousins in Altoona who looked after him. Eventually we concluded he could no longer live alone and so seven years ago we brought him to Panama. We bought a little Panamanian house for him in town just outside Valle Escondido which worked well when we lived in Valle Escondido. But getting him to live on schedule, take his medication and insulin and eat regularly was a challenge.

When we moved from Valle Escondido to our coffee farm we converted a caretaker cottage on our farm into a cute little *casita* for Ed. It was right at the entrance to our farm so we could keep closer watch on him. Our Indian farm worker woke him up every morning, tried to make sure he ate and took his medicine, and we tried to have him improve his diet.

Things went fairly well for about two years, but Ed would suffer from bouts of dementia. He would forget to take his medication or not eat, or just take medication at random and in varying amounts. We came up with a monthly calendar with little plastic bags of morning and evening pills, which worked for a while. But then Ed started to forget what day it was, so he'd just grab a couple of bags of pills at random and consume them. He was always pretty good with his insulin, until he started forgetting if he'd taken it, so would give himself a second injection. Then we noticed instead of 30 cc he would sometimes give himself 20 cc or 60 cc. Several times our Indian worker who lived next door to Ed found him going into a diabetic coma. We knew we were getting to the point where we had to do something.

We were able to find a home in a neighboring district run by a church group. While the home is beautiful on the outside, we developed serious concerns about the quality of the care. Ed lost over 60 pounds in the year was there. We tended to dismiss his complaints about the food and set about looking for a medical reason for the serious weight loss. The food was Panamanian and we assumed was just be a problem of Ed adjusting his tastes, since we didn't expect to change their menu just for him. Unfortunately, we discovered that the home was just poorly managed. Given his weight when he entered, his age and sedentary life, Ed needed about 2,000 calories a day. Several times I showed up unannounced at the evening meal time and each time his meal totaled around 300 calories. The standard evening menu appeared to be a hot dog roll, cut into thirds with either cheese or cheese and inexpensive lunch meat. No fruit or vegetables even though the home is in an area that produces most of the country's vegetables and fruit. Different times when we visited there was no water, not even water to drink.

The only other senior care center we could find was a home in David catering almost entirely to advanced Alzheimer patients. With nothing else available, we were forced to take my brother back to the States.

In Panama ongoing government regulation and supervision of such homes is severely limited. Panama does not have the type of senior living common in the States where you move from one level to another.

As more and more retirees move to areas like Boquete this is a definite need and an opportunity for someone to develop facilities to meet this need.

We've seen people come to Boquete late in retirement, perhaps for one last adventure, or perhaps intent on dying without the fuss and presence of family, only to be unable to care for themselves and very much alone. It is one thing to say you can hire a full-time caregiver at relatively low cost compared to the States, but what is this person's training, if any, and who supervises such a person when you are no longer able, and who deals with their Social Security and all the legalities and hassle of having workers in Panama?

For this reason a number of expats got together and started a Hospice program in Boquete. There is no facility, but the group does attempt to provide respite care and assistance to those who find themselves totally alone in the final stages of life. The demand exceeds the ability of this fledging group to provide the services needed and the likelihood is that the demand will grow.

The final exit

Dying in Panama is different than that to which you are probably accustomed. The result is the same, but . . .

- Panama does not have a "living will" like in most jurisdictions in the United States. So you may be brain dead but your family could be saddled with a hospital and medical professionals who are unwilling to "pull the plug," first because of legal and religious questions and second, because they continue to rack up income even although you are brain dead. This can go on for a long time and become a nightmare for your family. Some people have taken U. S. living wills and had them translated into Spanish, hoping that when the time comes, they will be honored.

- Your personal physician must pronounce you. Unlike in most jurisdictions where any physician may pronounce you dead, in Panama it must be your personal physician, which can result in quite a wait, particularly if your personal physician is in a different part of the country. If you are pronounced by another physician who does not know your history and hence supposedly cannot know the cause of death (and we won't even discuss the logic) the law requires an autopsy.

- Typically there is no embalming ... or refrigeration for bodies. So the process has to move rather quickly and a body must be buried within three days.

- There are funeral homes of a sort in the larger cities, but typically in most rural areas of Panama dealing with death is a personal, family matter and not farmed out to specialists or funeral directors.

- There is one crematorium in Panama City.

For poorer families the process is very personal, hands-on and a little like we seen in those Old West U. S. movies.

- The family waits with the body until the personal physician can be summoned, or in the case of a hospital death in a poor family that cannot afford a funeral home assistance, a family member goes to the hospital to pick up the body either with a friend, or in a taxi. The body is then loaded into the vehicle, sometimes just in the back of a pickup truck taxi, and taken home to be prepared for burial.

- At home the body is cleaned and dressed and placed in a casket, which may be open for the family and friends to view. Should the body have been held in the hospital for some time or required autopsy only a small glass window will be in the coffin so the family can see the face of the deceased. Members of the family and friends will remain with the body throughout the night based on the concept that maybe, just maybe, the person isn't really dead.

- During this time family and friends will dig the grave in a local cemetery. It's real dirt, a real hole, real hard work with no paid grave diggers, no backhoe, and no artificial turf.

- The next day, barring any unforeseen resurrection, there will be some kind of service in a church and the body will be taken to the burial site with family and friends walking behind an old hearse or pickup truck carrying the casket.

- At the grave site the casket is placed in the previously dug hole which hopefully is large enough for not only the casket but the friends who must get down into the hole to help lower the casket. No neat systems where the funeral director can unobtrusively tap a button with his foot to silently lower the casket into a hole lined with Astroturf. Once the casket is in place family and friends grab shovels, or stand around and watch and visit while the casket is covered and the hole is completely filled with dirt.

This is the reality and finality of death and, for me theologically and practically, it's not a bad way to go, if you have family and friends to take care of your remains.

Returning remains from one country to another is generally a frustrating nightmare. In this age of total examination prior to boarding a flight (you, your luggage and carry-on) it has become impossible to surreptitiously transport cremated remains.

My personal choice, should I make my final exit in Panama, is to be cremated and have my remains quietly and privately scattered either on Volcan Baru or in the Bay of Chiriqui. I have no doubt that the God who created man out of clay can get me back together for the Day of Resurrection.

All of us will make that final exit, and for some of us it will be in Panama, so it pays to be prepared and to let your family and friends know your final wishes.

I know many of us, particularly from the United States, chafe over big brother knowing everything, including exactly where in the world we are located. But you have a chip in your passport, the U. S. National Security folks are monitoring your telephone conversations and Internet use, so "they" already know. It is helpful to register your presence in Panama with your embassy, and also to know your countries warden in the area as a contact point with the embassy.

This can become incredibly complicated should both you and your partner die together, possibly in a car accident, and your family back in the States not only have to deal with your final arrangements, but also unscramble your financial affairs in Panama. So, the more information and direction you can provide, the better. And it is helpful if your heirs have met and have confidence in your Panama attorney who is going to be key in unscrambling the assets you own in Panama.

Our best friends are a couple. One guy is from Taiwan and his partner is from the States. One day sitting around and talking about Boquete gossip and news and the subject came up about a couple who had been killed in a car accident. We realized that our friends didn't have our kids' phone numbers and we didn't have the number of their relatives either in the States or Taiwan. The sad thing is that we know we should do this, and we still haven't, which is the case for most people when it comes to telling family and friends their final wishes.

Action Items and Points to Ponder

1. If you are thinking about retiring in paradise, your mind is probably running a mile a minute, making plans and weighing options for your new life. But have you thought about your own exit plan?

2. Likely your kids didn't like you always telling them what to do when they were kids and you don't always like them now telling you what to do. But ... what does your family think?

3. How willing and prepared would your children or heirs be to unscramble the remains of your life in Panama when and if it comes to that? What guidance could/should you provide?

4. Yes, it is your life, but what about the other lives that your life impacts?

Some of the most fantastic, and expensive, horses in the world
are raised at the Haras farm in Cerro Punta.

[52] River rafting in Chiriqui.

16. Legalities

When I do my "Beyond Johnny Depp: The History of Piracy" lecture on board ships, I like to have some fun with the audience and include some of the dumbest pirate jokes I know.

"Where did the pirate stop for breakfast?"

"IHOP."

Someone always yells this out and I respond, "Either you have a six-year-old grandson or the sense of humor of a six-year-old." It always gets a laugh, except when I was on a ship filled with folks from Great Britain who had never seen an IHOP [International House of Pancakes] restaurant.

My favorite dumb pirate joke: "What do you call it when you have 500 pirates in the same room?"

"A convention of lawyers."

We all grouse and gripe about inequities in the law, stupid laws, and the injustice that often characterizes the law in the United States or wherever you call home. Oliver Wendell Holmes commented on the U. S. legal system, "This is a court of law, not a court of justice." But before you decide to move off to another country, be it Panama or anywhere else, you need to take a look at the legal system of this new country, which may be VERY different from that to which you are accustomed. Sometimes the devil you know is better than the devil you don't know.

U. S. law is based on English Common Law and case law, which is why would-be lawyers spend so much time studying cases and quoting chapter and verse from cases which set precedent for future legal decisions. Panamanian law is VERY different because it is based largely on colonial Spanish law and Colombian law, since Panama was part of the Spanish Empire and, after Simon Bolivar's liberation of Latin America. a part of Colombia. Long association with the United States has added in a few things adapted from U. S. law and practice, but it isn't the same. In the end it is up to judges to make decisions based on the judges' understanding and interpretation of the law, not necessarily case law or precedents. This system, for someone used to a U. S. system of law, throws everything up into the air! From an outsider's perspective this opens the door for political and economic influence of judicial decisions, not that that same thing doesn't happen in the United States and elsewhere, albeit more surreptitiously.

From the U. S. Department of State

"Panama has a court and judicial system built around a civil code, as opposed to the Anglo-American system of case law and judicial precedent. In September 2011 Panama started a four year conversion to the accusatory system which is expected to simplify and expedite criminal judicial cases. Fundamental procedural rights in civil cases are broadly similar to those available in U. S. civil courts, although some notice and discovery rights, particularly in administrative matters, may be less extensive than in the United States. Judicial pleadings are not always a matter of public record, nor are the processes always transparent.

"Many lack confidence in the Panamanian judicial system as an objective, independent arbiter in legal or commercial disputes, especially when the case involves powerful local figures with political influence. For example, Panama ranked 133 out of 142 in judicial independence in the September 2011 World Economic Forum report. Over the last few years, the majority of disputes involving U. S. investors have been related to land purchasing and/or titling issues. Such disputes have been difficult to resolve due to the lack of adequate titling, inconsistent regulations, lack of trained officials outside of Panama City, and a slow and cumbersome judiciary. Some of these disputes have resulted from U. S. investors being unfamiliar with the Panamanian titling system. The court system is slow and prone to massive case backlogs and corruption. For this reason, Panamanian legal firms typically recommend that companies write arbitration clauses into contracts.

"Panama's commercial law is comprehensive and well-established. Its bankruptcy law is antiquated and remains under review to be adapted to modern business practices."

Even when it comes to something as simple as calling the police, it is different in Panama. Here's the word from the U. S. Embassy in Panama:

"The U. S. Embassy informs U. S. citizens living, working or travelling in Panama, that we are aware of concerns over crime against foreigners in various areas of the country. In addition to urging the U. S. community to take all necessary precautions to avoid becoming a victim of crime, the embassy encourages U. S. residents and visitors to Panama to immediately report crimes to the police.

"Police response in Panama is different than in the United States. The police will respond to provide immediate assistance and protection to victims, will arrest suspects if they are still on the scene or nearby (assuming they have probable cause that the suspect indeed committed a crime) and, if necessary, call for DIJ investigators (see more about DIJ below). *The Police will NOT take a report or conduct follow-up investigation.* They may take some data for statistical purposes, but they are not empowered to file reports or conduct investigations. If your call to the police is not timely (i.e. when the crime is discovered) there is little the police can do. If you delay in reporting the crime, or if it is minor, you should go straight to DIJ.

The DIJ or Department of Judicial Investigation) ["Dirección de Investigación Judicial"] is the bridge between the initial police response and the investigation for prosecution of a crime. They are actually an arm of the Attorney General's Office ["Fiscalía"].

If DIJ responds to the scene of a crime, they will conduct an initial investigation, however, they cannot conduct a full investigation or a follow-up investigation unless you go to the local *denuncia* center and file an official report. Filing a *denuncia* is the ONLY way to open a case and get a case tracking number. Once you have filed a *denuncia* and obtained a *denuncia* number, you can use that number to follow up on the status of your case.

"The Attorney General's Office ["Fiscalía"] - Matters are taken up with the Fiscalía once the DIJ investigation has begun. During this step of the crime reporting process, you will need a lawyer or a public defender to represent your case. On average, it takes two to four months to investigate a case, and prosecution can take years.

"In addition to reporting crime to Panamanian authorities, US citizens are encouraged to provide information on criminal incidents to the U. S. Embassy. This information will assist the embassy in tracking crimes against U. S. citizens in Panama, and to follow up with authorities."

There is a good online piece by the Hauser Global Law School Program, New York University School of Law, which is well worth reading before you embrace a devil you don't know. [Nyulawglobal.org/globalex/Panama.htm]

Here are two sad examples of how a different, and unfamiliar, legal system impacted two different expat families. In both situations the people came from countries with legal systems based on English common law and case precedent.

The expat in the first case was a retired policeman, so he knew, or thought he knew, something about the law. His neighbor was going away and asked the man to "watch" his house while he was gone. One night the retired cop saw someone break and enter the house and so he went over and confronted the would-be thief inside the house and in the act of burglarizing. When the burglar threatened the neighbor with a machete, the neighbor shot the burglar in the ass wounding him. The not-so-bright thief fled, but did not seek treatment and bled to death. The former policeman was arrested and charged with murder. Under Panamanian law he had no right to shoot the man because his neighbor had asked him to "watch" the house and not told him specifically to go "inside." Additionally the gun and the machete did not have equal weight as weapons. Had to former cop thrown the burglar an extra gun, and then had a shoot-out, and the burglar and not the cop died, then it would have been a "fair" confrontation of equal weapons. Fortunately the expat, retired cop was released pending his trial and was smart enough to "get out of Dodge" before trial.

The second story concerns a wealthy retired couple who came to Panama and invested their own money, to the tune of several million dollars, in a fantastic project which would have benefited Panama and the local community. One night they were coming home from the store and, after looking for oncoming traffic, pulled out onto the Pan-American Highway. They did not see another vehicle without any lights bearing down on them. One of the passengers in the oncoming car was killed. There were no witnesses to the accident. The driver of the oncoming car was intoxicated, but it was the expat driver who was held and charged with murder. As the trial date approached scores of witnesses began materializing out of the woodwork to testify against the expat driver. On the advice of counsel, the expat couple found a boat to take them to a neighboring country in the dark of night from which they were able to make their way back to their home country. Their dreams were shattered. Their project and investment was abandoned. But they escaped being in prison, perhaps for years, until the case was resolved.

Their car insurance company had a dogged attorney who would not give up, and kept pressing the case through the court system. After three years, it was determined that the "witnesses" had all been hired, the drunk driver of the oncoming car was totally at fault, and the expat couple were innocent. But in the meantime they lost everything.

Your new best friend

We used a lawyer in the United States to draw up wills and a family trust. That's it. When we had travel agencies I had a lawyer on retainer who, fortunately, I never had to use. When we purchased houses there were always escrow and title companies involved who had their own lawyers. In the church I usually had an attorney who was a member of the congregation who handled church legal matters. In the Bronx I was fortunate enough to have the senior partner of a Wall Street firm who was a friend of our ministry and did pro bono work for us including suing the City of New York, a case that went on for years after I was no longer the pastor, but this guy stuck with it, took it all the way to the state supreme court and won.

In Panama you need a lawyer by your side for almost everything, so plan on your lawyer becoming your new best friend.

It's almost, but not quite, true that lawyers are a dime a dozen in Panama. Finding a good lawyer, someone you can trust, someone who knows what they are doing, and someone who knows their way around, preferably with connections and someone who will return emails and calls, is a challenge. An even bigger challenge is finding someone who actually will get things done.

The path to becoming a lawyer in Panama is different than in the United States. Accreditation as attorney-at-law is granted to all Panamanian citizens that earn a law degree from a Panamanian law school (or a law school from a Spanish-speaking country recognized by the University of Panama) and apply to the General Affairs Section of the Supreme Court. Graduates from non-recognized foreign law schools must comply with a thesis requirement in Panama. Membership in a Panamanian bar association is a requirement to litigate, but not to practice law.

Go to school and become a lawyer. There seem to be more lawyers in Panama than any other profession, but not all lawyers are equal. This will shock most U. S. Americans: there is no bar exam in Panama. You have to pass your courses, but there is no final test to see if you learned what you need to know to practice law. So there are excellent lawyers and there are some who ... well ... it is a good idea to talk to many people and get a lot of feedback before you jump into a relationship with a lawyer in Panama.

You WILL need a lawyer, even just for day-to-day matters, matters which you may have felt comfortable handing in your own country. In a different country with an system with which you are unfamiliar, at least initially, you are safest to check with your lawyer.

Choose carefully. If you have the misfortune to end up in court, plan for the case to take years and the legal fees to soar. Should you have the terrible misfortune to end up in an accident where someone dies, expect that everyone except the dead person goes directly to jail, does not pass GO, and does not collect $200 and waits in jail while the lawyers and police decide guilt and innocence. So you'd better have a good lawyer.

That's why I have my lawyer's cards in the glove compartment and in my wallet and on speed dial. You never know! Forget getting "one phone call" or a quick and speedy trial, not that anyone actually gets those anyway, except in movies.

When we first came to Panama, and Panama was still in many ways a "second-world" country, we were driving the Pan-American Highway from David to Paso Canoas on the Panama-Costa Rican border to buy tires. There are lots of stores on the border which sometimes have good prices on things. The stores are unique because exit out one door and you're in Panama, go out another door and you're in Costa Rica. You can pay in either countries currency and get whatever receipt you want and sometimes avoid taxes. About half way between David and Paso there is a police and customs check point.

We were stopped at the check point on the way *to* Paso Canoas and did not yet have our permanent *Pensionado* visas, but *I* had paperwork from Immigration with me, saying that *my* application was being processed, which should have been adequate. For whatever reason, maybe they were looking for a "gratuity" or whatever, they had us pull over to the side and wait … and wait. Several times an officer came over to the car to tell us what a big problem we faced. I guess I had not been forthcoming with the gratuity. So I called my lawyer, and the next time the officer came back I let him talk to my lawyer.

We ended up having to follow a cop to the Immigration office on the Costa Rican border. I went into this tiny, tiny, ramshackle house that had two tiny rooms, no air conditioner or working fan. I sat at the desk with the Immigration supervisor in his office, furnished with an old desk, an antique big box computer monitor (which since nothing was computerized was just a decorative item), and a doorway with a flimsy curtain, no door, which led to the bathroom where a member of his staff was trying to quietly use the toilet. It was like a movie set! The guy in charge talked with my attorney, on my cell phone on my dime. And we waited 45 minutes until the ancient fax cranked out some additional paperwork. Meanwhile, Nikki sat huddled, quietly in the heat of the car, not sure she would ever see her husband again and fearful because she hadn't brought ANY paperwork!

The Immigration supervisor guy was very cordial, even offering me water out of the tap in a dirty glass, and it all ended well, BUT … Having a Panama City lawyer on call who was used to getting things done, and who had some influence and connections, and most importantly, spoke the language and understood the law, certainly helped.

It is important to establish a relationship with a lawyer early on. Not only will it help expedite your visa application, because you'll do things right the first time, but it will also give you someone who can assist you if necessary.

There is nothing "second-world" about Immigration today. The computers work most of the time and the offices are new and modern. Immigration and the National Police have access to their own data bases as well as the FBI, Interpol and other national police data bases. If you are stopped at a road check or for some other reason, the police will ask for your Panamanian ID called a cedula, or your passport. The policeman has his hand-held "Pele Policia" that connects to a computer that runs your number through Panamanian, Interpol, U. S. and Canadian data bases and if you are on the run from the law you will be arrested on the spot and possibly deported the next day.

A Way of Life

Don't assume things are the same in Panama as your home country. Don't assume that your lawyer has no conflict of interest or that he will disclose any potential conflict. A key aspect of U. S. law is that "time is of the essence," but this is definitely not the case in Panama. The culture is different. Things take as long as they take ... and with a lawyer longer than you might ever imagine. In Panama there is no sense of urgency ... ever.

What kind of visa?

Tourist Visa or Tourist Card

These requirements in Panama change frequently, so you will want to check with your Panamanian lawyer for the most current requirement. Many countries[53] hold treaties with Panama that permit their citizens to visit for up to 180 days without a visa.

Citizens from these countries can apply for an extension for another 30, 60 or 90 days. Petitions are approved or denied by Immigration on a case-by-case basis.

Although you don't need a visa, nationals from many countries[54] including the United States, Canada, and a few European countries, do require a tourist card, A tourist card is just a piece of paper or a simple form you fill out that costs $5 and is available from Panamanian embassies and consulates, airlines serving Panama, border crossings, or at the international airport: In most cases the airline takes care of buying the tourist card and the price is included in the price of your ticket, if not your can buy one at Tocumen International Airport just before going through Immigration.

Tourists are required to have a round-trip ticket when entering Panama, but maybe you aren't sure how long you will want to stay, or you are test-driving living in Panama and you don't want to pay for an open return or excessive airline change fees. You'd prefer to buy a one-way air ticket. There is a workaround! Your "round-trip" just has to take you out of Panama, not necessarily back to your point of origin. The cheap way is to buy a bus ticket from Panama City to Costa Rica for $25, fulfilling the requirement but without spending a lot of money.

Pensionado Visa

Most people retiring to Panama will be interested in the *Pensionado* Visa which gives you permanent residency in Panama. The *Pensionado* (Retired) visa requires you to prove that you have a lifetime pension income of at least $1,000 per month, or a pension income of $750 per month if you have purchased real estate valued at $100,000 or more. These numbers, like most things in Panama, often change so you will want to check with your lawyer. It is best if you start the process in your home country. The earlier you start working with a lawyer the better, as it will save you a lot of time and frustration.

The pension amount must be proven with documentation from the government agency or company providing the pension. This certification must be authenticated by the nearest Panama Consul or by apostille and generally translated into Spanish by a certified translator. Other documents may be required to prove legitimacy and solvency if the pension is not from a recognized government agency.

You will need a police criminal background report issued by a national police or investigatory agency where you have lived for the past five years. When we moved to Panama all they required was a letter from the police department in my home town of Ventura saying that I wasn't wanted and had no criminal record *in Ventura*. For all they knew I could have been an axe murderer wanted in Sacramento. As Panama has become more "first-world" things have become more complicated and Panama has had bad experiences with criminals from other countries, including the United States, trying to get lost in Panama. Now, you need an official apostilled report from your national police. In the case of the United States this is the FBI. There are very precise regulations regarding this document so you need your attorney's guidance before requesting it from the national police in your home country.

Other things you may need are a marriage certificate and/or birth certificates of children under 18. Ordinary copies do not work: you need the original or a certified copy, apostilled, and translated; but of course! The earlier you begin working on assembling the documents the better. And it is far, far easier to do all this while you are living in your home country rather than attempting to do it long distance from Panama.

Once your attorney has submitted all the documentation you will get a temporary *Pensionado* card, and after about six months your permanent Panamanian identification which is a plastic card known in Panama as your *cedula*. You will have to show and use your *cedula* frequently and provide your *cedula* number. Your *cedula* will be exactly like that of Panamanians except that it will have a letter "E" before the number indicating that you are an *extranjero* or foreigner.

The *Pensionado* visa gives you permanent residence in Panama but does not allow you to work in Panama or put you on a path for citizenship. However, after you have lived in Panama permanently for five years you can apply for citizenship.

Because Panama is growing and needs more talented people

there are several other attractive options for resident visas.

Panama Self Economic Solvency Visa

The Self Economic Solvency Visa requires an investment of a minimum of $300,000 in a Panama bank CD for a minimum of three years. The interest earned is not taxable in Panama and can be used as you wish. Or you can invest at least $300,000 into titled Panama real estate. Or you can do a combination of the above equaling $300,000.

Panama Reforestation Visa

The eco-friendly Reforestation Visa allows foreigners to invest in a government certified reforestation project in return for a permanent residency visa. You must invest at least $80,000 in purchasing a minimum of five hectares [about twelve acres] of a reforestation project certified by the Panama government. After five years you can become a citizen and get a Panamanian passport. I've watched some of these projects and seen the amount of timber, generally teak, culled out in only five or six years. Because demand for tropical woods is increasing and native trees are increasingly rare, a well-run reforestation project can not only be a good thing ecologically, but also a good investment.

Panama Agriculture Investor Visa

Persons investing a minimum of $60,000 in Panama aquaculture, Panama farms, or Panama agriculture can get up to six years temporary residency, but this visa does not provide permanent residency or lead to citizenship.

Panama Friendly Nations Visa

One of the biggest changes to Panama's immigration policy was introduced by President Ricardo Martinelli in response to the need for additional labor and professionals created by Panama's booming economy. Citizens of 47 nations[55] considered friendly to Panama who wish to start a new business, purchase an existing business, or be hired in a professional capacity[56] by a Panamanian company can be fast-tracked to get a work permit and temporary residency including dependents. You must prove economic solvency by depositing at least $5,000 into a Panama bank account plus an additional $2,000 for each dependent. Once the primary applicant is approved, a permanent residency *cedula* will be issued.

As with any government, things take time. Nothing happens overnight anywhere, especially in Panama. But the sooner you can identify an attorney specializing in visas and immigration the easier everything will be because you will do things right the first time.

Run for the border

There are expats who live permanently in Panama who play the "run for the border" game with Immigration. They enter on a 30-day tourist visa, and then go to Immigration to have the tourist visa extended. Prior to the expiration of the tourist visa they drive to the Costa Rica border, cross, and spend two or three nights at a Costa Rican resort, or even just a few hours in Costa Rica, and then return to Panama, purchase a new tourist visa and start all over again. You need to show a ticket out of Panama but it need not be an airline ticket. Just a bus ticket to San Jose, Costa Rica will do.

I know Costa Rica is a wonderful place to visit, but this has always seemed like a lot of hassle to me. If you screw up your dates you can be in line for a big fine, so why not just do it right?

Citizenship

Most countries, including the United States, permit dual citizenship. However be aware that when you have dual citizenship you are incurring responsibilities and liabilities to both countries. There are many Panamanians, even government officials, with dual citizenship. Many Panamanians had one or both parents who worked for the U. S. Canal or military and so have dual United States / Panama citizenship.

Anyone born in Panama, even in the U. S. Canal Zone, can become a Panamanian citizen. Because John McCain was born in the U. S. Canal Zone in Panama he could become a Panamanian citizen.

Once you have lived permanently in Panama for five years, and have no police record you can apply for a Panamanian passport and citizenship. You must understand Spanish at about a fifth grade level to take a test and be interviewed in Spanish. The test is given in Panama City and covers Panamanian government, history, geography and culture. The multiple choice test has 65 questions and to pass you must get 71 percent correct. The cost of obtaining citizenship is anywhere from $2,000 to $4,000 depending on legal fees.

Why might you want Panamanian citizenship?

As a citizen you can work or start a business in any field … doctor, tour operator, whatever … with no work or business restrictions other than those that apply to Panamanian citizens. You have the right to vote like any other Panamanian and after fifteen years can run for office. As a citizen you can never be deported unless you lied on your application.

As a Panamanian citizen there are no restrictions on bank accounts. Because of the FATCA regulations and administrative costs of FATCA for Panamanian financial institutions, some are refusing to open or maintain accounts for U. S. citizens. And, as one expat said, "In case your country goes insane, and starts clearing out personal bank accounts to pay off failed bank debts (like Greece just did)" you can have your money in accounts as a Panamanian citizen, although, if you are also a U. S. citizen you continue to have reporting obligations to the United States.

"TIP"

A frequent expression among expats living in Panama is "TIP" meaning "This is Panama!" It is not the U. S., Canada, Europe or wherever you are from, it is Panama. It is different! You just have to accept that fact and live with it. How different?

As I write this, a year into a new administration, the new administration is still in the throes of massive investigations of fraud and corruption alleged against the previous administration. The former President and many of his cronies have fled the country amidst allegations of corruption.

I mentioned that the judicial system in Panama is not what many are used to coming from countries where the legal systems have evolved from English law. Here judges make the decisions based on the facts of the case as the judges see it, and not necessarily based on precedents of case law. From a U. S. perspective this would appear to be a wide-open door for corruption and pay off. Recently *two judges of the Supreme Court of Panama, including the Chief Justice of the Supreme Court,* were charged with corruption and bribery and are now sitting in prison. This is Panama! It's different.

Action Items and Points to Ponder

1. What is your intent in possibly moving to Panama? Retirement? Working? Investment? Knowing clearly what you intend to do will help you select the best visa option.

2. If you are actively moving ahead on plans to relocate to Panama, do you have an attorney? The sooner you get one the easier things will be, but choose carefully. Consider experience, expertise in immigration law, accessibility (Do they return calls and emails?), language and cost.

17. Just Say No

"Just Say No" might well be the motto for retail business in Panama. (With apologies to Nancy Reagan; and we all know how well her "Just Say No" to drugs campaign worked in the United States.) Like it or not, if you decide on an expat lifestyle in Panama you are going to confront a way of doing business like you've never encountered before.

Banking in Panama is a nightmare. Forget the U. S. FATCA business: banking in Panama was a nightmare long before the United States government stuck its long nose into the banking tent. In the movies moving money around the world happens at the click of a few computer keys. Good luck with that!

I realize the days are long gone when the local branch bank managers in the States threw themselves at your feet offering incentives of free toasters and blankets to get you to open an account. In Panama I'd challenge the Obamas to try and open an account. You need this, you need that, and when you finally pull all the documentation together ... you wait. It all has to go to Panama City to be processed and for someone higher up in the food chain to decide if they want to accept your money. You shouldn't take it personally because "Panama City" needs to approve everything, including, I suspect, the local bank manager's potty break requests.

In Boquete we have a bank which the expats all call, "The Bank of Just Say No" because no matter what you need, or ask for, the answer is always no. Even simple things, like seeing your own bank statement (since of course they don't mail monthly bank statements) becomes a big deal. Panamanians spend a lot of time perfecting their signature which, almost like a Chinese chop, becomes a work of art unique to them. So every time they sign anything they use this artistic, time-consuming signature which is perfected down to every detail. Anyone from the United States, particularly someone who has been in business or conducted fund raising campaigns, has signed their name thousands, or millions of times. Their signature has evolved and it is never exactly and perfectly the same. North Americans value time and "time is money," so we're not going to waste time in order to create the perfect signature, let alone take an additional, totally unnecessary, thirty seconds when signing. BUT if your signature is not perfect, and I mean perfect, "The Bank of Just Say No" will return your check, unpaid, and charge you a fee.

If you're starting to feel like Alice in Wonderland, just wait!

The United States is convinced that Panama is a giant money laundering machine. In my opinion the best and most effective way to launder cash in Panama is to throw it all in the washing machine and let it run. Granted, there are a few folks on *both sides* of the law who want to launder their illegal drug proceeds in Panama and don't have a large enough washing machine.

So how do you launder money in Panama? If you've got enough money, and believe me the narco crowd of drug producers and law enforcement thugs have enough money, you accept that you are going to throw away some money in order to make the rest clean and useable. So you've got millions to launder. You build a giant, high-rise expensive hotel, or a tiny resort in Chiriqui. Then you manage to have nearly 100 percent occupancy of rooms rented even though on any night the hotel is virtually empty. All those rooms are conveniently rented for cash. Dirty cash money is shown as income from hotel operations and ends up as nice, newly cleaned U. S. dollars that can be invested in other operations, some of which are entirely legitimate.

There are other variations of the same game. Importers in the Colon Free Zone shuffle make-believe inventory and paperwork, or high-end brand stores that never have any customers, and even small resorts that appear to have high operating costs but rarely have guests.

That's the way the big guys do it and once in a while a big guy is snagged and brought down, like the few big-name international banks that have been busted and fined millions of dollars. But it's so much easier for the U. S. Treasury Department to pretend that the real problem is a bunch of elderly baby boomer expats who are struggling to make ends meet on pensions and Social Security. It's easier to go after the small fry than the big fish who are likely also to be big campaign contributors. Only when really pressured will they go after the big guys like HSBC or Morgan Chase.

Banking is different in Panama and so is the way of doing business.

Panamanian workers are great, if, and when they are allowed to excel. They can be creative, enthusiastic, and will work hard IF they are given the responsibility, training, encouragement, and reward by management. The problem is with management. Panamanian workers have been trained to only do what they are told by their *jefe* or boss. A Panamanian friend helped me to better understand the problem when he said, "The workers themselves are very efficient, which may sound like a joke, but they have been trained to imitate their bosses' attitudes. They say 'no' because that is what they have been taught by their supervisor. They are poor workers, because the wealthy class in Panama prefer them to be just that, only poor workers."

Some things are changing ... for the better. There are lots of Panamanian companies who "get it" and are making progress. The Panama Canal is the best-run company in Panama. I recently stayed at an all-inclusive resort in the Coronado Beach area, and I was impressed by the staff and their level of service.

Looking at all the growth and infrastructure development in Panama, and the changes that have taken place in the past ten years, one could conclude that things happen rapidly in Panama. Not so! Things will happen, but generally not on your, or anyone else's time schedule. Progress is made slowly, as it is in doing retail business, but progress is being made.

Here's the stuff about doing business they failed to teach me in my MBA course at Cal State Northridge. It took retiring in Panama to understand the way retail business is supposed to work, at least judging from my experience with *some* retail businesses in Panama who haven't yet gotten the memo about customer service.

The customer is the enemy. The customer comes only to steal and wants to walk out of your store with whatever your employees have not already stolen. There are a myriad of ways to keep the customer from buying goods and emptying your shelves or from returning to interrupt your employees' day.

The customer is always wrong. Period. No ands, ifs, or buts. Heaven forbid that the customer should return to shop with you again based on your customer service.

 lways promise way more than you can deliver. Your advertising must always create expectations that you cannot possibly deliver.

Never actually have advertised items for sale. Use loads of brand logos and pictures in your advertising for stuff you don't actually have. Maybe you can come up with it from the Colon Free Zone, maybe not, but advertising all those brands is impressive, even if you can't actually get the merchandise.

Unload whatever you can on the unsuspecting customer. If you know it doesn't work, by all means sell it. Even if it's last year's model or a floor sample, sell it at the higher price of the new model. Hopefully the customer won't know the difference. And if they find out feign ignorance. Everything is, after all, the customer's fault.

Have a "no returns" policy. Whatever you do, do not take anything back, defective or not. In small print on the 15 copies of your *factura,* state, in the smallest type font available, that there are "absolutely no returns after 26 minutes." It is perfectly OK if you deliver zinc roofing material to the customer that is all scratched and dented, but if the customer attempts to return anything to you, it had better be in pristine condition.

When a Home Depot wannabe hardware store opened in David my wife bought a lawn lounge chair for me on the Saturday before Father's Day. She told the manager it was a Father's Day gift and asked if she could return it if I didn't like it. Yes, he agreed. I didn't like it and the day after Father's Day Nikki took it back. They didn't want to accept the return.

"Yes, but you said I could return it," Nikki complained.

"Yes, but it has been used," replied the manager.

"He didn't use it! He got it yesterday as a gift for Father's Day and didn't like it."

We endured 45 minutes of consultations and phone calls, presumably to Panama City. I'm sure the idea was that if they took long enough we would just throw up our hands, leave, and not come back.

"But it is dirty." Here's where I lost it! Now in Panama you never want to "lose it." It's impolite, culturally inappropriate, it doesn't help, and usually Panamanians will feel that you are being rude, so will just dig in their heels and you've lost the game. But sometimes ... I walked over to the same chairs which they had on display, ran my finger through the accumulation of dust and dirt on their display chairs which were filthy compared to the chair I was returning. I made the point and grudgingly they refunded our money.

If something sells out, do NOT reorder. If an item sells out then there will be an empty spot on your shelves. Only order stuff that people are not going to buy. If an item sells out it means the customers like it, and if you restock it they might start coming back, which is not the goal of retail business in Panama.

Spend a lot on a logo. A logo is THE single most important thing for your business. Don't waste money on things like training employees, customer service ... just get a sexy-looking logo.

Have a website. It doesn't matter that nobody in your organization ever looks at or updates the website, nor that it has nothing of value to customers. Like a logo, just having a web URL is essential to your business. And be sure to include the Facebook and Twitter logo on all advertising ... even if you don't have an account because just having the Facebook and Twitter logos make you look hip and trendy.

Have uniforms. Everyone loves uniforms, especially employees who don't have to start the day by thinking what they are going to wear and who, if you are really successful in the retail business in Panama, have been trained not to think all day.

Have a cast of thousands. The more employees you have standing around, talking on their personal cell phones, and chatting with one another, the better you can ignore your customers.

Eliminate competition. Either through your family members in government, or by establishing uniform pricing in your sector of the retail business, do not compete. Competition is bad and divides the essential control of business by the few.

Paper is the essential element of business. Even if you have a computer system, in addition to the computer, write everything out on paper longhand, and also have a notebook in which you also write everything yet again in longhand. The reason for this should be obvious: you can't rubber stamp a computer. If you have 15 *facturas* to stamp for each purchase you will give your employees something to occupy their time.

Do not train your employees. A trained employee is dangerous and can turn against you.

Do not empower your employees. An employee should never, repeat never, be permitted to make any decision, no matter how small. The key to success in retail business is for every employee to have to check with his supervisor before making any decision. Thus it is important that all managers carry their cell phones at all times, leaving them turned on at all times even when they are having coffee, lunch or visiting a push. [A "push" is a place offering "temporary accommodation" by the hour for various interpersonal recreational activities.] If you empower your employees they will start to think and a thinking employee will destroy your business.

Do not incentivize your employees. If you reward your employees for service, they will start taking care of your business and treating customers knowledgeably, with enthusiasm, and respect, which is the last thing that you want!

Never have inventory. Whatever the customer wants must always be in Panama City or need to be imported from abroad, thus discouraging the customer from purchasing or coming back.

Never have adequate parking. If you do have a parking lot, assume that nobody drives a SUV or pickup in Chiriqui and that everyone arrives on foot or horseback. Therefore a three foot wide parking space is more than adequate.

Never trust a computer. Computerization looks good and improves corporate image, but it should never replace traditional hand written inventory and invoices, all of which must continue to be in triplicate and rubber stamped and signed by at least four other employees. [See "Paper is the essential element of business" above.]

Above all, encourage inefficiency. Efficiency is the bane of retail business in Panama. The more steps you can create to prevent your customers from emptying your shelves by buying your goods, the fewer goods they will buy and the less likelihood they will return.

And people want to say that Panama is becoming the "Singapore of Latin America?"

I feel sorry for Panamanians who have always had to deal with such a hostile customer environment. David is booming with lots of new stores under construction. I hope that retailers in Panama will realize that customers are the reason why they stay in business and the most valuable asset for keeping customers and making money are their employees. Most employees would do an awesome job if they were valued, trained, empowered, and rewarded. My gripe is not with the employees, but with management that needs to move into the 21st century. Panama is no longer a backwater "banana republic" but is emerging as a powerhouse of world commerce. Retail businesses need to start operating as such.

When our daughters were in grade school we owned travel agencies. Rather than throw away outdated brochures, forms, old rubber stamps, and office equipment, I'd bring it all home and put it in a box in the garage for the girls. They would spend hours and hours playing "travel agency" which was a very complicated game. A single piece of paper would be passed back and forth with notations being made, pieces of paper being attached, and being rubber stamped endlessly with each child going through all kinds of motions back and forth. It was the most complicated, involved system I thought possible ... *until we moved to Panama.*

Now I know that some folks will think that I am just being too negative, that they have encountered wonderful service in Panama ... *as have I!* ... but from a long-term, national perspective, if Panama is to fully realize and exploit its unique opportunities, there needs to be a national commitment to genuine customer service. It's one thing to just say "that's the way it is", but increasingly that is NOT the Panamanian way. This is a country on the move, growing and prospering. There are major initiatives towards improving customer service. There is a major government initiative toward teaching English starting in grade school. Learning to speak in a U. S. or British accented English is a big deal. Not because there are gringos here, or because we have some ties with the U. S. in our background, but because English is the language of business, navigation, and the Internet.

Action Items and Points to Ponder

1. It is one thing to say, "Yes, I know the culture is different," but how well are you able to cope with a culture where even the most basic things like going into a retail store, operate on entirely different concepts?

Panama Relocation Tour group enjoying the best passion fruit margaritas.

Original locks of the, Panama Canal, joining the world together for over 100 years.

18. This Isn't the Panama Canal

When things aren't done "right," or workmanship is half-assed or sloppy, you will often find it excused as not being the Panama Canal so therefore a lower standard of workmanship is acceptable.

There is a great deal of national pride around the Panama Canal and the fact that in many ways the Canal places Panama at the center of the world. In a way this is ironic since, although the Canal is located in Panama, the Canal was built by the United States. But it was Panama that managed to gain control of the Canal and the Canal Zone. It was Panama that turned the Canal from being basically a service operation with tons of vested interests into a highly profitable business. And it is Panama that is expanding the Canal, doing what the United States had wanted to do since the 1930s. So it is understandable that the Canal should be the focus of national pride and the standard against which things are measured.

What is not understandable is why the excellence of the Canal operation should be an excuse for doing other things half-assed.

When I was a student, back in the day, travelling around Europe on a shoe-string budget with a Eurailpass I wondered why it was that the trains in Switzerland and Germany always ran exactly and precisely on time while the trains in Spain ran more or less on schedule, give or take a few hours. I realize things have changed and that the trains in Spain are now as fast and efficient as anywhere else in Europe, but back then I wondered. Was it a difference in national temperament or work ethic? Was Calvinism and the so-called "Protestant work ethic" really that influential? Perhaps it was the weather.

Folks in Latin countries seem to be a whole lot more laid back and take life, and work, at a more leisurely pace. Maybe there is more incentive to work your ass off when you are freezing your ass off. Our lives have normally revolved around Boquete, about 1,097 meters high [3,600 feet], with a spring-like climate year round where it is never hot and uncomfortable. By contrast, when I started working on making a livable *casita* on our seaside property in Boca Chica, I was amazed at how much energy the heat and humidity drained from my body.

Walk into any department or grocery store and the checkout clerks might as well have a button that reads, "I'm here to take up space and be paid: that's it, period." The checkout person will sullenly push your items across the scanner, expect you to see the screen showing how much is owed and hand over that amount. Forget the friendly, chatty checkers from Vons or Safeway in California. There is no good morning, thank you, nothing. Usually there is a young guy who bags your stuff hoping that you will let him carry it out to your car and give him a tip. Meanwhile, the checkout person goes back to the daydream that you were so rude to interrupt when you placed your items on the counter.

Now I admit that I approach this work ethic situation with preconceived notions.

First, I have a theological belief that if you belong to God everything you do should be done to the glory of God, including work . Whatever I do, no matter how exalted or how humble the task, I do to the glory of God. Even if it's only turning screw number 215 on an assembly line, I do it well not because of the name on the product but because of the Name on me. I doubt that my local pastor friends preach many sermons with that take on 1 Corinthians 10:31 ["So whether you eat or drink or whatever you do, do it all for the glory of God."]

It is said that Saint Francis was out one day hoeing his garden and someone asked him, "Francis if you knew you were going to die tomorrow, what would you do?" Francis replied that he would continue hoeing his garden. *All* work is important and should be done to the glory of God. At least that's where I am coming from theologically. Barring theology, a person can just do his best out of self-respect.

Second, I come from a different culture. The United States has one of the most work-driven cultures in the world. The U. S. has fewer holidays than in most of the world. You are expected to get the job done and make sacrifices, particularly if you want to "get ahead." In the States you are lucky if you get two or three weeks paid vacation a year, and even then it is dangerous to use all of your vacation days lest your job be eliminated while you are away. In Panama every employee by law gets one month a year vacation. In the States you are expected to take your laptop home with you and work from home evenings and on weekends. In Panama when your shift is up, it's up. You leave! You may leave customers standing in line or tools scattered about to rust in the rain, but the work day is over.

Different? Yes! Perfect? No! But there is a lot that we work-driven North Americans can learn about the meaning and quality of life apart from the workplace. There is a lot we can learn about what *really* is important in life. There is a lot we can learn about how to relax and enjoy life as well as work.

It's rare to find an employee who takes responsibility. We get frustrated when our workers stand around and don't do anything when to us at least, there is obviously work that needs to be done. Why can't they just "see what needs to be done and do it?" But our way of thinking goes against the way workers in Panama have been trained. The system in Panama is set up to discourage employees taking responsibility or doing anything that they are not told to do. Taking initiative is discouraged at all levels and being proactive is neither encouraged nor rewarded.

Workers in Panama are a protected class, understandable given the history of Panama being exploited by everyone from the Spanish conquistadores to the U. S. Canal Zone. In Panama labor law the worker is always right. Guilt of the employer is assumed unless the employer can prove otherwise. Wages for various positions are set by the labor board. No one works at the will of the employer unless they are a day laborer or contracted worker, and even then it can only be for a limited time before you are involved with the labor board. You may get by with a gardener or maid for one or two days a week, but there is no guarantee that eventually that worker may get pissed off at you for one reason or another and take you to the labor board, where the worker will be right, you will be wrong, and you will end up paying.

Although these labor laws may have been implemented to protect the worker, in today's multi-national economic environment these very laws work *against* the Panamanian worker. It's hard to imagine Panama taking its rightful place in the world unless it can create a more effective work force.

When Singapore looked at its advantageous geographical position, somewhat akin to Panama's advantageous geographical position, and wanted to exploit that position and grow, Singapore realized that with China right next door it could not compete on the basis of low-cost labor. So it decided to educate its people and provide a highly educated and trained labor force, and as a result Singapore has become this model for success.

The United Arab Emirates and Dubai on the other hand decided to import workers from abroad creating a system where, if you wanted to do business in Dubai, you had to partner with a UAE national. In return for lending his name to the business, the UAE national would reap a generous share of the profits without doing any work.

Individual Panamanian workers can do incredible things. A Panamanian can make things work, and keep them working, long after most North Americans would have given up and bought something new. Given space and the ability to make decisions and think, Panamanian workers can be amazing. It's the system that sucks, not the workers!

Labor law in Panama protects Panamanian workers and businesses from success.

If you have a worker for more than a few days a week on a casual relationship, you are going to fall under the labor board. That means the labor board will tell you what you must pay, the paid holidays you must allow [currently around 12 days a year[57] and in some areas a few more], the number of paid sick days [currently around 16 days a year], and the number of vacation days [30 per year]. So if you're adding all that up you're left with about 10 months of work, having paid for 12 months. But not so fast: by law you must also pay for a "13th month." That's right, you pay for another month, not as an incentive bonus based on performance, but by law. So now you are paying for 13 months of work and only getting 10 months. Additionally when the worker leaves, for whatever reason, you need to pay a severance at a percentage determined by the labor board.

In a multinational labor market this outdated Labor Law puts Panama at a distinct disadvantage in spite of Panama's prime geographical location.

One of the "advantages" to legitimate employees who are part of Panama's Social Security system is that they will receive between 60 to 70 percent of their average monthly salary as retirement pension when they retire at the age of 62 for men and 57 for women.[58] Of course without a good postal service with home delivery, all of these Panamanian *Pensionados* must line up in enormous lines to collect their checks every month.

Unlike in the United States, Social Security in Panama also provides medical care while you are working. Panama has three medical systems: National Health providing low-cost care to mostly Indigenous and people without Social Security, Social Security for workers paying into the system, and private hospitals.

So our Indigenous farm worker pays 11 percent of his meager weekly salary into Social Security and we pay an additional 15.75 percent. If our worker has a dental problem and goes to the Social Security clinic or hospital, they give him some aspirin and tell him to come back and eventually they will pull the tooth. That's dental care! When he's sick he takes a day to go and sit at the Social Security clinic all day for a cursory glance by a doctor if he's lucky. If he's not lucky, he has to take another day, sit all day, and hope to see a doctor.

Being Indigenous he usually doesn't get seen until all of the Latinos have been seen. When he finally gets a quick look by a doctor and is given a prescription he discovers that the Social Security pharmacy is closed so he needs to come back yet another day to get his prescription filled. So day three, he's back off the job waiting in a long line to get his prescription filled by the Social Security pharmacy. After waiting he is told that they don't have that medication and that he must go to a private pharmacy to get it filled. He goes to the private pharmacy where the cost of his prescription is 30 percent of his weekly salary and since his family has to eat, he goes without the medication, or he buys a single pill hoping that one pill will cure him.

Does this bother anybody? Not really. "It's not the Panama Canal and he's just an Indian."

Unfortunately companies have the same, "It's not the Panama Canal" attitude.

Most roofs in Panama are just rusted zinc. But some folks pay extra for colored zinc roofs, usually red. It has always frustrated me to see someone's red zinc roof a year after it has been installed and to see one zinc panel that has discolored from the rest to be a lighter or different color of red as it weathered due to someone in the zinc factory deciding, "It's not the Panama Canal."

There are three big building supply houses in Chiriqui. One has the most surly checkout staff in Panama. The other, which has vinyl windows and pre-hung steel-clad doors that I like, delivered a hung ceiling material that was so scuffed up and unusable – "It's not the Panama Canal" – that I had to return it and go to "Plan G." (If you're even thinking you can get by with "Plan B" in Panama, forget it!) So when I decided on a blue zinc roof for my *casita* in Boca Chica I decided to try the third supplier which was recommended by a friend.

Purposely I bought the better quality and more expensive zinc which was offered in a darker "*marine*" blue and a lighter Caribbean "*azul*" blue. I had to choose from a quarter inch square in an old order book. I picked what looked like the darker blue and waited two months for my special order zinc to arrive. It came and amazingly only one piece was all scratched up. Well, my bad, I had incorrectly figured the amount of zinc I needed for the overhang at the ends, so I needed four more sheets. Never mind that these folks chose to deliver my zinc to a construction site at 5:30 p.m. on Saturday night, when everyone knows the workers in Panama all go home at 12 noon on Saturdays. I figured that if I wanted the same zinc I'd better go back to the same store.

So I reorder and wait two months and eventually the zinc comes. This time it is all scratched up and a different color blue. Not a color variance but totally the other color blue. So do I wait another two months with a hole in my roof and a blue tarp? This is Panama! And besides, it's not the Panama Canal, so in spite of my best efforts I end up with a roof of two different colors of blue zinc.

Fortunately ... I've lived here ten years and I know how things work ... unless you are flying over in a helicopter or out on the ocean looking into shore, you won't be able to see the difference and besides, it's not the Panama Canal. But I know the blues are different.

Action Items and Points to Ponder

1. Panama is over 500 years old. The system is what the system is and you are not going to change it. Can you live with it even if it is not that to which you are accustomed?

2. As we get older we become less flexible not just in our joints, but also in our attitudes. If you can't adjust to differences in cultural attitudes and systems you are not going to make it in Panama. Better to figure that out now, before you've cashed in your chips and moved, than later. How "flexible" are you ... really?

19. Due Diligence

I am amazed at folks who sell all, pick up and move to **Panama without really doing their due diligence.** What do I mean by due diligence? Studying, finding out all you can, communicating with as many people as possible and then when you've done all that, do it some more!

The Internet is a great resource for information but be aware that often information is posted and not dated so what you are reading online may be out of date. Follow bulletin boards on the Internet but, again, take everything you read online with a grain of salt. Aside from not always being current, some folks have axes to grind and others are just shills for one project or another. Take advantage of the opportunity the Internet provides to enter into the discussions, ask questions, and maybe even make connections and friends online with whom you can communicate offline.

Google and other online services will allow you to follow news from Panama (albeit they often throw in Panama City, Florida), Boquete and various outfits promoting Panama.

Of course you will want to visit. There are several ways of visiting and all can be helpful.

Come and visit as a tourist and spend two or three weeks traveling around Panama and taking in the sights. You will have an amazing visit. If you go away thinking, "It's a nice place to visit, but I wouldn't want to live there," at least you know and you will have had a great vacation.

Come on a tour that focuses on relocation. There are a number of outfits that promote Panama, as well as other areas as places to live and invest. Some of these offer seminars in big hotel ballrooms in Panama City where presenters, often folks who've paid to participate, share information and investment "opportunities." Obviously they are selling something. Usually there will be expats, carefully screened and prepped, who will tell you about life in Panama. There are other tours that are real estate investment tours and ... guess what? Of course, they want to sell you real estate! Sometimes you will find yourself in a delightful place but with a schedule so tight that you can't get away from the participating and sponsoring development to look at other options. And if the tour is sponsored by a real estate office, because there is no multiple listing service [MLS], you will see *their* listings.

I would look for a relocation tour that is a boots-on-the-ground tour where you are not in a fancy ballroom but traveling around Panama to see first-hand some of the places expats like to call home. You need a tour that gives you the opportunity to see the real Panama and meet real expats and see how they live, hear their experiences and pepper them with questions. If you decide that Panama is for you, you can always come back for the real estate tour, or you can come back, rent a place for three to six months and see how well you like it before making a major life change.

The more you know, the more you research, the more people you talk with, the better are your of having a fun, happy and successful expat life.

I'm always amazed at people who make the move before thinking things through and then end up moving back to wherever they came from. Like the lady who loved to shop at Nieman Marcus and got to Boquete and discovered ... no Nieman Marcus! Or the woman who every day had played tennis at the club and had lunch with the girls who moved to Boquete only to discover ... not only no tennis club, but at the time no tennis court! Another guy ... had to escape what he viewed as a vast conspiracy at home ... after all the expense of moving to Panama discovered that, at least in his mind, we were a backward country because we didn't have wall-to-wall carpeting! Or it rains a lot ... or we have mold ... or we don't have a favorite brand of canned tomatoes from Italy ... or you can't get your cat's favorite treats. It really is incredible!

By far the craziest story ... a woman bought a home in Panama, sold her home in the U. S., moved down a container load of all her stuff and bought a car. She moved into her new house and the first night encountered the ants. The next day she announced, "I can't deal with ants" and put her new Panama house on the market, sold her car and moved her and her stuff back to the U. S.

Any move is stressful and a big life change. Moving to another country and another culture is a tremendous change.

Of course, you need to look before you leap, but eventually you have to gather up the nerve to make the leap. No matter how much you study, and visit, and think you know, at some point you just have to leap.

Like Caesar, we came, we saw, we conquered. We came to visit Panama only to see if it should remain on the list of countries we were considering. We fell in love and bought a house. And we've been happy here now going on eleven years. I don't recommend that! But Nikki and I have successfully done that before, visiting an area that we liked, realizing the potential for the area to "pop" and gone ahead and invested, and it's worked well. When we came to Panama we had already worked through the exercises I described earlier and we knew what we wanted. We found it ... and we jumped!

For most people I think it is a far better idea to come and live here for a while and test it out before making a precipitous decision and doing something you may later regret.

In the meantime, while you are doing your due diligence, brush up on your Spanish skills or start taking courses. A number of people I know have come to Boquete to study

Spanish and test out local living before making the move. You don't have to speak Spanish, but the more Spanish you speak the more enjoyable will be your life in Panama.

And don't believe people who glibly say, "You'll pick up the language." These are people who have never learned a second language in their lives. At age 60, you do not "pick up" a language. Six-year- olds can do that., not sixty-year-olds!

Action Items and Points to Ponder

1. Admittedly different readers are at different stages in terms of considering living in Panama, but what is your *plan* to continue your research?

2. How are your Spanish skills? How do you feel about learning a new language? How well do you do in situations where everyone around you is speaking a language you don't understand?

20. The Devil You Know

The devil that you know is sometimes better than the devil you do not know. Think carefully before you jump from the embrace of one to another.

Every government has red tape, but at least you know the red tape where you live now. Every human government struggles with corruption and ineptitude, but at least you know that where you live now. Laws, systems, and philosophies of law differ. Many people thinking of adopting an expat lifestyle in Panama come from countries whose system of law is based largely on English common law. Panama's legal system is based on a combination of old Spanish and Colombian law. As I mentioned before, the legal devil you know may be better than the legal devil you don't know. Yes, it's difficult to sue in Panama: a nice plus. But it's difficult to sue in Panama and cases can drag on perpetually without resolution: a big pain.

Governments and politicians come and go. Nothing lasts forever! No world power is a world power forever. Things change. The government or head of state you detest now will be different in a few years. If you are fed up with your government, change it, or get out and forget it. When we moved to Panama ten years ago there were many who thought George W. Bush would be the death of the United States as we knew it, but Bush moved on to a quiet retirement and the Union survived. I've had visitors from the States show me a list of Bible verses proving, or so they claimed, that Barack Obama was the Great Satan and Antichrist.

Believe me, government in Panama isn't perfect! Talk to any Panamanian and they will detail the corruption of the political party that they didn't vote for and conveniently ignore the corruption of the party that hired their brother-in-law. Panamanians understand politics. Politics in Panama isn't a matter of expensive TV campaigns but a local matter of who gets what patronage after the election.

Panamanians have a handle on politicians. While they enjoy the political soap opera they don't take it seriously. Panamanians say that politicians are like vultures, the giant birds, AKA "the Panamanian Air Force," that circle overhead and keep the roads remarkably clean of road kill. People say that politicians, like vultures, "during the day fight over the same road kill, but at night all go home to the same tree to roost." They belong to the same prestigious families, social clubs , party together, and intermarry. In politics, in Panama as elsewhere, things are not always what they seem.

When Martinelli's party lost the last election and he boarded his private jet to escape to a paradise other than Panama ... some folks say Florida ... we don't think he took anyone along.

Escaping to ... not from

You will have a much more enjoyable and successful expat life if you are escaping *to* a better, more vibrant and adventurous lifestyle than escaping *from* something.

Just escaping to a new location isn't going to change things if you are bored or in a dying relationship. If you are unhappy where you are now, just changing the scenery isn't going to suddenly make you happy. If you are tired of the stress and pressure, know that moving to a new and different culture creates massive stress and pressure. **Wherever you go, you take yourself with you!**
Depending on where you are coming from, Panama *may* be cheaper, but not necessarily so. You can probably live a lot cheaper where you are right now if you adjust your life style.

The reason to come to Panama is not to escape the high cost of living at home, but to escape *to* what I consider to be a healthier and better lifestyle.

If you decide on Panama you will enjoy it most, and others will enjoy you, if you leave your political baggage behind and just explore and enjoy a new culture and life style, which, I admit, at times can be very challenging and demanding.

We see some folks who come to Panama because they were fed up with government and life back home. They brought their "color" loyalties with them, not in the sense of color of skin, but color of politics, i.e. for those from the States either "Red" or "Blue." Once they got to Panama, rather than jumping in, exploring, and struggling with the local culture, they chose a self-contained existence only associating with other expats of like mind, instead of trying to speak Spanish and associate with locals. They are angry, uptight and as unhappy here as they were back wherever. They could be in almost any country for all they know or seemingly care about where they are actually living.

Such a shame! Everyone has something to share and contribute. We all have things to learn. Yes, the culture is different, and may be at times frustrating, but that's what makes expat life interesting!

Action Items and Points to Ponder

1. So, are you escaping *from* or escaping *to*?

2. What are you looking forward to discovering?

Zip lining at Boquete Tree Trek.

Kayaking at Boca Chica.

21. To Like & Not to Like

If you are looking for the perfect paradise you probably **won't find it.** This book is about escaping to paradise, not escaping to the perfect paradise. Big difference!

Thanks to the screw-up by our first parents, Adam and Eve, you're not going to find perfection or paradise this side of heaven. Accept it. Nothing is perfect. No one is perfect. No place is perfect, but, as far as we're concerned, life in Panama is damn close, at least for us.

Folks decide to move to Panama for a lot of reasons: escape, adventure, discovery, start a new life, remake themselves ... whatever. For many people it is an excellent choice, as it has been for us. So there is a whole lot to like ... make that LOVE! ... about living in Panama, and, given as nothing is perfect , there are some things not to like.

Top 10 Things I Like About Living in Panama

10. Adventure

When we first moved to Boquete it was an adventure.

We were sitting recently at Central Park Café in Boquete town having breakfast and overheard two recently arrived *gringas* at the next table. The one lady was complaining that the store in David only had three brands of food mixers and none were the name brand she preferred. Nikki just rolled her eyes, remembering that when we first moved to Boquete you were lucky to find a mixer without going to Panama City.

Yes, it still can be an adventure moving to Panama,

particularly if you go off the beaten path and get away from the built-up, developed areas which have become more and more like living anywhere in the "developed" world, albeit with better weather and more beautiful surroundings.

For a tiny country Panama has a wealth of fascinating areas to explore. It's not just the physical opportunities of adventure, but also the adventure of living. You can look at some aspects of life in Panama as frustration, or, if you choose, adventure. It's up to you. Part of that adventure, is another thing that we like about living in Panama …

9. Panama is someplace different

Both Nikki and I like "different." If everyone was the same, thought the same, looked the same, did the same things in the same way year after year, that life would be incredibly boring. If you like "different" you are a good candidate to live an expat lifestyle. If you don't like "different" then maybe you should stay put in your familiar surrounds.

Interestingly, although we like "different," it is the flip side of this coin that often creates frustrations. The differences in cultural traditions and mores are often the things that reach up and grab you when you least expect it.

8. Country Living

I lived in New York City for six years and I've been fortunate enough to visit many of the great cities of the world. I love visiting cities, but I prefer living in the country. Those who love city living will thrive in Panama City. There are suburban areas around Panama City, some of them left over from the U. S. Canal Zone days, where suburban living, complete with giant shopping malls, approximates suburban living in North America.

But, we like country living, so we call a beautiful coffee farm in the mountains home. Over the past ten years there have been many changes and Boquete has become a much busier little mountain town. One of the things that has changed I call the "horse factor." When we first came to Boquete you'd find people riding into town on horseback and tying up their horse in front of the store. Then, as the town grew, you'd see people riding their horses in town on Sundays. Now you only see horses for parades and town is so crowded with new pickup trucks and big SUVs, most of which are driven by Panamanians, not *gringos,* that a horse would be out of place.

7. Outside Living

One of the great advantages of living with our near-perfect weather is the ability to spend much of your time outside. When we designed our home we specifically designed it to be open to the breezes with a huge back porch or "terrace" where we spend as much time as possible. I dislike being cooped up inside or dependent heating and air conditioning.

6. Food

I don't personally find Panamanian cuisine very exciting. We joke that typical Panamanian cuisine is "chicken, rice and beans, salad and bananas" and for variation, "bananas, salad, rice and beans and chicken." Panamanians eat rice morning, noon and night. Unlike that of their neighbors to the north in Mexico, Panamanian food is rather bland. But, since people have migrated to Panama from all over the world, there are lots of ethnic restaurants in cities and towns, and in Panama City there is every kind of food, including fine dining.

Most beef is Brahman which is notoriously tough, but there is lots of chicken, pork and seafood. You can get freshly caught ahi sushi-grade tuna for $8 a pound, or giant prawns for $12 a pound. Vegetables are locally grown, incredibly fresh and delicious. Carrots actually taste like carrots and not Styrofoam. Most towns have daily farmers' markets where you can buy vine-ripened tomatoes and other fresh vegetables. Our coffee, in my somewhat prejudiced opinion, is the best in the world.

Yes, apples and grapes are imported, but all kinds of citrus, melons, tropical fruit and pineapple are all locally grown. Melons and pineapples are big export crops. Panamanian pineapple is incredibly sweet and a pineapple costs about $1.25 *gringo* price, or at the market in David 50 cents. In the lowlands there are mango trees everywhere.

So in Panama we definitely can eat better for less, particularly if we eat like Panamanians. When we first came to Panama Nikki was searching without success for canned crushed pineapple. Finally a Panamanian neighbor said, "Nikki, why would you pay $3.50 for a can of crushed pineapple, when you can buy a fresh pineapple, throw it in a food processer and have crushed pineapple for a month?"

Processed U. S. food, such as cereals and the like, must be imported so obviously cost more in Panama than in the States. But, if you want Haagen-Dazs ice cream you can find it, and actually it is imported from France. If you want fast food, in Panama City and in the larger towns you can find the same fast food outlets that are all over the rest of the world.

5. Positive View of Life and Future

The way in which people in a country view their lives and future, a national psyche if you will, is often the result of economic and political forces over which ordinary citizens have no control. There are countries where the national attitude is aggressive based on fear (the United States and North Korea would come to mind), or pessimistic based on economic struggles (Greece especially), or uncertain based on political and ideological struggles (like Syria and Egypt). Some countries have a certain smugness that is often based on wealth (like Germany, Switzerland and Monaco). There are countries which were once colonial powers with vast influence whose national identity is based primarily on past glory (such as Great Britain, France and Spain).

Although its been around for over 500 years, Panama, since the fall of Noriega and the turnover of the Panama Canal, is kind of the new kid on the block, with a booming economy , a positive national outlook, and a renewed sense of importance in world trade and commerce based on its geographical location and Canal.

Panamanians by en large view life and the future in positive terms. Political parties may fight prior to an election, but in the end they are all Panamanians, dedicated to God and country, and willing to work together for the common good despite the ongoing political *telenovela*.

4. Weather

As I write this much of North America is fighting winter weather. The only white Christmas I dream about is on a white, sandy beach. I've done Wisconsin winters where you'd wake up, look outside at the bright sunshine and think "a nice day" only to step outside and discover the temperature was well below zero degrees Fahrenheit. I've had more than enough snow, slush, and ice, thank you very much. It looks nice in pictures, and it's nice for skiing vacations, but I don't want to live in snow and ice.

I have what I call the "bougainvillea standard": if the brilliant colored bougainvillea vine will grow there, I'll grow there, if not, count me out.

Boquete and the Chiriqui Mountain towns represent the best of all worlds with spring-like temperatures year-round, meaning you don't spend money on heat or air conditioning.

Panama is outside of the hurricane belt and although we do get strong northerly winds sometimes in January and February, it is a small aggravation compared to five months of winter.

3. Cost of Living

Although due to inflation, the devaluation of the U. S. dollar, development and a booming economy, the cost of living in

Panama has increased significantly over the past ten years, the cost of living in the States has gone up as well. **We are still able to live better for a lot less in Panama than we could in Southern California.**

2. Beauty

Panama is incredibly beautiful. Sitting on our front porch watching the sunrise, listening to the birds, looking out over coffee, banana and orange trees, as well as several flowering trees while sipping a cup of our home grown coffee, is truly a heavenly[59] experience. In the evening I can sit in my spa on the back terrace, sipping wine, watching the sun sink behind Volcan Baru. I feel blessed to live in such a beautiful country.

As I write this my daughter from California is visiting with us. This morning we had breakfast just off the plaza in downtown Boquete and since it was such a spectacular morning decided to take one of the "loop" drives out of downtown Boquete. You can hardly get lost in Boquete since all of the roads eventually loop back downtown. We drove along a road lined with flowers, coffee trees, along a sparkling mountain stream, past a waterfall, up a narrow road into what is called the Grand Canyon of Boquete, where steep volcanic rocks rise up from the valley.

As we were taking that ride, enjoying the beauty of the tropical landscape and the weather, Nikki and I were reminiscing about when we lived in Milwaukee and to escape frigid temperatures and piles of snow would escape to Mitchell Park Horticultural Conservatory, "The Domes", where, for a few magical hours we could "experience a desert oasis, a tropical jungle and special floral gardens." Now we live in a tropical jungle surrounded by our own year-round floral gardens.

John le Carre summed it up perfectly when he wrote, "We've got [in Panama] everything God needed to make paradise. Great farming, beaches, mountains, wildlife you wouldn't believe, put a stick in the ground you get a fruit tree, people so beautiful you could cry." (*Tailor of Panama*)

1. People

The beauty of Panama is found not just in the stunning natural surrounds, but as John le Carre noted, in "people so beautiful you could cry."   Today's Panamanians are from Latino and Indigenous stock, coupled with people from all over the world who've come through the centuries to call Panama home. People are not black or white, Latino or Indigenous or Anglo, but Panamanian.

My friend, Jubal Atencio. a Panamanian now living in Europe, observed, "Panamanians are open, not extreme people. A great example is the presidents we have had, five years from one party, and the next five years from another party, each with completely different ideas. Yet everyone adjusts and works together for the greater good.

"We are very adaptable to the reality of our country, yet most Panamanians, especially those living in the countryside, don't know anything but their own town. For them travelling abroad is visiting Panama City. Of course they have TV and are influenced by what they watch, however, they still have some of that state of innocence that people living in the so-called 'first world' don't have.

"It's tricky with Panamanians: you have to get to know them first to experience the warmth and openness. But they are open and welcoming to foreigners. And, by the way, after ten years, 'Panamanians' includes you, and the others who have chosen to make Panama their home."

The very best way to appreciate the people is to get involved. If you set yourself apart and only associate with other expats, you miss the grand opportunity of getting to know and appreciate the people. It's important, I think, to get in touch with "salt of the earth" people in addition to the wealthy Panamanians who live as well, or better, than the North Americans we lived with before coming to Panama.

I could write a book, and maybe someday I will, about the memorable moments we have enjoyed in Panama when we were involved with the people. Involved not as people who thought we knew better, or wanted to change something, but just as people relating to people.

One of Nikki's most memorable experiences was when the power went out ... for days. Knowing that all the meat we had stored in the freezer was going to spoil, Nikki took it and distributed it to our Gnabe Bugle Indian neighbors, many of whom help us to harvest our coffee. The Gnabe cook over open fires and don't have refrigerators or microwaves, so being without electricity is no big deal. Nikki still gets kind of choked up when she remembers those neighbors coming up the driveway having made dinner for her, making certain she had enough to eat.

It's a touchy balance, trying to share what we have, without coming across as the wealthy *gringos*. We are always touched when our neighbors, many of whom have so little, come to share special treats with us.

If you come to Panama you can surround yourself with other expats and live in a mostly *gringo* world, but, if you do, you miss out on the best that Panama has to offer, her people.

Top 10 Things I Don't Like About Living in Panama

10. Dirty Propane

Panama runs on propane. We use it for cooking, washing, and on demand water heaters. You can opt for convenience, like we do and buy big tanks for $80 or, if you don't mind running to the corner store frequently, you can buy the small tanks (about the size of a propane tank for a barbeque grill) for the government subsidized price of $5.37. But don't assume these tanks contain the same gas you buy in the States for your grill because what you get in Panama is not really propane. As I understand it, what we get is "dirty propane" more like butane, so things are always burning out. Like many North

Americans we were used to hot water tanks so that's what we installed. After two burned up (Yes, burned up, flames and all!) we switched, to on demand gas water heaters. They cost about $200 each and since most are made in China they stop working in two years and the part to repair them is naturally unavailable. We tried switching to an electric on demand hot water heater and it, although made in the U. S., burned out in one year. (Panamanians, many of whom don't worry about hot water, don't have these problems!)

9. Ants and Creepy Crawlies

Ants are a constant struggle. They are everywhere! There is more mass of ants in our house than there is mass of people and dogs! Don't get me wrong. If bug flies into the house and happens to die and lay legs up on the tile floor, don't worry. In thirty minutes a zillion tiny ants will appear and in an organized manner dispose of the carcass.

There are tiny, tiny ants that get into everything. I've even had them set up housekeeping in my laptop keyboard. So, should you find typing errors, know that the ants are to blame.

Outside in the garden, leaf-cutter ants can strip a bush overnight. You can be trimming a bush and suddenly find yourself covered in tiny ants.

Then there are the red ants that bite. I learned the hard way to watch where you step or stand. When we first came to Panama and were looking at real estate we were out with a real estate sales person looking at a beautiful property. I was standing by the fence when suddenly I was being bitten up and down my legs. I looked down and I was standing on an anthill. Travelling "commando" I could only run behind the truck and strip off my clothing and fight off the ants. My wife still thinks that was funny.

You always keep a can of Baygon insect spray handy and do the best you can.

It's the rain forest! We have a house designed to be open, so bugs and creepy crawlies get inside the house. It is a fact of life in the tropics so you accept it and get used to it or YOU go bugs! We have an exterminator come in every other month, as you do in most warm areas in the States, but we still cope with fly season, ant season, and roach season. When it starts to rain and roaches who are usually at home under leaves in the jungle decide to come in out of the rain. There is also June bug season (although not necessarily in June, these heavy shelled little buggers sound like pebbles bouncing off the walls and the dogs love to snatch them out of the air and eat them like jelly beans), and gnat season (those tiny flies that love to take a swim in a good glass of merlot adding a degree of protein to the mix).

There is even a scorpion season. Our scorpions are mostly harmless aside from stinging and, if you have a ultraviolet flashlight, you have the added joy of going scorpion hunting since they glow under ultraviolet like a white T-shirt washed in Tide.

The good thing about the bugs is that you are always finding a new bug you've never seen before and many of them are unbelievably beautiful.

I said earlier that one of the things I like about Panama is outside living and that to achieve that we keep our house as open as possible. That means that ants and creepy crawlies are a fact of life.

8. No Home Depot

Don't laugh: it's one of the things I miss the most. When I go to visit my kids in the States I always get them to take me to Home Depot and they keep telling me I'm embarrassing them by fondling the power tools in public. When we came here ten years ago, it was hopeless. Now we have Do It Center and Novey in David but they are nothing like Home Depot. Locally we have the two Chinese hardware stores, Ivan's and El Dorado, both of which are almost like the old hardware

stores we used to have in the States. It can be pretty
disorganized but they have almost everything. Unfortunately,
it's all made in China. At least at Home Depot there was the
possibility of finding something not made in China and
therefore providing a reasonable expectation that it would
work.

I'm told Home Depot isn't what it once was. What you're
looking for probably is in some other bin somewhere and you
may not find it even though it's there. I'm told that the days
when I'd go in and buy whatever I thought I might need, and
then return what I didn't need only to have my money
cheerfully refunded without a receipt, are long gone. I'm told
that if something just doesn't work that you can still return it
back because it's no skin off Home Depot, in fact they *make*
money for handling returns. Believe me, it's not that way in
Panama.

Maybe worse yet, no Costco, Sam's Club or Walmart. We do
have something called PriceSmart run by the same family that
used to run Price Club in California before it merged with
Costco. There is a look and feel about PriceSmart and a layout
that is familiar, but don't be mistaken, this is not the old Price
Club or Costco.

Let me count the ways:

- Buying in bulk is not cheaper. Believe it or not, the
  idea here is that may pay more for the convenience of
  buying a larger size – incredible, but true.

- The employees lack the enthusiasm and ownership
  that they used to demonstrated in club stores.

- If something sells it is frequently discontinued. Why?
  Now, I know this will be tricky, but try to follow. If it
  is a popular item people remove it from the shelves
  and buy it, making it difficult to keep the shelves
  neatly organized and full, therefore it has no place in
  the store.

- Customer service – say what? If a popular item, say dog food, is sold out, you'll have to chase down someone to find someone else who will get a forklift and bring another pallet of dog food down for the masses … if they have it, and chances are they don't.

Nevertheless we use PriceSmart faithfully because it comes closest to what we are used to. Hopefully with the new Free Trade Agreement with the Unites States we will see more of the familiar Kirkland brand products on the shelves. PriceSmart doesn't have it all down yet, but it is getting better and there are more and more Panamanians who are shopping PriceSmart in David.

7. Microclimates

OK, microclimates can be wonderful when it comes to fine wine and great coffee. But a place like Boquete has so many microclimates it boggles the mind.

During the dry season, some places can be as dry as the desert with dusty winds howling like the Santa Ana winds in California, or the Chinook winds in Colorado, while just few miles away, it is pouring rain, and other areas, like downtown Boquete, are getting their late afternoon mist called *bajareque*.

This is a good reason to spend six months, and preferably a year, in Boquete or anywhere else before you jump and buy or build. At least spend a few months and talk to as many people as you can. True, we are in the tropics and don't have the traditional four seasons, but we do have definite seasons and they are different. Add to that all the microclimates in an area around Boquete and you understand why you need to ask a lot of questions and do a lot of research.

6. Forced Overnights in Panama City

Living in Chiriqui, as I do, if you want to fly to or from the States or Europe, you almost inevitably end up with a forced overnight in Panama City coming and going because of flight schedules. People have been hoping for years for a direct flight to the States from the David Airport. The runway, radar and terminal have all been upgraded and all that remains is for an airline to figure a way to make such a flight profitable. The new international airport at Rio Hato initially is primarily intended for charter flights from North America and Europe serving the large resorts around Coronado on the Pacific Coast.

Now, with Copa ... a great airline by the way, despite a frustrating Web site ... flying from David [DAV] to Tocumen Airport [PTY] it is possible on some routes to avoid an overnight, and to avoid the taxi transfer between the national airport at Albrook and the international airport at Tocumen.

5. Mold

During the rainy season it is a constant battle with mold. Mold gets inside dressers on the backs of the inside of the dressers, so you need to pull out the drawers and clean the inside of the dresser. It gets on books. It gets on the inside and outside of kitchen cabinets. Leave an extra leather wallet or purse, or the leather dress shoes you only take with you for formal nights on a cruise and they end up moldy. It usually wipes off, hopefully without much damage and vinegar seems to be the best mold-buster.

We've even had mold on serigraphs and lithographs. I pulled the pictures apart and carefully wiped off the mold with a tiny bit of vinegar. With that and a very light application of Pledge I've been able to save most pictures without damage. I've discovered that all the layers framers in the States put on the back as part of their framing process just breed mold, so after cleaning I put as little on the back of the picture as possible. And I put little blocks of wood on the corners of the frames to keep the artwork from touching the wall and allowing air to circulate behind the art work.

If you have dressy clothes, or North American clothes that you seldom use in Panama, and you leave them hanging in your closet, when you are getting ready to travel and go to pack the clothing you find colored mold that will not wash out, so the item is ruined. It's not just mold but also condensating humidity which after several years will corrode and destroy.

Panamanians have discovered that the best way to prevent mold is with lots of airflow. Traditional Panamanian houses have windows that are made from open cinderblocks and not glass for a reason: to prevent mold. A good Panamanian closet or cupboard doesn't have doors and has shelves that are actually slats instead of solid wood, thus allowing airflow. You can keep the lights on in closets, or in the rainy season we use de-humidifiers in our walk-in closets to deal with the humidity. Ceiling fans and windows aren't a bad idea in walk-in closets. North Americans and Europeans like nice windows that we can shut tightly to keep out bugs and so instead of bugs we end up with mold.

When we designed our home we specifically designed it to be open and encourage airflow, and if we get a few bugs, so be it.

4. Communication Infrastructure or Lack Thereof

OK, it's MY list.

Some folks may find the communications infrastructure in Panama great, passable, or to their liking. I don't! Perhaps it is because I like to think that I live in the "real" Panama out in the country. Sometimes I think two tin cans on a string would function better than either cell phone service or the Internet.

When we moved to Panama ten years ago, Valle Escondido promised high-speed Internet. We fought for four years trying to get any decent Internet service and then we moved to our coffee farm. As soon as we moved Cableonda came to Boquete and Valle Escondido now has reliable and inexpensive Internet for about $20 a month. Since I now live on the mountain above Boquete town in a more rural area, I pay $65 a month for 1 MB mobile Internet which doesn't always work during heavy rain or fog.

Panamanian President Ricardo Martinelli wanted the whole country wired with free Internet access and even gave laptops to students in rural schools. Since Panama has never had school books the idea was to skip ahead a whole generation by putting everything online. Problem was where lots of these kids lived there was no Internet, sometimes their homes didn't have electricity, and no one knew how to unscramble the inevitable computer issues. Now Mark Zuckerberg, who invented Facebook ,has partnered with the current President Juan Carlos Varela promising free Internet access. Promises or reality? Time will tell.

I just don't happen to live in one of the areas with great Internet access.

Telephone service? Scratch "service." Scratch: "telephone."

I'm sorry but the best phones ever created were the heavy black ones that sat on the corner of your desk. You never had to yell, "Do you hear me now?" Calls were never dropped. There were no buttons to push designed for the hands of five-year-olds. If you wanted to talk with me you simply used the rotary dial to dial MOtt Haven 6-5643. You knew you were calling the Bronx, and Mott Haven area. If you saw people on the street seemingly talking to themselves, you just walked on the other side of the street.

The major telephone company, with the government's blessing, is Cable & Wireless and they no longer do land lines, which, I guess, is OK because it seems like every Panamanian comes out of the womb with at least one cell phone in hand and talks on it constantly for the rest of his or her life despite the threats of the traffic police, who are busy talking on their own cell phones. In Panama you either struggle with a cell phone, use smoke signals, or remain incommunicado.

So what's wrong with cell phones aside from the fact that they aren't waterproof? I get the cheapest phone I can buy since I know whether it's a $39 phone or an expensive iPhone that plays games with me and meets all my personal and interpersonal needs, eventually it's either going in the river, the spa, or as in the case of my last phone, the washing machine.

Never mind that every phone likes to pretend it is a miniature super computer designed to foil attempts to use it as a damn telephone. Never mind that even if you do choose "English" the phone company only speaks Spanish. Never mind that the cell phone provider sends you commercial messages which beep and grunt and ring 24 hours a day promising that if you buy another $5 cell phone card you will get a zillion free minutes ... which expire thirty minutes after you get them.

Every cell phone company promises the best signal and they do this by painting everything in sight across the country with their logos and often horrible signature colors. If they just invested a fraction of the advertising budget in actually improving their signals, it wouldn't be so bad. Yet across Panama, cell phone towers spring up like weeds during the rainy season.

Where we live, you really need three cell phones, one from each of the competing companies, in the hope that when you need to make a call one of the three might actually work.

I'm retired. I don't need a cell phone and I don't want one. You want to contact me, send me an email ... and we'll both hope my Internet service works. Besides, I spend half of my life cruising around the world. Show me a connectivity service that works world-wide at a reasonable cost, and I'm in. It's coming and who knows, I might live to see the day.

Culturally, I know, I'm very disconnected. Even the Indigenous teenagers next door have smart phones. This is one of the serious disadvantages of my grandsons living in Seattle and me living in Panama.

3. *Spanish*

"Dude! It's a Spanish-speaking country, what do you expect? You're a guest, so don't start dissin' the locals' language!"

Spanish is a romance language which can be very beautiful unless it is slurred rapid-fire like a machine gun, which is the way most Panamanians speak their language. I live in a Spanish-speaking country so I should speak Spanish, although it would be nice if all those Panamanian companies who love to take *gringo* money would be considerate enough to add, "Press 2 for English."

The problem isn't that Panama speaks Spanish, but that I don't speak Spanish, at least not fluently. Here's my hang up with languages. I went to a private junior high school where we had one required language choice: Latin. A "dead, dead language, as dead as dead can be, it killed the ancient Romans" and came close to killing me. Two years. Get through. Get the grade.

Then high school. Guess what. Spanish! *El Camino Real* was the text book. I never knew that in California I would actually live on El Camino Real, the royal highway and trail of the Spanish missions, nor in my wildest dreams did I ever think I would live in the South Bronx [AKA Puerto Rico Norte], or the Republic of Panama. We had a Spanish teacher who was forever sexually propositioning half of the girls in the class and generally was a world-class jerk, but I did learn some Spanish. Not much, but enough to get the grade and get out.

College. French. Mainly because I thought that a woman singing in French was about as sexy as language can get. I worked my way through college as a night watchman so I could study on the job. After working all night, I would head into the language lab and do my French. So I struggled just to stay awake and never did find the sexy women singing in French. I learned enough to get the grade and get out.

Language was always a requirement to be fulfilled without any really "live" purpose.

On to seminary. More languages. Really useful ones: ancient Hebrew and Greek. Two years of each. Passed. True confession: I passed Hebrew only by memorizing vocabulary words using the most graphic pornographic images imaginable. Requirement fulfilled. I guess the idea was that in the church everyone was going to inundate you with questions about the meaning of the text in the original Greek and Hebrew. Thirty years in the ministry: nobody ever asked or seemed to care.

Something did happen in seminary. I spent three months one summer in Europe and encountered people actually speaking different languages. Too late, I got it. Yes, the French laughed at me but I usually managed to get the room (never the girl), the road, the train, or the entree I wanted.

Out of seminary for six years I was pastor of an all-black church in a Puerto Rican area of the South Bronx. This should have perfected my Spanish, and in a sense it did. If I ended up in prison on Riker's Island I could communicate fairly well in street Spanish. I knew enough street Spanish to insult your mother and her various romantic liaisons and I could do pretty well putting down your particular sexual habits. Once I left the Bronx for a staid, old, emphasis old, very traditional, emphasis very, church in Milwaukee, Wisconsin, the only time I really got to use my Bronx street Spanish was when the Xerox machine wouldn't work.

So I have this long history with languages ... and I can't communicate.

In the ten years we've been in Boquete, thanks to many Panamanian friends with unbelievable patience and the ability to "dummy down" their language for my benefit, I can get by with some basic Spanish communication. My tenses are wrong. Feminine words are masculine and vice versa. Lots of the locals are trying to learn English and the *gringos* are trying to learn Spanish and when we relax and are willing to make fools of ourselves in the other person's language, amazingly, communication takes place.

But ... when you want to get beyond the basics of "How are you?" and "How is your family?" and the weather and you want to share feelings with friends, and ideas and talk about life, and meaning in life and all the stuff that friendships are made of ... then you need to be able to really communicate. And that's my frustration.

So I have decided to bite the bullet and learn Spanish. Immersion? I'm already immersed living in Boquete. I need to move on. Like a lot of folks I looked at the most expensive packaged Spanish program, the one sold at airports around the world, assuming that because it was the most expensive it must be the best. Then I discovered how much they spend on commissions and advertising to reinforce that image. And I talked to folks who'd used the most expensive program available ... and unhappily sent it back to get something else, or let it just sit ... like most of us do with exercise machines. Unfortunately just owning the exercise machine doesn't improve cardiovascular function, and placing even the most expensive Spanish program under your pillow at night doesn't help you learn Spanish.

Not only does my age make learning a new language difficult, but when I was in grade school some brilliant educator had the idea that you shouldn't teach children grammar, just teach them to speak and write so it "sounds good." So I need to learn English grammar in order to learn Spanish grammar. And what can you say about a language that has twice as many tenses and every other word is "irregular"? I've actually awakened from nightmares about Spanish grammar.

Whether or not I will ever succeed is an open question, but I can assure you that the more Spanish you know, the better you will enjoy life in Panama.
I work on ships with 35 different nationalities, all of whom speak multiple languages. My Ngabe farm worker speaks

Ngabe, Spanish and is learning English faster than I'm learning Spanish. Unfortunately communicating in multiple languages just wasn't part of my growing up experience in the U. S.

2. Frustrating Differences in Culture

Yes, the food preferences are different ... more rice, less potatoes, more fish and chicken, less beef. The music may be different and louder and go all night. And, as a whole Panamanians, as most Latinos, seem to know how to enjoy life and seem less uptight and "driven" than many of their North American and European cousins.

Panamanians are beautiful, gracious, and polite people. Where else would folks entering a crowded waiting room or a restaurant feel compelled to greet the room upon entering? Can you imagine stepping on a crowded elevator in New York and saying, "Good morning!?" But by the same token, as a whole Panamanians have some traits which many expats find irritating.

You either accept these cultural differences or you go nuts, or move back to wherever you lived originally.

Many are not dependable ... at least by North American standards. It's almost a national trait. Part of the politeness is to tell people what they want to hear, which may or may not be what they need to hear, and may or may not be an accurate representation, what we might call "the truth." If someone says they will take care of it, or do it, or be someplace at a given time, they may actually mean it or, more likely, they are just telling you what they think you want to hear.

People keep information, like card players, close to their chest and don't volunteer information. What do you need most as an expat moving into a new culture and community? Information! North Americans love to share their knowledge, insights and know-how, whether the world wants it or not. Getting the information from Panamanians can be like pulling teeth. You have to ask, over and over and over again. People don't volunteer what you need to know.

North Americans are a pretty trusting lot. Generally we like to trust people and tend to trust them until they prove that they cannot be trusted. Panamanians aren't very trusting of each other, which I guess tells you something.

There are Panamanians who live by the way of *"juega vivo"*, which is defined as "getting over" or "pulling a fast one." These folks will screw you at every opportunity and for them it is a way of life. It is just part of the cultural fabric of Panama, known to all Panamanians, and practiced by many.

Example: We owed money to a guy who had helped us initially as a consultant on our coffee farm and said we would drop it off at his house and give it to his mother if he wasn't there, but he didn't trust his mother. Our relationship with this guy grew and we let him use a car and eventually "sold" him the car with a small down payment and the promise to pay over time.. *Gringos* who've lived in Panama a while are now on the floor laughing because they know exactly how the story will end! He screwed us out of $8,000. His sister was the Panamanian equivalent of our justice of the peace, and his mother worked for the Panamanian equivalent of the FBI. Everything was in his mother's name, so his "So sue me!" response meant nothing.

"Not to trust anyone" has been a tough lesson for us to learn. We've learned it ... at a cost of almost $50,000 overall if you count my conniving contractor. Know that if you move to Panama, rightly or wrongly, you are perceived to be fabulously wealthy and of course there are folks who will assume that the reason why you came to Panama is to spread that wealth around.

Even within Panama there are different cultural idiosyncrasies between Latinos and the Indigenous. The Indigenous always assume that you will pay, for everything. And what you are already offering is never enough they always want more. But then you are the rich *extranjero*.

1. There Is No Escape

I know that the title of this book is *The New Escape to Paradise* ... we "escaped" to Panama and we love it! But ... there is no perfect place in the world, because, unfortunately, we aren't perfect. However, Panama comes damn close!

There are folks who think that if they change jobs, change partners, or change locations, that all of the problems will go away and life will be good. Unfortunately it doesn't work that way. Sometimes you need to change *you*. Don't get me wrong: I am a big proponent of change. But change just for the sake of change ... or thinking that moving to Panama is going to make everything right is a big mistake. *Por ejemplo*: if you have problems in your relationship deal with them before moving to Panama. The stress of a new culture will only make things worse. It seems nary a week goes by but the latest "Coconut Telegraph" gossip is who is breaking up this week.

If you're going through some midlife, late-life, retirement, "senior citizen" crisis, deal with it. Picking up and moving to Panama ,buying a Harley and becominga senior-citizen-Hell's Angeles-wannabe is not going to solve your crisis.

Now this is directed mainly at my fellow U. S. citizens. Much of the world is dreaming and scheming to get a U. S. Passport. Yes, everyone in the States hates the Federal Reserve and the IRS. We, as well as the rest of the world, know that the United States has a totally dysfunctional government. We know things are screwed up beyond recognition. We inherited something precious and we are leaving something tainted and tarnished to our grandchildren.

But if you are a U. S. citizen, Uncle Sam is going to chase you everywhere to claim his pound of flesh ... well now, pounds of flesh. There is no escape from the IRS: just accept it. It's a cost of business, the price of citizenship in the United States. You're not going to find a sandy island anywhere where you are off the radar because there is a chip in your passport and within 15 years, the way things are going, I predict a chip will be embedded in your arm. So what are you going to do? Are you going to give up your U. S. passport for Dominica? Good heavens! Or a passport from St Kitts and Nevis, when Nevis is already looking to break away? Get real! There is no escape.

Try travelling the world on a passport from Dominica or St Kitts. I travel around the world on a ship with a crew from some 35 different nationalities. You would not believe the confusion folks with other passports endure which you don't have to put up with if you have a U. S. Passport.

I didn't drop out in the '60s, but now that I am in my 60s I'm dropping out and Panama is as good a place as any to live in exile. Should you need it, Uncle Sam is here to help you. The IRS has just added a bunch of additional agents in Panama, not to help you with your taxes, but to put you in handcuffs. But it's helpful to know our spendthrift Uncle is not far away. In the second Carter-Torrijos Panama Canal Treaty, the United States agreed to protect the neutrality of the Canal in perpetuity and ipso facto the neutrality of Panama. There are times when it's nice to have a big brother.

OK, so Panama isn't perfect and it isn't for everyone, but it's worth taking a good look at Panama. It's been great for us, and my only regret is that we didn't make the move sooner.

Action Items and Points to Ponder

1. Those are my lists. What about yours? Wherever you live there are things you love and things that drive you nuts. Identifying these will help you better evaluate places you consider for relocation.

2. What are the top things you like and don't like about your life right now?

3. How will moving to Panama, or elsewhere, change those things?

The great spider vs. scorpion fight out on the bathroom floor.
Well, it doesn't happen every day.

A day with friends on a deserted white sand beach on one of
the many islands off Boca Chica

22. A Place to Call Home

You can live anywhere you want in Panama, but there are places that expats seem to like to call home,.

An advantage or disadvantage of places where there are other expats, depending on how you look at things, is that there is a community of people, *extranjeros*, who can offer support, encouragement and opportunities to socialize.

Panama City is, of course, a big, growing Latin American capital city with lots of activity, people, traffic, stores, restaurants, and cultural attractions, which is appealing to many expats. Others are looking for a more *tranquilo*, rural atmosphere. Some like it hot and others prefer the cool climate of the mountain highlands. In Panama there is pretty much something for everyone.

If you've followed my recommendations in Chapter 3, "Finding Paradise," you should by now have a good idea of what you are seeking.

Foreigners, or *extranjeros,* can own property in Panama everywhere except for a few areas along the borders with Costa Rica and Colombia where you probably wouldn't want to live anyway.

The Isthmus of Panama links North and South America running east and west and north and south between the Caribbean Sea and Pacific Ocean. It's the 118th country in size comparison, a little smaller than South Carolina. It is tropical, located between latitudes seven degrees and ten degrees north, so we usually just say nine degrees. Because it is tropical it is hot and humid year-round and there is very little variation in the hours of daylight. There are cool areas in Panama, like the highlands, but this is because the tropical lowland temperatures are moderated by the altitude.

Even within a small area like Boquete there are many microclimates, each with significantly different characteristics, which is one reason why I suggest doing a trial run of three months to a year actually living in a place before making a move.

Panama has nine provinces and five *comarcas* or territories of various Indigenous groups who were here before Columbus arrived in 1502.

Panama has about 3.7 million people with the Panama City Metropolitan Area serving as home to around 1.6 million. David, the capitol of Chiriqui province, is the second largest city with a population of around 150,000. Colon, sitting at the Caribbean entrance to the Panama Canal and home to the world's second largest free zone, and Santiago between David and Panama City, would tie for third place at around 80,000 each.

The main artery of Panama is the Pan-American Highway which at points is a four lane superhighway and in other areas is a narrow two-lane road winding through the jungle. The fabled highway runs around 48,000 kilometers [30,000 miles] from Alaska to, at least in theory, the tip of South America. However there is a 100 kilometer [60 mile] gap through the Darien jungle in Panama so it's not really possible to drive from North to South America.

Since the road passes through many countries, climates, and ecological areas there is no uniformity. The road through Panama varies from good to just OK, but is far better than through some other Central American countries. Aside from crazy and crazed drivers, and giant semi trucks with so-so tires swerving to avoid potholes, it is safe to drive even at night.

Jake Silverstein may have written the best description of the Pan-American Highway saying that it is a "system so vast, so incomplete, and so incomprehensible it is not so much a road as it is the idea of Pan-Americanism itself."

Panama City

If you like big city life this is it. Panama City is a vibrant Latin American capital city; just think Miami on steroids. Whatever you need, whatever you want and maybe a lot that you may not want, like traffic, is in Panama City.

Originally founded in 1519 by Spanish conquistadores, Panama City was the starting point for expeditions to Peru and became the most important city on the trade route for gold from the New World being shipped back to Spain. In the last half of the 16th Century, Panama City was the richest city in the world. Gold would be shipped to Panama City and from there carried by mule train across the Isthmus to places like Nombre de Dios and Portobelo on the Atlantic side to be shipped to Spain.

Naturally such a lucrative target captured the attention of pirates. Sir Frances Drake successfully captured Nombre de Dios on the Atlantic side in 1572 and a year later captured a mule train carrying silver across the Isthmus. Drake climbed a mountain to become the first Englishman to see the Pacific Ocean. He later would sail up the Pacific as far as California, although not stopping in Panama City, becoming the first Englishman to sail around the world. Drake would go on to defeat the Spanish Armada and be knighted. In his 50s, he returned to unsuccessfully attack the El Morro fort at San Juan, Puerto Rico. His ship limped back to Panama where, off the coast of Portobelo, Drake died of dysentery and was buried at sea in a lead coffin off Portobelo.

The pirate most associated with Panama City is Henry Morgan. Morgan operated as a privateer under a letter of marque from the British Crown authorizing him to attack Spanish ships and possessions. Morgan attacked and captured Portobelo, the third richest city in the world in 1668. He went on to attack the Spanish stronghold of Maracaibo in Venezuela in 1669. Emboldened by his victories in Venezuela, Morgan set his sights on the richest city in the world, Panama City.

January 6, 1671 Morgan came back to Panama and captured
Fort San Lorenzo on the Atlantic side. Leaving 300 men to
guard the fort, on January 19 Morgan set out for Panama City
sailing up the Chagres River with seven small ships and 36
boats and canoes. As Morgan moved across Panama, the
Spanish generally fled rather than fight. January 28th Morgan
arrived at the gates of the city of Panama with around 1,500
men. The Spanish defense force of around 1,200 infantry and
400 cavalry fell apart and by mid-afternoon Morgan's men
were following fleeing Spanish soldiers into the city. The
fighting that ensued left much of the city in flames.

The privateers tried to put out the fires as they searched for
the city's gold, but much of the wealth had been loaded onto
ships that managed to sail in the confusion of the attack or
was hidden in the Bay of Panama. Morgan's men stayed four
weeks poking through the smoldering remains of the city
looking for treasure. In the end they managed to plunder so
much that it took 175 mules to carry the loot back across the
Isthmus.

The remains of that original city are known as Panama Viejo
or "Old Panama" and today it is a UNESCO World Heritage
Site. You can walk across what remains of a 500-year-old
bridge or climb to the top of the iconic tower, all that remains
of the old cathedral. The tower has been restored and today is
the symbol of Panama City.

What Morgan didn't know is that during his voyage, England
had signed a treaty with Spain and his attack on Panama City
violated that treaty. Morgan was taken back to England, tried,
and during the trial he managed to prove that he didn't get
the "email" about the peace treaty, so was knighted and made
Lieutenant Governor of Jamaica.

Morgan settled down in retirement with his buddies in
Jamaica, was a heavy drinker, and died in 1688 in his early
50s.

So why, inquiring minds want to know, would you name a
popular and delicious brand of spiced rum Captain Morgan?

Alas, Captain Morgan Spiced Rum is good, but too expensive for me, so I've come up with my own recipe for "Captain Richard's" Spiced Rum. I'll share it with you, and if you like spiced rum, this will more than cover the cost of this book!

> 1 liter golden rum or dark rum
> 1 vanilla bean cut up or ½ teaspoon vanilla
> 3 cinnamon sticks (3")
> 4 whole allspice or a pinch of ground
> 1 whole nutmeg crushed
> 3 star anise
> Pinch anise seed

Let stand one week, more or less, depending on strength of flavor desired. You can experiment and get exactly what you like. This is best consumed looking out over one of our two oceans, or sitting in your spa in Boquete watching the sun set over the mountains.

The pirates are pretty much gone from Panama, except for the few disreputable real estate agents, and developers of high-rise buildings, in Panama City, who lure investors with tales of fortunes to be made by flipping million dollar condos.

After Morgan's attack, with their city in ashes, residents of Panama City decided that the original location of the city really wasn't that good due to the swampy, mosquito-ridden surrounds, so they moved their city to a more attractive peninsula that enjoyed sea breezes. So the second Panama City was born, which today is known as Casco Viejo, or the old town center.

Casco Viejo

Casco Viejo is the area of the old colonial city, heavily damaged during the U. S. Invasion of Panama. It is lovingly being restored and is the jewel of Panama City. Here you will find national treasures like the National Theater, the *Palacio de las Garzas* or "Herons' Palace"[60], the Museo del Canal Interoceanico de Panama or "Panama Canal Museum" housed in the building that was headquarters for both the French and

U. S. companies during the Canal construction, the House of
Simon Bolivar, and numerous public buildings and beautiful,
historic plazas graced with cafes. St. Joseph church is home
to Panama's famed golden altar, one of the items saved from
Morgan in 1671, successfully hidden and moved to the new
city.

I think if I were ever to live in Panama City, I'd probably want
to live in Casco Viejo. I love the history and the architecture
and it is becoming a very hip and trendy area. You can get
nice breezes off the Bay of Panama depending on where you
live and you are close to the city with all that it has to offer.
You can walk to the National Theater and there are often
outside cultural events and performances.

But there are challenges living in Casco Viejo. Living in the
restored buildings, if you can find a place, is very expensive,
like around $3,210 a square meter [$300 a square foot]. There
is really no local shopping for necessities. There are lots of
tourists and, although traffic is restricted, lots of noise. Air
conditioning, even just for control of street noise, is essential.
And unless you have a rare off-street parking spot or garage
you wouldn't even want to think about owning a car.

The metropolitan area of Panama City, which includes some
areas on the opposite side of the Canal, is called a district. The
district is divided into thirteen neighborhoods or
corregimientos [San Felipe, Santa Ana, El Chorrillo, Calidonia,
Curundu, Ancon, Bella Vista, Bethania, San Francisco, Juan
Diaz, Pueblo Nuevo, Parque Lefevre, and Rio Abajo].
Corregimiento is an old Spanish term referring to
administrative subdivisions. As you might expect in a large
city each area has distinct characteristics.

The El Chorrillo neighborhood, which many would describe
as a slum, consisted mostly of old wood-framed buildings
dating back to the 1900s that were destroyed by fire during
the U. S. Invasion. Eventually the United States financed
construction of large low-cost cinderblock apartment
buildings to house the displaced population. These are now

an urban slum with high crime rates. As you would expect in any large metropolitan area, there are areas of Panama City that are quite safe and areas that you want to avoid.

Most of the area's expats would find interesting feature apartments and high rise buildings. Punta Paitilla is home to Trump Tower and many of Panama City's newest and most expensive high-rise apartment buildings and is very popular with expats. Throughout much of Panama City you will find small communities of older single family homes nestled between high-rise towers. Some of the popular residential areas, many with high-rise buildings, are Balboa Avenue, Costa del Este, Marbella, Punta Pacifica, Coco del Mar, Punta Pacifica and San Francisco.

Panama City has everything: theater, night life, multiple grand shopping centers, the best doctors and hospitals. Panama City has a vibrant international community. Tocumen International Airport, as well as the national airport and bus terminal, make traveling easy. Panama City is a Latin American business and banking center: if you want to do business in Panama, or even Latin America, Panama City is the place to be.

The price of living in a large city is that it is expensive. Most things cost more in Panama City than they do in the rest of the country. It is always hot and humid so air conditioning is essential. There are lots of people, traffic, and congestion.

Panama City is not an easy city in which to get around. The new public bus system and Metro are designed to move masses of locals but are not always convenient for expats. Driving your own car in Panama City is a challenge. There are times of the day when you can get from Tocumen International Airport across the city to the Bridge of the Americas in 45 minutes or less. At other times of the day the same trip can take several hours. Fortunately there is a sea of licensed and more-or-less regulated yellow cabs. A sea of yellow cabs in Panama City looks pretty much like a sea of yellow cabs in New York, but with a few exceptions. Probably more cab drivers in Panama City speak more English than their counterparts in New York, and Panama City cab drivers were all born here so they know a zillion back ways around the congestion. Sometimes when trying to drive around Panama City, I've just hired a cab as an escort and then followed the cab to where I wanted to go. You'll pay more if you have a cab to yourself. Usually cabs in Panama will pick up other passengers going somewhere near to your destination unless you specify you want the cab all to yourself. Cab drivers like to charge *gringos* more than the established fare if they can get away with it. After you've been in Panama a while you learn to insist on the correct fare and the cab drivers are fine with it, but you have to take the initiative and not just automatically pay the *gringo* rate.

The amazing thing about Panama City is that because of the U. S. Canal Zone history there are some fantastic areas right in the city where you can feel like you are a million miles away. Ancon Hill has some residential areas where you are surrounded by trees, monkeys and toucans. The Balboa area, once the center of life in the Canal Zone, has residential areas where old U. S. Canal and military houses have been remodeled and you can feel like you are in a suburban area of the States.

Somewhat unique to Panama City is the Parque Natural Metropolitano, a tropical dry forest of over 232 hectares [573 acres] within the city limits. Unlike New York's Central Park, the Metropolitan Natural Park really is a jungle with 284 species of trees, 45 species of mammals, 254 species of birds, reptiles and amphibians. The monkeys, ocelots, margays and macaws here are not in a zoo but in the wild. It's so wild that if you want to go off the marked path in the park known as "Panama City's lung" you'd better have a licensed guide or you may get lost in the jungle and never return.

There were about 20 U. S. forts and military installations in Panama that were returned to Panama starting in 1979 as a result of the 1977 Panama Canal Treaty. The areas of the old U. S. Canal Zone are known as the "reverted areas" and consist of 5 miles on either side of the Canal. What was once Fort Clayton is now known as The City of Knowledge and is a center for high-tech businesses and industry. There are housing areas in and around the Clayton area that have a delightful suburban feel.

Howard Air Force Base, on the western side of the Canal opposite Balboa, was the bastion of U. S. air power in Central and South America for over 50 years before being turned over to Panama in 1999. Since then it has been relatively unused except, perhaps notably, as an airport in Bolivia for filming the James Bond movie "*Quantum of Silence*". The base is being transformed into a new, suburban, planned community known as Pacifico with an industrial area and a Free Zone, all within a short commute to downtown Panama City.

Many U. S. retirees who at one time either worked for the U. S. Canal or served in the U. S. military [See the listing of Former Panama U. S. Military Installations 1904-1999] have chosen to retire in and around Panama City.

The Pacific Golden Beaches

Drive roughly an hour West of Panama City on the Pan-American Highway [three to four hours on holiday weekends] and you come to one of Panama's prime Pacific beach areas centered around Coronado. There are residential areas, sometimes built around golf courses and/or resorts, several all-inclusive beach resorts, private houses of wealthy Panamanians and expats, and high-rise condos, many of which have at least some units overlooking the beach and the ocean.

This area is becoming highly developed which has both advantages and disadvantages. There are shopping centers and malls along the Pan-American Highway with a wide array of stores, restaurants and services. There are golf courses and a vibrant expat community. Most areas have a mix of generally well-off Panamanians and expat retirees, some of whom are snow-birds coming to Panama only during winter months in the Northern hemisphere. Many of the Panamanians live in the city and come to the beach for weekends and holidays.

A big advantage of the Gold Coast area is its proximity to Panama City with all the benefits of the big city within a reasonable drive, except on holiday weekends when it is best to just stay put.

The airport at Rio Hato was originally built by the U. S. military in 1931 and used until 1948, after which it was used as an auxiliary landing field for Howard AFB until 1990. After the U. S. Invasion of Panama and the dissolution of Panama's military, the landing strip at Rio Hato was deserted and used mostly for drag races. In 2011 Panama decided to rebuild Rio Hato and create the new Rio Hato International Airport in order to provide additional airlift to Panama, initially aimed at charter flights to deliver tourists to the beach resorts. For residents and investors in the Gold Coast area it offers the potential of future scheduled flights abroad as well as additional development, jobs, tourism revenue and real estate demand.

El Valle de Anton

El Valle de Anton is actually located inside the flat caldera of an inactive volcano that last erupted 300,000 years ago. Once you get to the beach resorts it is still about an hour ride from the Pan-American Highway up a winding road to reach El Valle. Because it is higher than the lowlands it is usually cooler and so is an attractive weekend place for people living in Panama City. Sometimes thought of as an alternative to Boquete and Volcan that is closer to Panama City, it really isn't the same. El Valle is only 600 meters [about 2,000 feet] above sea level, whereas Boquete is 1,200 meters [around 3,900 feet] and Volcan is 1,400 meters [around 4,600 feet] above sea level, so El Valle does not have the year-round spring-like climate of the Chiriqui mountain towns.

There are about 5,000 people living in El Valle and many of these are people who only come in from the City on weekends. There is a new Rey supermarket and a "Chino[61]" general store, but for most other services it is an hour or more drive down a very winding two-lane road. Because so many of the residents are part-time Panamanians, El Valle does not have the vibrant expat community of say Boquete, Coronado, Bocas or some other areas.

Altos del Maria is a private residential community often thought of as being in or near El Valle. Although there is a private mountain road between the development and El Valle, so at least residents can get to the few restaurants in El Valle. To get to shopping and services it is almost a 45-minute drive on a hilly and curvy road to get to the Pan-American Highway and even longer to the Coronado area shops.

Azuero Peninsula

The Azuero Peninsula is that big hunk of Panama that juts out into the Pacific with the Gulf of Montijo to the west, and the Gulf of Panama to the east. The Azuero region was settled more than 10,000 years ago and was cultivated thousands of years before the arrival of the Spaniards. Nearby at Parita Bay, at the end of the 19th Century, heavy rains caused the river to flood and change course, washing away ancient burial sites and revealing spectacular pre-Columbian gold artifacts. In the late 1930s a scientific archeological expedition uncovered some of the most spectacular pre-Columbian gold ever discovered in the area often called "The River of Gold."

When the Spanish *conquistadores* came, they heavily settled the Azuero peninsula, conquered the jungle and chopped down rainforests to graze cattle. Because of the heavy Spanish colonization, still visible in the architecture of many of the small Azuero towns, there are virtually no Indigenous groups living today on the Azuero Peninsula. Unfortunately the destruction of the rain forest helped to create a dry area known as the Sarigua desert, an 8,000 hectare [19,768 acre] national park. Although not technically a desert because it gets more than 1 meter [39 inches] of rain each year, the wind-blown sand and cacti look more like a desert in Arizona than what was once a rain forest in Panama. It is preserved as a mute testimony of the result of poor land management and destruction of the rain forest.

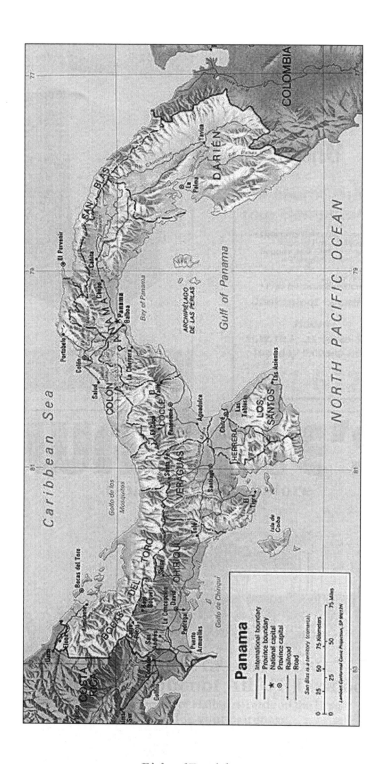

To get to the most popular communities on the Azuero you turn off the Pan-American Highway at Divisa, not far from Santiago. Midway on the Peninsula are the towns of Chitre and Las Tablas which, because of their proximity to the water and lower cost, have recently become attractive to many expats.

Las Tablas literally means "the boards" and legend has it that the town got its name because planks of wood salvaged from a grounded Spanish ship were used to construct the first houses. Las Tablas is best known for its carnival which attracts more people than carnival in any other town in Panama except Panama City. Carnival in Las Tablas is hot, wet and wild as participants in the street dances are sprayed with water to cool them down.

The real pearl of the Azuero is the tiny town, almost at the end of the peninsula named Pedasi. The tiny town of Pedasi has been described as "Panama's most attractive small town," in part because it benefited from being the home town of Panama's first woman President, Mireya Moscoso , who invested heavily in the town during her term in office. There is great fishing, snorkeling, beautiful beaches and nearby some of Central America's best surfing.

There are some beautiful developments of expat and resort housing, but it is a good hour to grocery stores and services. Pedasi is about four hours from Panama City, and five hours from Boquete. We seriously considered buying a place in Pedasi because we loved it so much, but four hours from Boquete was just too far for us. One afternoon we were sitting on the thatched *bohío* of a property we were considering that looked out over the ocean and a huge whale fully breached up and out of the water better than at Sea World.

Santiago

When we first came to Panama, Santiago had the dubious distinction of being midway on the Pan-American Highway between David and Panama City and having a McDonald's with a clean restroom, so it was the place where all *gringos* stopped when driving to Panama City. It also had the most hair-raising section of the Pan-American Highway in Panama, just before Santiago, so by the time you got to Santiago you needed a bathroom stop.

Although it is growing rapidly, Santiago is not typically a city that draws expats. It is hot, sprawling and for people who don't actually live there it is mainly a stopover point. There are some beautiful new hotels and a new shopping center.

Chiriqui Beach Areas

If you want the best of the cool mountain highlands and the Pacific beaches you will want to look at Chiriqui province, home to Boquete, Volcan, and David, as well as some beautiful beach areas.

Chiriqui beach areas are comparatively undeveloped, some might say more "pristine" than the Huntington-Beach-style development of Coronado or the touristy high rise beach developments closer to Panama City.

Playa Las Lajas

If you like a beach pretty much to yourself and dream of walking along the beach "forever," you will find the ten-mile sandy beach at Las Lajas appealing. Las Lajas is just a few miles off the Pan-American Highway and about two hours from Boquete. It doesn't have an anchorage but if beach is your thing, Las Lajas just might be your future home. It's about 20 minutes to a large "Chino" general store and an hour and a half from shopping and services in David, the second largest city in Panama. There are a lot of expats who've found home in Las Lajas and some Boquetanians who have weekend homes at the beach.

Boca Chica

OK, I'll tell you right off I'm prejudiced because this is where our tiny beach *casita* is located. Unlike Playa Las Lajas, the really great beaches in Boca Chica are off the mainland on the barrier islands that dot the Pacific. To get to those beaches you either need a boat or use one of the water taxi boats that depart from the tiny fishing hamlet called Boca Chica.

In my opinion, Boca Chica is pure Panama. The fishing village itself is one tiny loop, but it does have an increasingly busy dock where fishing boats bring in their catch and several dozen small boats are available for hire to take you out to island beaches, hotels, dolphin watching, or whale watching in season. Everything is low-key in Boca Chica ... VERY low-key. If you stay in a resort here choose wisely because that's where you are going to eat. It's best if you stay at a place where meals are included because you are a captive audience and there is really no other place to eat, well, hardly.

There is a place in Boca Chica where you can keep your boat ... a boat yard where a lot of Boquetanians store their boats. Just in front of my little *casita* there is a protected anchorage where a number of people keep their sail boats at anchor. There are several fishing lodges offering some of the best fishing in the world. More deep sea world fishing records have been set in this area of Panama than anywhere else. A week at one of these lodges, including fishing, can run from $5,000 up to $13,000.

Just a few miles off shore is the Chiriqui Gulf National Marine Park. If I can quote from Frommer's, "At Boca Chica, the closest town to the park, there are no high-rises, golf courses, or gated communities, just a couple of lodges and a tiny fishing community -- and a lot of thick vegetation and crystalline water. The Marine Park was founded in 1994 to protect 14,730 hectares [36,400 acres] of extensive coral reef, mangrove swamps, and marine meadows -- the park's most salient characteristics. Another significant feature of this park is its dozens of picturesque rocky outcrops sprinkled across the gulf, as well as its idyllic islands carpeted in forest and lined with slender coconut palms. Several of these islands boast tropical-paradise white-sand beaches lapped by turquoise waters (unlike the Pacific Coast beaches on the mainland), especially Isla Gamez and Isla Bolanos. While out in the gulf, you can see the purple silhouette of Volcan Baru rising high in the background. The air is fresh and balmy, unlike the interior humid lowlands.

"The sea is rich in marine life, providing scuba divers and snorkelers with the opportunity to see huge schools of colorful tropical fish, as well as large pelagic fish like white-tipped sharks. Scuba divers and snorkelers will need to book a boat tour to get to the offshore islands, where visibility is better than it is near shore (expect up to 15 meters/50 feet off shore)."[62]

The nearest real shopping, aside from small "Chino" stores, is in David, about an hour drive from Boca Chica. Ice and a few staples are available in the nearby tiny town of Horconcitos.

On the nearby islands there are fishing lodges, small bed and breakfast hotels, howler monkeys that I can hear in the distance: "in the distance" is important with howler monkeys since they can make a lot of noise. There are also private homes in and around Boca Chica and the islands. There is a giant luxury development promised at Isla Palanque at the end of Boca Brava. On the 400 acre property the master plan calls for 220 homes and 80 hotel rooms. A 137 square meter casita [1,470 square feet] will run you around $400,000 and if you want the grand first house, with a tiny pool and ocean view plan on a cool $1.5 million.

We actually looked at a number of properties on Boca Brava long before Isla Palanque and those kinds of prices. The only way to get to Boca Brava or Palanque is by small boat or helicopter if you happen to have one. We decided against island living one afternoon when we were coming back to Boca Chica by boat after spending time on Boca Brava looking at property. We got caught in a late afternoon squall and when we got back to the car soaking wet, we looked at one another and asked some serious questions. Did we really want to drive an hour back from David with our groceries, get in a little boat in the rain and go thirty minutes to our house? And what about electric, and water? Water can be a big problem on these islands, especially near the end of the dry season when some island hotels have been forced to turn away clients because they had no water. Then and there we decided that as romantic as island living sounded, since we weren't like Richard Branson or Mick Jagger, island living was not for us.

So my little *casita* is right off the main road to Boca Chica, with electric and between two resorts. Yes, I had the expense of digging a well, but I've got a better chance of having water all year long than folks do out on the islands.

What do I like about Boca Chica? It's Panama, the real Panama. When we first came to Boquete ten years ago you'd still see people coming into town on horseback. Then you'd only see horses on Sundays when people rode around. Now everyone has a giant SUV, no horses, and there is no place to park. When I drive through Horconcitos and see folks going around on horseback, and horses sitting saddled up in the front yard, and typical folks of a little country town, I feel that I've rediscovered the Panama I came to find. This is nothing against Boquete with a convenient four-lane highway, a thriving community of expats, and lots of big SUVS ... to each his own, but when I'm in Boca Chica I feel like I'm in Panama. Would I like to live full-time in Boca Chica? Probably not, but the jury is still out on that one, the only other juror being my wife. But, I am enjoying escaping to Boca Chica AND enjoying coming back to the cool breezes of Boquete.

Las Olas

Las Olas is the beach nearest to David. It is a beautiful mostly dark sand beach that goes for miles. There is a resort and a development right on the beach consisting of some beautiful homes. You see the ocean on one side and the Chiriqui mountains in the distance on the other side. Next to the beach resort is a protected area where sea turtles come to lay their eggs. But the beach is steep and there is often a dangerous undertow and riptides so it really isn't a place for swimming. Shopping and services would be in David, about thirty minutes away.

Puerto Armuelles

Puerto Armuelles is just five miles from the Costa Rican border, right by that little finger of land that juts out into the Pacific called Charco Azul, a small sliver of which is actually part of Costa Rica. Panama City is 378 kilometers [235 miles] away, about eight hours drive on the Pan-American Highway. Once the center of Panama's banana industry and United Fruit Company, Puerto Armuelles today struggles. There are two deep water ports, one for bananas and the other for oil. The oil port was once used for giant tankers like the EXXON VALDEZ to offload oil that was then pumped across the Isthmus to ships on the other side. There was talk of a giant oil refinery in Puerto Armuelles but studies were put on hold when the world economy tanked.

There are some adventurous expats who have found a home in the old United Fruit Company housing areas and there have been a couple of beachfront developments appealing to expats. Armuelles is on the Bay of Chiriqui and there are some nice beaches near town and driving out the Charco Azul peninsula. Foreigners are not allowed to own land close to the border so that is something you need to keep in mind should you fall in love with property on the Charco Azul.

The Chiriqui Lowlands: David

David is Panama's second largest city and the commercial center of Western Panama. The city is growing rapidly and it is the place to go for services and shopping. But the Chiriqui lowlands are hot, really hot, and humid. Like Panama City you need air conditioning in David. While there are some expats who enjoy calling David home, for most folks it is just too hot and humid.

The new "International" airport in David is beautiful, but presently the only flights are to the national airport in Panama City, and occasionally to San Jose, Costa Rica.

South of David is mostly low-lying farm land and mangrove

with winding waterways that are only navigable at high tide so the growth of David is mostly north towards Boquete, thus the new four-lane highway linking David and Boquete. Along the way there are numerous low-cost subdivisions springing up, mostly of smaller, Panamanian-style homes. The government guarantees low interest loans to Panamanians to encourage the growth of a middle class. If you are working, the monthly payment … which may be as low as $50 … is automatically deducted from your paycheck. For around $135,000 you can buy a simple, but small Panamanian tract home.

The Chiriqui Highlands: Boquete and Volcan

The four areas of Panama where you will find the most expats are Panama City, the Coronado beach areas, Bocas del Toro and the spring-like Chiriqui mountain cities of Boquete and Volcan.

Volcan Baru is the highest point in Panama 3,474 meters [11,398 feet] high and is about 35 kilometers [22 miles] from the border of Costa Rica. On a clear day you can see both the Pacific and Caribbean from the top of Volcan Baru. It is possible to climb to the top of Volcan Baru or take a tour on an all-terrain truck but it can be windy and cold on the mountain with nighttime temperatures dropping to 0 degrees Celsius [32 degrees Fahrenheit].

Volcan Baru is an active stratovolcano and the youngest in Panama. The large eruption of the volcano around 700 AD wiped out life and settlements around the volcano and ruins of those civilizations have been found near Volcan. The only recorded historical eruption of Baru was in the mid 16th century although carbon dating indicates activity as recently, well, recently in geological terms, as 500 years ago.

The mountain I see while sitting in my spa on the back porch, just outside Boquete, sipping chardonnay and reading a good book, is a fraction of the original mountain. The original mountain was about 500 meters [1,640 feet] higher, but around 50,000 years ago volcanic activity caused the mountain to partially collapse and created an enormous landslide.

Sometime in the next 5,000 years or so, it is likely that Volcan Baru may do something, but being Panama "5,000 years" may mean 10,000 years or 15,000 years, or never. So in the meantime I enjoy living on the slope of an active volcano[63], having a wonderful view of the mountain, and enjoying the year-round spring-like climate of living at 1,127 meters [3,600 feet].

Panama has relatively frequent earthquakes ... most of which are hardly felt[64]. Having lived in Southern California for almost 20 years, and lived through the 1994 Northridge quake, earthquakes are nothing new for us. The earthquakes here, when you are aware of them, are rarely the rolling kind we used to experience in Southern California. Usually they feel more like a jolt, like a car backed into the corner of the house. Most of the quakes are out in the Pacific where three tectonic plates come together. Sometimes we do get quakes you can really feel and once in a while a swarm of quakes related to the volcano, which is when those of us who live around Volcan Baru sit up and take notice.

A lot of small quakes, even ones you don't feel, are actually a good thing, allowing the earth to release pressure gradually.

Theologically I appreciate small earthquakes because it indicates to me that God is not finished with his creation, and if he's not finished with the earth, maybe he's not finished with me either.

Boquete

Boquete is the emerald in the crown of Panama with its cool spring-like climate year-round, often with rainbows arching over a town that's nestled snugly in the mountains. Boquete has always been not only a place where wealthy Panamanians could escape the heat, but also a place that has attracted international travelers and expats.

Boquete refers to a district within the province of Chiriqui. Within Boquete there is the town of Boquete, called Bajo Boquete ("Lower Boquete") and Alto Boquete ("Upper Boquete') and there are surrounding communities or townships like Palmira, Caldera, Jaramillo, and Los Naranjos.

Various Pre-Columbian Indigenous groups lived around the volcano. On the Volcan side of the mountain remains and rock carvings were discovered at Sitio Barriles, and on the Boquete side near Caldera. Pottery remains have been found that give insight into these civilizations. Technically, any Pre-Columbian pottery or objects belong to the State and discoveries should be turned over to the appropriate government agency. However, knowing how much museum-quality material mysteriously disappears from government museums and storage facilities[65], a lot of people feel their finds are safer if they just keep them quietly at home. We've seen amazing gold jewelry found by farmers digging holes for fences and many Panamanians have their own collections of genuine Pre-Columbian pottery.

Often tourists will be approached by someone with a bag full of "Pre-Columbian" pottery wrapped in newspaper. If the price is right and you have no illusions about authenticity, these replicas make nice souvenirs and collectible items. One guy approached me on the street in Boquete with some pottery they "just dug up on my uncle's farm last week." He neglected of course to say that they had just buried it last month. I asked if it was genuine Pre-Columbian pottery and he assured me that it was. I protested that I thought it was illegal to buy, sell or remove from the country the real thing. Thinking quickly he responded, "Yes, it is, but I have a cousin who will write a letter for you saying it is a fake." You've got to love Panama!

The Guaymi or Ngabe-Bugle are an Indigenous people who were here in Chiriqui before Columbus. Although Spanish conquistadors encroached on Ngabe territories, many Ngabes retreated into the mountains to engage in a seven year struggle with the Spanish, never to be defeated.

The first Anglo, Latin and European people started coming to the Boquete area around the end of the nineteenth century. Interestingly around Boquete you will find families with names like Watson and Collins, because some of the first settlers were English. "JR" Watson's great-something grandfather was an English sea captain who jumped ship in Panama and fell in love with an Indigenous woman. They were some of the first settlers in Boquete. Watson tells of his ancestors having to go to David for supplies, only then, without a four-lane highway, by ox cart it took three days instead of thirty minutes.

In the early 1900s a train ran from David to Boquete. The train was discontinued by the mid seventies and the rails ripped up and used for bridges. What a tourist attraction the train would be today! There is one more-or-less authentic train car that remains today preserved in front of the municipal building in Boquete and the municipal building itself was once the train station.

What attracted the first settlers was not only the beauty of Boquete, but the incredibly rich *tierra negra* or black volcanic soil which still is tilled to provide onions and tomatoes for the entire country and produce some of the finest high altitude, shade-grown Arabica coffee in the world.

Boquete's first hostelry, the Panamonte, opened in 1914, is still standing and is still a wonderful place of hospitality. It was purchased in 1946 by the Collins family and is still family-owned and run, presided over by the Grande Dame of Boquete, Inga Collins. It is a charming hotel with a great bar, complete with fireplaces, and a very European-style dining room with excellent food. Dinner for two here with wine, tax and tip will probably set you back around $75 but it's worth it. If you have a *Pensionado* visa it will run around $60. Some of the notable names of folks who've graced Boquete and the Panamonte with their presence include Teddy Roosevelt, Charles Lindberg, Admiral Richard Byrd, the Shah of Iran, Ingrid Bergman, Richard Nixon and Sean Connery.

Bajo Boquete, or the town of Boquete, was once described in a guide book as a "little nondescript, mountain town." Now Boquete runs the danger of becoming a *big* nondescript, mountain town. Unfortunately Boquete has grown without a plan and without any architectural unity, which, frankly, is a shame. For the Panamanians who live here, this is their home. They look at the new modern-looking buildings with pride and a sense of accomplishment. I'm a guest, but I imagine what might have been and what, with some architectural planning, it could have meant for the tourism industry, which is an important part of Boquete's economy as well as and the quality of life. It may not be too late.

There are lots of expats living in and around Boquete. Nobody really knows how many and guesstimates vary wildly. There is a vibrant expat community which, for the most part, rather than function as a separate entity, has built on relationships and created projects which are joint projects of locals and *extranjeros*. Things like Bid4Boquete, which raises thousands of dollars for local charities like Animales, which sponsors spay/neuter clinics, charities helping disabled Panamanians, the local children's home/orphanage and families in need of food. Expats have been instrumental in creating and developing the Boquete BCP[66] Event Center, and the Boquete Jazz Festival. The Price and Susan Peterson family, Rotary and other service clubs made possible the new Boquete library.

A vibrant expat community is one of the great advantages of Boquete. In Boquete you can be as active in expat and community events and programs as you want. You can almost be out and doing something every night of the week going to events, trying out new restaurants[67] and having dinner parties with friends, if that is what you desire, or, like me, you might prefer to sit at home in your grubbies with your spouse and dogs by the fire and talk, read or watch old TV series. [68]

There are four grocery stores and basic services, although many people prefer doing major shopping in David which is thirty minutes away.

The cool, year-round spring-like weather in Boquete is the clincher for many people. Even during the dry season, Bajo Boquete or Boquete town, gets an afternoon misting called *bajareque* which keeps everything green and creates fantastic rainbows arching across the valley.

When we first moved to Boquete there was a hand-lettered sign, in Spanish, about midway on the two-lane road between Boquete and David. If you were stuck behind a truck carrying construction materials in a no-passing zone there was plenty of time to read signs. The sign said, "If you want to see Boquete look fast." There is a sense in which that sign was right. Boquete has changed and most folks, including natives, would say it has changed for the better.

In and around Boquete there are a number of planned residential communities, most notably Valle Escondido which was the first such community in Panama. We lived in Valle Escondido for four years. Our house was one of the first built in "the Valley." It is a private, gated, guarded community that surrounds a private resort. It is a reality, unlike some such projects that evaporated once the world's economy crashed. Some are gone for good, tied up in litigation which will likely last years. Others are making a comeback. Interestingly some of the homes most in demand are the more expensive properties.

Volcan

On the western side of Volcan Baru is Volcan with the surrounding hamlets of Nuevo Suisse, Bambito and Cerro Punta. Volcan is about an hour ride up a winding road from the Pan-American Highway surrounded by spectacular scenery and farm land that runs up the sides of mountains.

Volcan is 1,400 meters [4,617 feet] above sea level, about 305 meters [1,000 feet] higher than Boquete. The cool, spring-like climate and rich volcanic soil make the Volcan area the market basket of Panama. Dairy farms and vegetable farms around Volcan provide much of the food that is shipped to supermarkets in Panama City. Birders make their way to Cerro Punta hoping to catch a glimpse of Panama's spectacular, yet elusive Resplendent Quetzal. It is also the home of Finca Dracula[69] described as the largest collection of orchids in the world with around 2,200 species.

Expats enjoy the beauty and climate of Volcan and many prefer it to Boquete because there are fewer expats. Volcan is about an hour from David but the sprawling little town has basic services. Volcan lacks a town center like Boquete and does not have as large of an expat community as Boquete.

Bocas del Toro

On his fourth voyage to the New World, Columbus sailed for two months along the Caribbean coast of Central America from the coast of Honduras to Panama where he put in at Almirante. It was here that Columbus heard the Ngabe people talking about another ocean several days journey South, later to be seen by Balboa and named the South Sea[70]. The Indigenous gave Columbus evidence of Panama's rich supply of gold. Leaving the Northern Islands of Bocas del Toro, Columbus encountered the worst storm he had ever seen and was forced back to Panama.

In January 1503 Columbus built a small fort at the mouth of the River Belen and pulled out three of his ships for repairs while he explored the area. The Ngabe attacked the fort and Columbus managed to hold off the attack, losing one ship in the process, and fled Panama with the three remaining ships still in need of repairs.

Bocas del Toro is the name of the province in the Northwest corner of Panama, and is also the name of the group of islands located off shore. Bocas Town is the name of the main island community located on Isla Colon.

Bocas is best described as a cross between Panama and the Caribbean with an at times crazy mix of Latino, West Indian and expat cultures. The last time I was in Bocas Town with a relocation tour group I walked up and down the main street in the morning for 45 minutes waiting for the group to check out of our little hotel right on the waterfront. No fewer than four guys riding bicycles asked me if I wanted "weed," "ganja," or "pot." Bocas has the reputation as a let-loose party town. Even if you escape to your own Caribbean dream home on one of the outer islands, it's likely that at night, and especially on weekends, you will hear the boom-boom-boom and thumpa-thumpa of the giant speakers at dance clubs on Isla Colon.

Bocas is a very international town with a mix of traditional Latin Panamanian culture, a heavy dose of Panamanian West Indian culture, and lots of *gringos* and Panamanian Chinese who've chosen to call Bocas home. There is an expat community but because many expats live on the small islands away from Bocas town, it is not as cohesive as perhaps in Boquete.

The pluses for Bocas are it's a wonderful place if you have a boat. It is on the Caribbean with that incredible azure water, white beaches, and great snorkeling and diving. It's hot, casual, and the uniform is shorts, T-shirts, and sandals. But there are some downsides, apart from the counter-culture druggy atmosphere, the biting flies and oppressive heat. Everything, everything has to be brought over from the mainland. There are some small convenience stores and "Chino" stores, but many of these stores are buying goods at PriceSmart in David, trucking them over the Continental Divide then onto a ferry boat to get them to Isla Colon and Bocas town. So expect to pay as much as $1 per more per item in the little grocery stores because you are in Bocas. It adds up. Not just food but also building supplies need to be brought in from the mainland.

Land ownership on islands and properties with ocean frontage is VERY tricky in Panama. In years past, much of this land was held by rights of possession and was not titled. Because there was so much confusion, and sometimes outright fraud, especially over land sales in Bocas and on islands, and to increase tax revenue, the government has created new rules for land possession and ownership. Many of the homes and businesses that are built on or over the water in Bocas Town will never own the land or space over the water, but occupy it only on the basis of government leases or concessions. So if you consider purchasing property in Bocas, it is important to have a good lawyer who is experienced in real estate matters and, even then, the watchword is "*Cuidado!*" or in plain English, be careful!

Welcome Home!

Wherever you choose to call home in Panama, you will find the locals and local expats to be warm and genuinely friendly and welcoming. Yes, the culture is different and can be at times frustrating and threatening because it is new and different, but most Panamanians are anxious to help you cope and adapt.

So how do you know which is the right place for you to call home? Study, study, and study some more. Back in California, dreaming of Panama, I was dreaming specifically about Bocas. We weren't considering moving to Panama but moving to Bocas. But once I got to Panama things changed. For a number of reasons I wouldn't be happy living in Bocas.

You can use an exercise similar to what I described in Chapter 3, "Finding Paradise," not only in your search for countries, but also in your search for a place to call home within your chosen country.

And nothing, nothing, can beat the boots-on-the-ground experience of actually visiting the places you think might interest you. Spend a couple weeks and see how it feels. How might it feel not as a tourist, but as a resident? What supplies are available and what do they cost? What are options for rentals? What do properties cost? How friendly and helpful are the locals and expats?

Action Items and Points to Ponder

1. We've looked at some of the places expats choose to call home in Panama. You have my brief descriptions and thoughts and if you've been doing your own independent research you have some of your own. You may not know everything about these places, but ... you know everything about YOU. Based on your limited knowledge about the places, but your extensive knowledge about yourself, what places or kind of places might interest you and why?

Many expats who worked for the U. S. Army and Canal and fell in love with Panama have come back to retire in Panama City.[71]

"Green acres is the place for me. Farm livin' is the life for me": Cerro Punta outside Volcan in the Chiriqui Mountains.

23. *Addicted to Coffee*

"*O* Coffee! Thou dost dispel all care, thou art the subject of desire to the scholar. This is the beverage of the friends of God." ["In Praise of Coffee," Arabic poem, 1511]

Even though we already were "friends of God," we discovered coffee late in life. Aside from occasional cappuccinos on board ship back when free after-dinner cappuccino was still a hallmark of Princess Cruises, or once in a while a stop at Starbucks, neither Nikki nor I were coffee drinkers before coming to Panama. So how is it that we became not only coffee addicts but drug growers?

Happy goats

We know coffee originated in the highlands of Africa in what is today Ethiopia. No one is certain how coffee was discovered but there are some wonderful legends. My favorite is the story of Kaldi and his happy goats. Kaldi was a teenage goat herder off in the mountains of Ethiopia, certainly not the best circumstances for a teenage boy. But Kaldi was smart and very observant and noticed that when his goats ate the leaves from a certain bush, or tree if you will, they became frisky and danced around. So being a teenager ... no, he didn't smoke it, but he tried eating the leaves of the plant himself and sure enough his life looked better and he felt more alive. Soon Kaldi was dancing around with his goats. We're not sure exactly what happened next, but according to the legend, eventually Kaldi came down off his mountain and shared this new discovery with his father. Word spread and eventually people began figuring ways to enjoy this new discovery.

Caffeine is in the entire plant, not just the beans. Perhaps foreseeing the day when harried commuters would line up at Starbucks for a morning fix before settling down in their cubicles and realizing that sitting at your desk chewing a bunch of leaves might not be very chic, it was quickly decided that the best way to enjoy coffee was to brew a mixture of seeds, leaves and husks in water and eventually, the focus was solely on the coffee seeds or beans.

Coffee became a fixture of Ethiopian life and it still is. Unlike a quick stop for a latte with a double shot of espresso at a corner coffee shop, Ethiopians serve coffee in an elaborate ceremony often taking almost an hour.

From Africa, coffee spread across the Arabian Peninsula where it had a very practical and religious function of keeping people awake during lengthy prayers. The Prophet himself is supposed to have said that with coffee he could "unhorse forty men and possess forty women." But, as you will see in our story, many years later, the good ladies of London would disagree with this assessment. Whether the tale about the Prophet is true or not, not all in the Muslim world were enamored with coffee.

"As the drink gained popularity throughout the sixteenth century, it also gained its reputation as a troublemaking social brew. Various rulers decided that people were having too much fun in the coffeehouses. 'The patrons of the coffeehouse indulged in a variety of improper pastimes,' Ralph Hattox notes in his history of the Arab coffeehouses, behavior 'ranging from gambling to involvement in irregular and criminally unorthodox sexual situations.'"[72]

"When Khair-Beg, the young governor of Mecca, discovered that satirical verses about him were emanating from the coffeehouses, he determined that coffee, like wine, must be outlawed by the Koran and he induced his religious, legal, and medical advisors to agree. Thus, in 1511 the coffeehouses of Mecca were forcibly closed.

"The ban lasted only until the Cairo sultan, a habitual coffee drinker, heard about it and reversed the edict. Other Arab rulers and religious leaders, however, also denounced coffee during the course of the 1500s."[73]

Of course, something so stimulating, and sometimes forbidden, could not be kept under wraps. It wasn't long before interest in this magical bean spread across Europe. Following the Ottoman Turks occupation of Yemen in 1536, beans from the Yemen port of Mocha spread across the Turkish Empire. To protect their market, the coffee beans, which are in fact seeds, were not allowed to leave unless they had first been roasted or boiled to prevent germination. But it wasn't long before beans were being smuggled out, quite possibly first by a Dutch sailor. In the mid 1600s the Dutch smuggled beans to their territories in the East Indies, and "Java" eventually became almost synonymous with coffee.

Coffee quickly became the rage across Europe with coffee houses springing up faster than Starbucks. It wasn't long before this came to the attention of the church, and, as the church is often wont to do it proposed that coffee should be banned as sinful. (Remember when many churches declared Rock and Roll to be the "music of the Devil?" And now it is semi-classical music for old farts like me!) Fortunately Pope Vincent III decided to taste coffee before banishing it and he enjoyed it so much instead of banishing it, he baptized it saying, "Coffee is so delicious it would be a pity to let the infidels have exclusive use of it." And coffee has been an essential part of church meetings ever since.

Coffeehouses spread quickly across the European continent and crossed the Channel taking London by storm.

"By 1700, there were more than two thousand London coffeehouses, occupying more premises and paying more rent than any other trade. They came to be known as penny universities, because for that price one could purchase a cup of coffee and sit for hours listening to extraordinary conversations – or, as a 1657 newspaper advertisement put it, 'PUBLICK

INTERCOURSE.'"[74]

There was only one major problem. It seemed that coffeehouses were the exclusive preserve of men, and the men were always hanging out with the boys at the coffeehouse, causing the good women of London great anxiety and distress. It seems the lovely ladies of London weren't "getting any" ... coffee, that is! So in 1674 the frustrated ladies got together "The Women's Petition Against Coffee Representing to Public Consideration the grand inconveniences accruing to their sex from the use of that drying, enfeebling liquor," which was presented to the "Right Honorable Keepers of the Liberty of Venus."

The good ladies argued for the abolishment of coffeehouses because, "Excessive use of that Newfangled, Abominable, Heathenish Liquor called COFFEE, which Riffling Nature of her Choicest Treasures, and Drying up the Radical Moisture, has so Eunucht our Husbands, and Crippled our more kind Gallants, that they are become Impotent, and as unfruitful as those Desarts whence that unhappy Berry is said to be brought."

Obviously these gals had not heard of the legendary assessment of the Prophet. But Great Britain survived and eventually tea replaced coffee as the drink of choice.

Coming to America

It is hard to imagine how valuable these original coffee plants were. In 1714 the Dutch presented a single coffee plant as a gift of state to Louis XIV of France. Louis built a special greenhouse in Paris just to propagate the coffee plants with the intention of growing coffee in French territories around the world, just as the Dutch had done in Indonesia.

In the Western Hemisphere, we are indebted to the French for coffee. In 1723 a French Naval officer by the name of Gabriel Mathieu de Clieu sailed to the French island of Martinique with a single coffee tree. The trip across was the voyage from hell with storms, attacks by pirates, the ship becalmed for days on end, and running out of water. De Clieu used his own water ration to keep the plant alive. His fellow passengers, anxious for a caffeine fix, tried to rip off the leaves and de Clieu had to fight them off to preserve his plant.

Much of the original coffee stock in the Caribbean and Latin America came from de Clieu's plant. But by the time de Clieu was harvesting coffee on Martinique, the Dutch were already growing coffee in Dutch Guiana [today Surinam] and the French in French Guiana.

To grow coffee, you need abundant sunshine, moderate rainfall, year-round temperatures averaging 21 degrees Celsius [70 degrees Fahrenheit] and no frost, which pretty much describes the tropics which is where the producers of coffee are located. The big producers are countries like India, Indonesia, Ethiopia, Brazil, Colombia and Mexico, and the smaller producers are countries like Costa Rica, Jamaica, Panama, and the U. S. State of Hawaii. Interestingly some of the finest coffee in the world comes from these smaller producers. Putting Panama into perspective, Brazil exports 42 million 60 kilogram [132 pound] bags, whereas Panama exports only around 100,000 such bags. But much of what we grow is called "specialty coffee" or "gourmet coffee," shade-grown Arabica coffee with no defects and a cut above the rest.

Coffee and Boquete

Ken Davids, writing in *Coffee Review*, says . . .

" ... Boquete Valley resembles California's wine-growing Napa Valley. The Boquete terrain is more precipitous than Napa's, its river more sparkling, its farms less pretentious, but the feel of an entire community focused with passion and sophistication on a single specialty crop is familiar . . ."[75]

There are many similarities between wine and coffee. Both crops are very complex and the quality of the product is determined by a host of variables, many of which are not in control of the grower. The soil, the exposure, the microclimate, the amount of moisture and how it is delivered, the additives, chemicals and fungicides that are used, the method of harvest, processing of the fruit, and storage, to say nothing of the host of diseases and bugs that can attack the crop all affect the final taste of "the cup." Once you have the finished product, coffee tasting is just like wine tasting: slurp, swish, spit. And the flavor wheel is much like the wine taster's wheel of flavors. Many of the adjectives used to describe wine are also used to describe coffee. Coffee, like wine, is often blended to achieve the desired flavor. Just like with wine, any misstep at any point along the way, however tiny, can destroy everything.

The old coffee farmers in Boquete can taste a cup of coffee and tell you the *finca* where it was grown ... solely by the taste. Even in a tiny area like Boquete there are many microclimates that impact the taste and quality of the final product.

Specialty or gourmet coffee is defined by the Specialty Coffee Association of America as "a coffee that has no defects and has a distinctive flavor in the cup ... Like wine and honey, specialty coffee has a unique flavor thanks to the micro-climates that produce it."

As American, Asian and European tastes in coffee are becoming more sophisticated, there is renewed interest in Panama-grown coffee and particularly the high mountain coffee of Chiriqui grown in Boquete and Volcan. Our coffee is becoming a unique, distinct, and increasingly recognized specialty coffee which is helping coffee production in Chiriqui and helping to maintain price levels where it may again be as profitable to raise coffee as sell off land for real estate development. However as land becomes more and more expensive, it becomes harder and harder to grow coffee and make a profit.

The fame of our coffee has been helped immensely by the introduction of Geisha coffee by my neighbor, Price Peterson. His Hacienda La Esmeralda Geisha coffee continually sets records as the second highest priced coffee in the world, second only to the coffee from Indonesia, kopi luwak or civit coffee which I will talk about in a moment.

Price is a scientist and botanist and went to Ethiopia to find old heritage trees from which he could cultivate his Geisha coffee. It stunned the world when it first went on sale at auction and sold for over $131 *a pound*! Since then, others in Boquete have been growing Geisha, but you should know that all Geisha coffee is not the same. The microclimate and indeed the farm on which it is grown can make a great difference.

A year ago another neighbor, who manages several big coffee farms and is a certified coffee taster, invited us to a tasting in which he included some of our coffee. There were at least a dozen coffees on a round turntable all identified only by number. A cup of each was brewed and we duly broke the crema, inhaled, sipped, swished and spit. All of us agreed that one coffee was superior to all of the others. Hands down, no question. We tasted and discussed all of the samples before the great reveal. Our own coffee was somewhere in the lower half. Frankly it had a kind of slight chemical taste which, we discovered, was because we were storing it in an old storage shed that, although it had been thoroughly cleaned, had once held oil and chemicals. There is no room for error anywhere along the way with coffee. The coffee we all thought was superior was in fact Geisha. But there were two other coffees that were both near the bottom of our lists. They were both Geishas as well, but grown on different farms. Apparently the best Geishas are grown at higher altitudes, and … just like wine … soil, exposure, shade, not just by trees but also cloud cover, make a difference.

Price continues to grow exceptional Geisha coffee. I can only describe it as being like drinking black velvet. He now auctions it himself on his own website.

I doubt those in the line at Starbucks, impatiently scrolling through messages on their phones while they wait for their coffee drinks, have any idea all the work that goes into a cup of coffee even before the beans hit the roasting plants.

Jaguar Java

At one time we thought of trying to market our coffee under the name Jaguar Java. We call our farm Jaguar Java and since, in Panama, everyone has nicknames, some of the guys who work on our farm, "Tigre," "Tigrito," and "Cobra," have given me the nickname of "Jaguar." But I realize that I am retired and I don't have the desire to spend all the money and do all the work necessary to market our coffee, so we sell it in the cherry to other local producers.

As I write this we are in the middle of our harvest season. It is the first week of December. "Looking a lot like Christmas" around our farm in the coffee growing area above Boquete, means that the coffee trees with their dark green leaves glistening in the sunlight, are laden down with brilliant red coffee cherries. The coffee cherry is the fruit, so called because it looks like a cherry. Inside are two seeds or beans from which you eventually will get in your cup of coffee.

This is a wonderful time of year. The heavy rains at the peak of the rainy season are mostly over. The cherries on the coffee trees, or bushes, look like red holly in the Pacific Northwest, and our Ngabe Bugle neighbors who pick for us are hard at work, the women in their brightly colored, hand-made traditional dresses. The folks pick all day and at 4:00 p.m. bring bags of coffee cherries to the little covered *deposito* where their pickings are counted. Usually their kids and dogs are also hanging around so it is somewhat festive. Nikki always brings giant bottles of soda and appoints one of the kids to be the *jefe* or boss of the Coca Cola.

After the count is completed the bags of coffee cherries are loaded onto our pickup to go to the *beneficio* for processing. Because we are paid by weight it is important to sell the cherries the same day to avoid any loss in weight by waiting overnight.

And all of the coffee certifications – "Fair Trade," "Rainforest," "Bird Friendly," etc. – are marketing schemes that all cost lots of money, which no truly small grower in Boquete can afford. I admire people who are willing to shell out $1 more per pound for coffee with one of these certifications thinking that they are helping the small grower and making life better for the Indigenous people who pick coffee. It is good when people do what they think is the right thing, but these marketing schemes help big growers and large cooperatives and are of no benefit to the truly small farmers like us and our neighbors. In fact, assuming some of that money eventually does trickle down to the person picking the coffee, it raises the rate that must be paid to coffee pickers for everyone, actually making things more difficult and less profitable for the truly small farmer who isn't a member of the big cooperative or grower consortium that was able to afford to buy into the branding scheme. Costa Rica has a lot of big coffee farms that have bought into the Fair Trade scheme and they pay pickers more than what we can pay in Panama. Indigenous can cross the borders without problems, or even identification, so a lot of pickers from our area go to Costa Rica, and we have a hard time getting pickers, and have to pay more, so Fair Trade is actually hurting genuine small farmers and workers in Panama.

Our neighbors, the Petersons, don't need any marketing label or association to encourage them to do the right things for their workers and the community. Many of the same people come in from the Ngabe Bugle community to pick for them every year. When there is a food shortage on the *comarca*, Petersons send truckloads of food to their workers and their families. Susan Peterson herself, without any fanfare or notice, drives eggs and bread down our road to one of their Indigenous housing areas so the kids have a good breakfast before going to school, and they have a day care, and give their workers food in addition to their pay.

A hobby farm

When people on the ship ask about my "coffee plantation" I assure them it is not a "plantation" and is actually a "hobby farm." When they ask the difference I tell them, "My wife promises that some day we'll break even."

That's not quite accurate, but we're not raising coffee primarily to make money. For us coffee is a hobby, a way to participate in the life of the community and a way to enjoy our own, home grown fantastic coffee. I can sit in the barber chair for my $3 haircut and talk coffee, or if the talk is in Spanish at least know what is being said. Nikki can chat with the old guys who've been growing coffee in Boquete for years and enjoy them praising the *gringa* lady's beautiful coffee. Because our neighbors work with us we know them and we look out for each other. Coffee enables us to be a part of the Boquete community in a very special way.

"I thought you said you guys didn't drink coffee"

That was then; this is now. We've both become addicted to really good coffee: two to three tablespoons of coffee to a cup of water just off the boil and of course, black. Why would you mess it up with milk and sugar? Definitely it should be 100 percent high-octane, because otherwise you are just drinking hot brown water. Decaffeinated coffee; why? You should know that coffee decaffeinated by whatever method still has some caffeine. Really high quality Arabica coffee has less caffeine[76] than the cheap, big can stuff that's loaded with fillers and sometimes even sprayed with MSG.

Earlier I mentioned the highest priced coffee in the world, kopi luwak from Indonesia. This is the coffee that is eaten by the civet, a cat-like small mammal that typically lives in palm trees. The civet eats the coffee cherries, excretes the beans in its poop, someone digs through the poop, rinses the coffee and sells it to you for an ungodly price. As civet coffee has become more of a high-priced novelty item, the civets are now farmed in cages to mass produce the coffee. When I was in Indonesia I saw it for sale for $40 for 31 grams [1 ounce] of ground coffee. To make a good cup of coffee I'd need at least 62 grams and, curious as I was, I wasn't ready to pay $80 for a cup of coffee made from coffee pulled out of shit! But it did give me an idea.

We have four dogs – stay with me here, folks! – and two are Dalmatians. For whatever reason, maybe because they've always liked to follow the pickers around during harvest, I don't really know, but the Dalmatians like to pick the ripe red cherries off the trees. They won't touch the green fruit and carefully pluck off the red ripe cherries with the expertise of our best coffee pickers. And of course the coffee beans come out the other end in piles of poop on our driveway. So I thought ... well, if people will pay $40 ... well, you get the idea! So if you see Dalmatian Coffee from Boquete ... add that to your "Bucket List" and drink up!

Our coffee harvest is usually November and December, sometimes spilling into January. At higher altitudes it is usually December, January and February depending on the altitude. Coffee grows on trees, although generally trees that are actually more the size of bushes. A coffee tree can live for over a hundred years, although usually after fifteen years or so the trees need to be replaced for maximum yield. It takes about three to four years for a tree to produce.

The coffee trees bloom over about a two-month period with a major bloom and several smaller ones, which is why the coffee doesn't all ripen at the same time and it takes several pickings to harvest the entire crop. When the coffee blooms it looks as if snow has fallen on all of the trees. Because coffee is self-pollinating we don't have a lot of bees doing the work. Coffee flowers smell like honeysuckle or orange blossoms, although not as cloying. When the coffee blooms, along with our orange trees, the farm smells like a perfume factory in France.

In past years we sold our coffee cherries to a big Panama producer who sold a lot to Starbucks. The big coffee companies like to use Panama coffee to boost the flavor of their various blends. I would tell folks on the ship that if you bought a cup of coffee at Starbucks, every billionth bean or so was mine. Now we sell to a small local producer, a neighbor who is also a pilot on the Panama Canal. His private label coffee is exceptional and sold in and around Panama and the Panama Canal. If you're on a Canal cruise and you see his Eco Green Mountain Farm Café Arauz coffee snap it up. I can tell you that the crews of ships from around the world fill their suitcases to take this stuff home.

Follow the bean

So how does the coffee get from the tree to your cup. Once it is sold in the cherry to the *beneficio* or processing plant it goes through a machine that removes the cherry husk and leaves only the bean. At plants like Eco Green Mountain the cherry husks are used as fertilizer and the water is recycled and then treated before being released into the streams where otherwise it would suck up all the oxygen in the water and kill off the fish. Next the beans are dried, both in the sun and in large dryers that look like over-sized clothes dryers. When the beans are sufficiently dried they have to just sit and rest for two or three months. After resting they are put through a machine that removes the hard outside shell of the bean as well as the thin, almost tissue-like "parchment" surrounding the actual bean. The beans that are left have a straw-green color and so are known as green coffee. The green coffee is then exported to be roasted around the world, or, as in the case of Arauz it is roasted and sold locally.

Every step along the way is important and roasting is one of the most important steps. Coffee roasting is at once an art and a science. The beans are roasted anywhere from 11 to 15 minutes during which the temperature of the beans can rise as high as 232 degrees Celsius [450 degrees Fahrenheit]. There is a color progression during which the beans move from straw-green to a rich chestnut brown. During the roasting process the beans pop open and double in size while losing 18-25 percent of their weight. The roasting process releases volatile flavor oils within the beans. The precise moment to stop the roast is based on the roaster's eyes, ears and nose and the taste the client wishes. In the coffee-Mecca of Seattle, home to Starbucks, there are many coffee aficionados who derisively call Starbucks "Charbucks" because of Starbucks distinctive roast which pushes the roast almost over the top to often give a slight hint of being burnt. Obviously there are millions of people around the world who prefer the distinctive Starbucks flavor.

Coffee, like wine, is a matter of personal taste. I tell people on cruise ships, "If you like Ripple wine, be my guest, but while you are on the ship you really should explore the wine list and let your palate explore because you may discover a whole new world of wine." The same thing is true with coffee. You may have been drinking the cheap, big five-pound can coffee that's sat around in a coffee maker all morning at work all of your life. But you owe it to yourself to explore the taste of coffee. Stores like Trader Joe's, Starbucks and your local coffee roasters make it easy to sample coffees from around the world.

The drug of choice

Yes, coffee is a drug. It contains caffeine which stimulates the central nervous system, temporarily wards off drowsiness and restores alertness. We get this drug in lots of ways other than coffee. It's in tea, cola, energy drinks, chocolate … even many of the pills you take for headaches. Like any drug it has symptoms of withdrawal: headache, fatigue, drowsiness, depression, irritability, difficulty concentrating, flu-like symptoms. And it is the drug of choice for 90 percent of North Americans. Just so you can compare your drug habit with that of others, North American drug use breaks down like this:

- Caffeine – 90%
- Alcohol – 61%
- Nicotine – 22%
- Marijuana and illegal drugs – 8%

Becoming Farmers

So how did we happen to start growing coffee?

I was looking for land in and around Boquete just as an investment. We had looked at a lot of places until I found the place we call home. It had been a coffee farm and like many coffee farms in Chiriqui it had been all but abandoned. After the Vietnam War the Vietnamese government gave farmers millions of coffee trees with which to replant destroyed land. A few years later that coffee started pouring onto the world market and much of it was high-altitude, really good Arabica coffee and the coffee market tanked. People in places like Boquete could no longer afford to grow coffee and so they just let their farms grow over. What is today Valle Escondido was once a huge coffee plantation which ended up being sold for real estate development.

So we bought this property and my wife looked at all these old coffee trees, overgrown by jungle and asked, "Do you think we could turn this place around and make it a productive coffee farm?" So, not knowing anything about coffee farming and without much of a "green-thumb," Nikki started cleaning, clearing, trimming, and fertilizing, re-planting doing everything necessary to transform this run-down farm. We enjoyed coming up to the farm and as Valle Escondido where we were living became more and more developed, we decided to build our dream house on our farm.

Today, thanks to Nikki and the Indigenous guys who've helped her, we have a beautiful *finca* producing outstanding coffee. It is a hobby farm. Pretty much we manage to break even, but the rewards of truly being part of the tradition and community of Boquete far outweigh even the reward of enjoying our own, fantastic coffee every morning.

Action Items and Points to Ponder

1. We all get the point about coffee, but do you get the point about using coffee as a way to embrace the local culture and tradition? It might be coffee, or vegetables, or horses, or the spay/neuter clinics, or Hospice or whatever, but if you can embrace and enter into the culture of a place, you are going to be happier in your new life style.

Counting out at the end of the day during coffee harvest.

Coffee tasting or "cupping."

24. Leaving Paradise

*I*t has always interested me to know not only what brings folks to Boquete, but why they leave. I wish someone would do a study on this, but here are some of my own observations and those of others.

Perpetual Adventurers

Let's face it, picking up and moving to a foreign country requires a certain sense of adventure. Some folks we know have left Boquete and moved elsewhere because that's just the kind of people they are. They are always looking for another place ... maybe another spot of the world that hasn't yet been "discovered" and where the cost of living and price of property are still ridiculously low.

There are some folks, who, the moment they move to Boquete, are already scouring International Living and the Internet, looking for the next "hot" place to move.

Relationships On The Rocks

Moving is always a high stress event, and moving to a new country with a new language, new customs, and new mores makes it even more stressful. Folks who may have thought that making a new start in a new country would fix things in their relationship soon find out it doesn't work that way. With greater stress, like tiny cracks in a car windshield, the cracks in the relationship are soon splintering off in multiple directions.

For a lot of people, moving to Panama is breaking out of the rut of the traditional commute, the nine to five job, social obligations, and family expectations – whatever. Suddenly, feeling free, and with a sense that this may be the last big adventure of life, folks break loose ... one stays, one heads back to the States, or they both move on elsewhere in different directions.

Folks who didn't do their homework

If you came to Panama looking to shop every other day at the Galleria, or expect museums, openings, Broadway, and symphonies in Boquete, or want a tennis club, U.S.-style country club, shopping at Pavilions or Bristol Farms, or a 30-screen Cineplex ... you aren't likely to find all those options, particularly if you are planning on living outside Panama City. So why are folks surprised when they move here and don't find those things? They didn't do their homework.

The novelty wears off

You chuck off everything in the States and move to Panama. It has a certain excitement and novelty to live in a new country where everything seems different. All the folks back home want to hear about your new adventure. But after two, or three, or four years the novelty wears off, and you begin to miss the familiar and the comfortable feel of wherever "home" used to be. You get homesick for Home Depot, Bed Bath & Beyond, Walmart and even the bureaucracy of the DMV where at least they – usually – speak English.

Looking for A Fast Buck

There are those who came to Panama to make a financial killing ... and didn't, or maybe did. For some, Panama was seen as an opportunity to get rich quick as the world's attention focused here and real estate and condo speculation was manic. Everyone saw the opportunity for instant cash: just buy a farm cheap, throw in a road and sell lots to unsuspecting foreigners. Well, things rarely work out that way. There are folks who were intent on making a killing in real estate, only to burn through their cash and be left with empty dreams as the world's economy tanked. The answer to the question, "How can you leave Panama with a million dollars?" is, "Come to Panama with two million dollars!"

There is still great opportunity in Panama, but the day of the "fast buck" is disappearing. Scam artists are gradually being sent elsewhere, either by being rooted out by Panamanian authorities or being extradited back to authorities in their own countries.

Rain, Rain, Go Away

There are those who don't like the weather ... not having bothered to check the weather before they moved. Living in a rain forest is incredibly beautiful, but, guess what? It rains. And it rains a lot, particularly at certain times of the year and that isn't for everyone. The high humidity means not having to worry about dry skin, but it also means dealing with mold, sometimes mold everywhere. There have been a lot of friends for whom Boquete is too cool and too wet and so they have left, not to go back to the States, but for beach areas in Panama where it's a lot hotter and there is less rain.

Been There, Done That

A lot of expat retirees, "baby boomers" looking for a better lifestyle in their retirement years, have come to Panama intending to stay. But interestingly we are getting a lot of younger people, people who did well and retired early, sometimes even families with kids, who are looking for a new and different experience. These folks come, enjoy Boquete for a few years, and then move on to other adventures.

We built the dream house, now what?

Most people have this dream of the house they'd like to have someday. So they retire, maybe cash out of their home country and move to Panama where the cost of building is still a lot less than it was back home and, for the moment at least, they are flush with cash ... so they build the dream house.

"Mea culpa!" When we moved to Panama we "downsized"[77] from a 1,680 square foot [156 square meter] house on the hill in Ventura, which by the way was very adequate for two people, to a 3,000 square foot [279 square meter] house in Valle Escondido and from there to a 4,500 square foot [418 square meter] house on a 3.5 acre [1.4 hectare] farm.

We have some neighbors who sold the big estate-sized house in the States and bought a 3.000 square foot [279 square meter] house while they built their 11,000 square foot [1,021 square meter] Boquete mansion. Over drinks the wife said to us, "I love our little house and I have no idea why we are building this mansion for the two of us."

Other friends built this incredibly well-designed and well-built French country chateau with a killer view and every amenity in the book. They bought a condo back home in Phoenix for a song in a depressed market, and are looking for a condo in Boquete. I bumped into the guy in the restaurant the other night and he said, "Richard, I'm tired of the upkeep and all the work. I just want a place where we can lock up and walk away for a few months."

I understand. Don't get me wrong: I love the farm and I love our house, but it is a lot of work and responsibility, especially when I'm on the ship half of the time.

Another couple moved to Panama and bought a very nice home, and then proceeded to add anything and everything that could be added spending money like water. When the rest of us were paying gardeners $8 a day they paid their gardener $21 a day and naturally upset the order of things since he had to brag to all the other gardeners and then they wanted the same thing. The guy bought the big Harley and every other toy and the wife lavishly decorated the house. Now after a few years of being in Boquete off and on for a few months, they are back in the States and all the gardeners now expect $21 a day.

Whatever happened to "free and easy?"

Panama isn't the "tax haven" some people thought it was. Panama, like every place in the world, has taxes. The taxes may come in different forms, like fees, the value-added ITBS tax on almost everything but food, corporation and property taxes, etc., but they are there nonetheless. Income from the Panama Canal alone can't pay for all the infrastructure improvements that are underway in Panama, so taxes have gone up. Where in the past a lot of taxes were never collected, as Panama becomes a more "developed" country the government is becoming more computerized making it harder for those who would just forget to pay their taxes. There are ways to legally minimize your taxes, but there are taxes.

A big plus for retirees and expats is that Panama does not tax on income earned outside Panama, nor does it tax interest on savings accounts. Panama's Assembly, like most representational government bodies, sometimes comes close to shooting themselves in their feet, and occasionally actually do aim AND fire. In the closing weeks of 2013 a piece got slipped into a bill that would have taxed all income if you lived in Panama, even income generated from outside of Panama. Perhaps everyone was too involved in holiday celebrations to actually read the bill, but it passed. Then after New Year's when everyone returned to work with clearer minds, the bill was quickly killed.

If you're a U. S. citizen and thought you were going to escape the IRS here's a news flash: for U. S. citizens there is no escape from the IRS. No matter how many seminars you've attended or books you've purchased, short of renouncing your citizenship there is no way out. It has even become difficult to give up your U. S. citizenship because the government wants your money. You will pay until the day you die, and then your heirs will continue to pay.

However, there are legal ways to reduce your U. S. taxes. If you are a U. S. citizen and your permanent residence is outside the United States you do get to deduct up to $100,800

[2015] of *earned* income if your permanent residence is outside the United States.

"I'm not ready to retire … what I really needed was a Sabbatical"

My wife helped me define this after talking with a friend who was returning to Atlanta saying, "I enjoyed life in Boquete and an extended break from work, but I still have ten years that I could be working." Nikki has sometimes said, "I feel guilty … like I should be doing something … like I should be contributing." I found myself scouring potential cruise jobs, not that I wanted to leave Boquete, but sometimes just wanted to be back in "action" for a few months of the year … which is how I ended up working part-time on ships. This isn't anything unique to living in Boquete but is just a challenge of retirement; perhaps more of a challenge to boomers than it was to past generations.

"It's about the grandkids."

I grant you grandkids are a life-changer. When we moved here we didn't have grandkids and now we have two wonderful grandsons whom we dearly miss. Thankfully with a combination of Skype and iPhone we can visit with them regularly. Both my wife and I are preacher's kids, so neither of us lived near our grandparents. And since I was a minister much of my career, my kids never lived near their grandparents and we didn't have Skype back then. Did we and our kids miss out on something? Absolutely! Did we cheat our parents out of watching our kids grow up? Yes. But even if we did live nearer to our kids, we are not the kind of parents who would want to be intruding into their lives. Our kids love to visit us in Panama and we love to see them. Hopefully as our grandsons get older they will want to spend some time exploring Panama. Everyone's different, but before you make the move you need to figure out how the rest of the family fits into your plans.

Life Changes

Life can take many dramatic turns. Aging parents back in the States suddenly require more direct attention and involvement. Properties back home don't sell as expected. Businesses you thought you left in good hands suddenly need direct involvement. Spouses die and what was once your dream of a life together in Panama now rings hollow. One or another partner develops a medical condition best faced in the company of family and familiar medical resources and/or Medicare assistance.

Our new house is on the road to a tiny cemetery. My wife has informed me that she is "not moving again!" She has made it clear that her next move will be in a pine box, where she doesn't have to pack anything, to the cemetery down the road. Well, that's our plan ... now. But, as Heraclitus pointed out, "We are living in a world of constant change." Things do change. People change. Plans change. And because of that, not everybody will stay in Boquete.

I posed this question on my blog and received a number of interesting responses.

From Scott and Belinda ... "The North Americans that I know who left Panama came here with little or no money and little to no continuing retirement income. They typically had exaggerated expectations of earning a living in Panama, a bad idea in my opinion. When that didn't work out, they had no choice, but to go back to their former jobs in the United States. If someone wants to have a business to keep them occupied or for fun or to employ locals, fine, but don't count on making a living or getting rich. Come to Panama with sufficient income or assets to pay your bills, which will be higher than you expect."

From Diana ... "From my observation, it is not until you have made the move and experienced the lifestyle, experienced the differences for more than a few months, and endured the real challenges of life in Panama that anyone can judge and accept or reject the way of life here in Panama.

"Boquete (if considered as a separate entity, which I think it should be) seems on the surface to be the paradise that so many retirees are looking for. The climate is cooler and the views of Volcan Baru and surrounding landscape are stunning. Boquete is marketed as the place to be. It is where so many have invested a lot of money, time and patience. It is where so many have made their home, or invested for the future. It is the place that boasts many housing developments, hotels, sporting and leisure activities and is one of the biggest tourist destinations here in Latin America.

"It is a place where many people have chosen to live in the safety of numbers, behind bars and security gates, in gated communities and advertised that they had something the local people could only dream of. As a result many fall victim to 'gringo bingo' where they end up being charged greater sums of money for products or services than locals. Many local people see us as an opportunity and feel there is much money to be made or just a little to supplement a pitiful income, as rich Americans and Europeans flaunt their previous lifestyle expectations in their faces. *[RD: However the Panamanian weekenders are the ones who really do have money and are the ones with the really big houses in Boquete.]* Many come here with the thought that they can have their cake and eat it but will not change or adjust to a new way of living. We expats share responsibility for how things progress and should realize that before we try to change this country into the one from which we escaped ... There is the need for patience here and many are so used to the fast pace they left behind, that the exceedingly slow pace here is intolerable. I think the reality, for many of us, is that we find ourselves way out of our comfort zone where the old rules no longer apply."

From Roger ... "I've observed that many come here with little or no knowledge of what to expect, assuming it'll be like it was from whence they came. Sometimes they try to recreate their 'comfort zone' here, but eventually give up. Many make little or no effort to learn Spanish, understand the people, customs and how things work here, or involve themselves into (not onto) the Panamanian community. Sometimes they retreat into their homes, like a turtle into its shell and, after they get bored doing nothing, despite everything there is to do, they leave. A foreigner here has to be proactive and friendly to be accepted and make a new life in a new land. Sometimes it's a matter of culture shock and sometimes just a lack of commitment."

One expat who has been here a while said, "I have a sense that people don't really take into account the radical difference in culture. Panamanians don't do this or that the way they were accustomed back wherever they came from and eventually they just get tired of trying to cope without ever really adjusting to the fact that it *is* different. After four or five years they come up with some excuse – grandkids, health, finances, whatever – and then head back to what is familiar."

One size does not fit all.

But even those who, for whatever reason, choose not to stay have at least for a time broken out of the rut of the familiar, experienced a different culture, and lived the adventure.

"Different strokes for different folks." Panama is not for everyone. Nor is Boquete, Coronado, Bocas, Ventura, Panama City or wherever. For us Panama has been wonderful. We only wished we had made the move sooner. But, like anything in life, it can become routine. We moved here to retire and to escape the rat race. And yet, as my wife noted the other day when we drove over to Volcan to buy plants, we may be as busy now as ever. Granted, for the most part we have chosen the busyness we have now. We're working because we want to. As I tell the cruise line, "When this isn't fun anymore I'm out of here."

A number of folks we know are moving back to the States, some who've been in Boquete as long as we have, or longer. So Nikki and I had this big discussion as we drove the winding road up to Volcan.

What did these couples have in common?

Well, with the latest three couples who've left, the men all seemed to love Panama, but the gals had gotten bored with the "adventure" of it all and missed the familiar accoutrements of home. Face it, going out for lunch with your friends at Tammy's isn't quite the same as lunch at the Cheesecake Factory. And shopping at La Reyna isn't Nordstrom. Have these folks had a good time in Panama and great adventures? Of course! But for them it was an experience and after a while it was time to move on and seek new experiences.

What I've tried to do in *The New Escape to Paradise* is provide you with information and raise some of the questions you need to consider if you've ever thought about moving to Panama or anyplace else that is radically different from that to which you are accustomed.

If there are two factors which you must take into consideration if you are considering adopting an expat lifestyle, they are these:

- Your attitude toward CHANGE

- Your attitude toward RISK

When you move from one country to another, one culture to another, there is going to be change – a lot of change and a certain amount of risk.

Action Items and Points to Ponder

1. How well do you cope with change? Is it something you avoid or something you embrace? Do you find change threatening or stimulating.

2. Moving to another country and culture and adopting a lifestyle involves a lot of risk. What is your risk tolerance?

"Community" – Christmas Day at the house of our neighbors
who regularly pick coffee for us.

Panama may not be perfect, but it is still pretty damn good!

25. What People Won't Tell You And Can't Tell You

*T*here are a lot of things you should know that nobody will tell you ... at least in print.

"If you can't say something nice, don't say anything at all." I can hear my mother saying this and it can, at times, be very good advice. But what if there are things about life in Panama that you really need to know ... stuff that could hurt you if you are not in the know?

Turns out that in Panama my mother's advice is not only good advice for being nice and polite, but good legal advice as well. Panama does not have "free speech" in the same sense as in the United States. Libel laws are much more onerous in Panama so you have to be careful what you say. In the States, generally, if something is true, then it's not defamatory or libelous to say it. Not so in Panama! While Panama may not be as litigious as the United States, it is actually quite easy to sue someone for saying something about you that you don't like, true or not. It will all eventually – meaning eventually in the sense of *"mañana,"* i.e. sometime in the future, which may be years, get sorted out in court but in the meantime the person suing you can have all of your assets in Panama tied up and sequestered. So people are very careful, particularly saying things against individuals and companies in public.

There is, however, a very effective and "uncensored" source of communication known as "The coconut telegraph."

If you are looking for a builder, a maid, a hospital, a doctor, a supplier, an insurance company, a bank, whatever ... ask around and you will get positive as well as unfiltered negative opinions. Panama is a small country and you need to understand that people are all related, by blood, marriage and friendships. Panamanians are often too polite to say negative things even if they need to be said. Sometimes Panamanians will say one thing and while they are saying it roll their eyes. Read the eyes! *Gringos* are by nature more direct, one might even say "blunt" and will generally in person tell you exactly what they think: the good, the bad and the ugly.

For example, had we talked to more people and maybe listened more carefully and read the eyes of locals as well as listening to what they had to say, we might have picked another builder.

You may want to come to Panama, avoid other *gringos* and go native, but you need to keep in contact with other expats to be in the loop on the "coconut telegraph." Don't count on just what you read online in chat forums, etc. The Internet is public and saying the wrong things online or something that could be interpreted as libelous can get you in trouble.

26. If I Had to Do It All Over?

Now that we've lived in Panama for over ten years, people often ask what would you have done differently?

If we could have, I would have made the move earlier. Thankfully we made the move when it was comparatively easy to get your money out of the U. S.

We have thoroughly enjoyed the adventure of living in Panama. Have there been hassles? Of course, but it's all been, and still is, part of our great adventure.

We live better in Panama for less. We eat better. Yes, we miss fresh blueberries and corn on the cob. [Corn in Panama is tougher, what we would call in the states "cow corn."] Once in a while I long for a real, corn-fed, tender steak. But we grow our own bananas which taste *so* much better than the ones shipped halfway across the world. Panamanian pineapple is the sweetest in the world especially when you are eating pineapple that had ripened in the field too far for export. Of course we grow, process, and drink our own coffee which is far superior to what you get most places in the States. We grow our own oranges and lemons. In the ten years we've lived here our blood pressure and weight has dropped, we eat healthier, live outdoors, and are more active.

Panama is rapidly developing and a lot has changed in ten years. When we came there were few existing U. S.-style houses, so we built our own. Today there is good inventory and with the increases in the cost of building you can often buy an existing house for less than it would cost to build today, so today I wouldn't think about building. Even if you can't find exactly what you want, it is cheaper and less hassle to buy an existing home and renovate it to your taste.

I wish I had mastered languages as a kid. **You don't have to speak Spanish to live in Panama, but the more Spanish you know the better your life will be, the less hassle you will encounter, and the easier it will be to develop friendships and relationships with Panamanians, even if they do speak some English.**

When we came many of the resources that are available today weren't available. If I were moving to Panama today I might not bring along a forty foot container since most of what you need is available. I wish there had been something like Panama Relocation Tours which could have given me an overview of possible places to live. We probably would still have ended up in Boquete, but I would have seriously looked at Cerro Punta and Pedasi, and, although I really doubt we would have opted for city living at this point of our lives, I still find the Casco Viejo part of Panama City appealing, if outrageously expensive.

At the time we chose to basically self-insure for medical issues taking the only limited coverage we knew about through a local hospital. Today there are a several good international health insurance plans that cover you all over the world, some including the U. S. and Canada. Usually these have upper age limits and I have aged-out for most of them or because I'm now ten years older they are prohibitively expensive. Since I still spend four to six months a year working on cruise ships where I need international health and evacuation insurance. It would have been much better if I had taken out an international health insurance plan when we came. This is an area where I should have done more research. If there's a moral to this story it is that you can't do too much research, but, on the other hand, there comes a time when you need to take the leap.

Lots of folks tell me I have the "ideal retirement" ... living in Boquete and spending four to six months working on luxury cruise ships seeing the world. How that happened ...

I've always been a speaker and communicator. When we had lived in Panama three years I signed on as a Guest Lecturer on Celebrity Cruises to talk about Panama and the Canal in exchange for a free cruise. I started doing this for Holland America and ended up doing frequent cruises. Holland America hired a former college dean to work on their enrichment program who, unfortunately, had never actually been on a cruise. They were developing a new position in the entertainment department called "Travel Guide." We ended up chatting frequently on the phone with her asking, "Richard, how does this work on the ship?" etc. Gradually the job description the new position emerged. When it was finalized she asked, "Richard, would you ever be interested in doing this?"

I said, "No, I'm retired. [Pause] How many weeks are you talking about?"

"It would be six months."

I just thanked her for the offer and laughed. When I told my wife and kids they said, "Dad, you'd never last six months."

At the time I was reading *Grand Jury* by Philip Fiedman and there was a sentence that almost jumped off the paper: "*... he was poised on some unforeseen cusp of his life he could either leap into the unknown or slide back down to where he had been stagnating, where he would continue to stagnate, sustaining himself on illusions of renewal.*"

I went for the leap! I called the cruise line and said "Yes!" and have been sailing for seven years.

Research all you want, but there comes a time when you need to jump and, in the words of Nike, "*Just do it!*"

Acknowledgements

Just like it is a bad idea to be your own lawyer or doctor, I learned it was a bad idea to be your own copy editor, a fact which some readers of the original *Escape To Paradise* were quick to point out. So this time around I've enlisted other expats to review, correct, improve, and provide additional valuable insights.

My special thanks to Ida Freer[78] who helped me rethink the organization of the book and helped to edit and to Jubal Atencio, a good Panamanian friend who helped me to rethink some of my own experiences. Ellen Bolton is a superb editor and any remaining mistakes are strictly mine.

The New Escape to Paradise became a collaborative effort. I want to thank those who reviewed, edited, and contributed to making this a better book including my wife, Nikki Steele; Phil Beecher; Jim Fletcher; Judy Sacco; Allison Guinn; Kristin Stillman; Chris Labute; Sarah Reynolds; Doug Tyler; and Kathy Donelson.

I hope you enjoy the result. As always I welcome your comments, suggestions, and hearing of your experiences. You can follow me and share with me on at my website at RichardDetrich.com.

If you enjoyed the book and found it helpful *please* write a review on Amazon! Thank you and I hope one day to meet you in Panama!

Starting to Learn Spanish

You are already starting to know and think in Spanish.

Look at all of the Spanish words you've already come to know and love.

- *bajareque* – a late afternoon misting that frequently happens in some areas of the Chiriqui highlands such as Boquete
- *beneficio*- in Panama a coffee processing facility
- *bohío* – in Panama an outdoor covered area for shade, usually covered with thatched palm branches
- *casita* – a small house
- *cedro* – literally cedar, but not the type of cedar wood typical of North America
- *cedula* – the Panamanian national ID card
- *comarca* – region of Panama set aside for Indigenous peoples
- *conquistadores* – Spanish conquerors of Panama
- *corregimiento* – an administrative subdivision of a district
- *cuidado* – be careful
- *denuncia* – report or formal complaint
- *deposito* – storage area
- *descuento* – discount
- *escritura* – written document, deed
- *esposa* – wife, *esposo* would be husband
- *extranjero* – foreigner
- *factura* – invoice
- *finca* – property, often property in the country
- *fogón* – stove or fire, in Panama frequently refers to outside cooking fire or roadside restaurants that cook over open wood fires

- *frontera* – the border, in Panama sometimes used to describe the rest of the country outside of Panama City
- *gracia a Dios* – "thanks be to God" used frequently if you ask someone how things are or about family or health and people respond, "*Bien, Gracias a Dios!*"
- *gringo* – although in some Latin American countries *gringo* is a pejorative term, in Panama it is just a description of what is, namely, a foreign person who does not speak Spanish, or at least not very well
- *gringo bingo* – practice of charging *gringos* more for the same item or service than Panamanians
- *hermano* – brother
- *jagua* – a tropical fruit used for traditional body art
- *jefe* – boss or supervisor
- *juega vivo* – to "get over" or "pull a fast one"
- *macho* – male, manly, tough-guy
- *mañana* – morning or tomorrow, but in actual use in Panama means "not today, sometime in the future"
- *más o menos* – more or less
- *nada* – nothing, not anything
- *pensionado* – a retired person receiving a pension
- *piragua* – in Puerto Rico it is a shaved ice cone with fruit juices, but in Panama it is a canoe made by hollowing out a tree trunk, a dugout canoe
- *por ejemplo* – for example
- *regalo* – a gift or present
- *renacer* – to be reborn
- *seco* - a clear liquor which, like rum, is brewed from cane sugar, sold at seventy proof
- *se vende* – for sale
- *sociedad anónima* – or SA, stock company with usually anonymous stockholders
- *telenovela* – soap opera
- *tierra negra* – rich black soil left behind by volcano
- *tortillas* – in Panama thick corn cakes baked or fried
- *tranquilo* - peaceful
- *transito* – Panama's national traffic police
- *un poquito* – a little bit

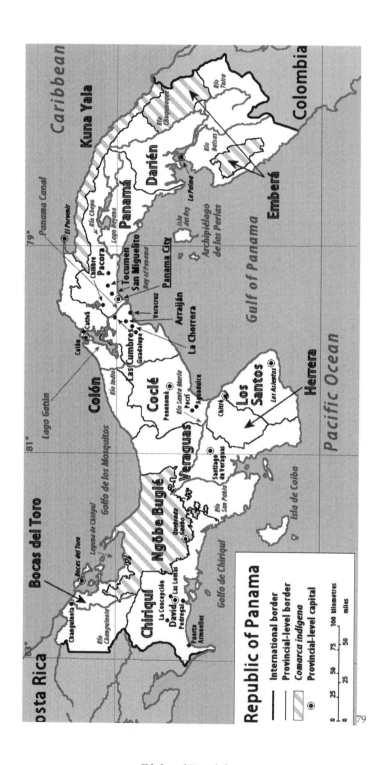

For Further Reading

Banks, Mary et al. *The World Encyclopedia of Coffee*. London, Lorenz Books, 2005.

Detrich, Richard. *Panama Canal Day: An Illustrated Guide to Cruising The Panama Canal*. Boquete, Create Space-Amazon, 2014.

Detrich, Richard. *Escape To Paradise: Living & Retiring In Panama*. Boquete, Create Space-Amazon, 2010, 2011, 2012.

Dinges, John. *Our Man In Panama: How General Noriega Used the US and Made Millions In Drugs And Arms*. New York, Random House, 1990.

Doggert, Scott. *Panama: Lonely Planet*. Melbourne, Lonely Planet Publications.

Frair, William. *Adventures In Nature: Panama*. Emeryville, CA, Avalon Travel Publishing.

Freer, Ida. *Panama Girl, Cry of The Jaguar, In The Depths of The Darien and The River Weeps*. Create Space,-Amazon, 2011, 2012, 2013.

Galbraith, Douglas. *The Rising Sun*. New York, Atlantic Monthly, 2001.

Green, Julie. *The Canal Builders*. New York, Penguin Press, 2009.

Harvey, William C. *Spanish For The Construction Trade*. Haupphauge, NY, Barron's, 2007.

Heidke, Dianne. *The Boquete Handbook*. Boquete, Heidke, 2010.

Independent Commission of Inquiry on the US Invasion of Panama, *The US Invasion of Panama: The Truth Behind Operation Just Cause*. Boston, South End Press, 1991.

Kempe, Frederick. *Divorcing The Dictator: America's Bungled Affair With Noriega*. New York, G. P. Putnam's Sons, 1990.

Koster, R.M. and Sanchez, Guillermo. *In The Time of Tyrants: Panama 1968-1990*. New York, W. W. Norton & Co., 1990.

Lindsay-Poland, John. *Emperors In The Jungle: The Hidden History of The US In Panama*. Durham, Duke University Press, 2003.

Mc McCullough, David. *The Path Between The Seas: The Creation of The Panama Canal 1870-1914*. New York, Simon & Schuster, 1977.

Noriega, Manuel and Eisner, Peter. *The Memoirs of Manuel Noriega: America's Prisoner*. New York, Random House, 1997.

Parker, David. *Panama Fever*. New York, Doubleday, 2007.

Pendergrast, Mark. *Uncommon Grounds: The History of Coffee and How it Transformed our World*. New York, Basic Books, 1999.

Perkins, John. *Confessions of An Economic Hit Man*. San Francisco, Berrett-Koehler Publishers.

Ridgely, Robert S and Gwynne, John A. Jr. *A Guide to The Birds of Panama*. Princeton, NJ, Princeton University Press.

Snyder, Sandra T. *Living In Panama*. Panama City, TanToes, 2007.

Key Dates in Panama History

Colonial

1501 -- Rodrigo de Bastidas, sailing west from Venezuela was the first European to sail along the coast of Panama

December 1502 -- Christopher Columbus, on his fourth voyage to the New World, lands in Bocas del Toro

January 1503 -- Christopher Columbus built a garrison at Rio Belen

1509 -- Spanish colonization began in what is today Colombia, Ecuador, Venezuela and Panama

September 25, 1513 -- Balboa claimed the "Southern Ocean" (later renamed the Pacific) for Spain

1519 -- Panama City was founded

1538 -- Royal Audiencia of Panama, a judicial court with jurisdiction from Nicaragua to Cape Horn, established in Panama City

1572 -- Sir Frances Drake successfully captured Nombre de Dios on the Atlantic side

1573 -- Drake captures a mule train carrying silver across the Isthmus

January 27, 1671 -- British privateer, Sir Henry Morgan, captured Panama City

1698 -- Creation of the ill-fated Scottish colony of New Caledonia in he Darien

1713 – Creation of the Vice Royalty of New Granada

1819 – Liberation of New Granada from Spin

November 10, 1821 -- "The Cry of Freedom of The Village of Los Santos"

November 28, 1821 -- Panama declares independence from Spain and joins New Granada and Venezuela in Bolivar's recently founded Republic of Colombia

December 26, 1848 -- California-bound gold seekers began arriving in Panama

1850 -- Colon founded as the terminus of the Panama Railroad

1855 -- Panama Railroad opened

The Canal

1880 --- Ferdinand de Lesseps began the French effort to build the canal

May 3, 1881 -- Compagnie Universelle du Canal Interocéanique incorporated under French law

February 4, 1889 -- The French effort was abandoned and Compagnie Universelle du Canal Interocéanique was declared bankrupt and dissolved

1894 -- Philippe Bunau-Varilla became stockholder and spokesman in the New Panama Canal Company, offering to sell the company's assets to the United States for $109 million, asking price later reduced to $40 million

June 19, 1902 -- U. S. Senate voted in favor of Panama as the canal site

June 28, 1902 -- The Spooner Bill authorized the United States to construct canal and purchased concession from France for $40 million

September 17, 1902 -- U. S. troops sent to Panama to keep railroad open as local Panamanians struggled for independence from Colombia

January 22, 1903 -- Hay-Harran Treaty with Colombia giving the United States right to build a canal was passed by Senate, but not ratified by Colombia

October 10, 1903 -- Philippe Bunau-Varilla met with U. S. President Theodore Roosevelt warning him of imminent rebellion in Panama

November 3, 1903 -- With USS NASHVILLE standing by in Panama and Bunau-Varilla standing by in Washington, Panama proclaimed independence from Colombia with the only casualties being a shopkeeper and a donkey

November 6, 1903 -- Panama officially declared its separation from Colombia

November 7, 1903 -- The United States officially recognized the Republic of Panama

November 18, 1903 -- Claiming to represent the newly created Republic of Panama, the Frenchman Bunau-Varilla granted the United States a strip of land across Panama and the rights to build a canal and in return the United States agreed to protect the new country

February 3, 1904 -- U. S. Marines clashed with Colombian troops attempting to re-establish Colombian sovereignty in Panama

February 23, 1904 -- The United States paid Panama $10

million for the Canal Zone

May 4, 1904 -- The United States began Canal construction

1904 -- Panama adopted U. S. dollar as its currency calling it the "Balboa"

1904 -- Dr. William Gorgas took over as chief sanitary officer

November 8, 1906 -- U. S. President Theodore Roosevelt visited Panama becoming the first U. S. president in history to leave the country while in office

1907 -- George Washington Goethals took control of the Canal Zone and construction

August 24, 1909 -- The first concrete was poured in the locks

1912 -- The Chagres River was dammed

October 10, 1913 -- U. S. President Woodrow Wilson pushed a button in Washington triggering an explosion in Panama, exploding the temporary Gamboa Dike and allowing water to fill Gatun Lake

August 15, 1914 -- With the world occupied by a World War, the Panama Canal quietly opened with the ANCON making the first official crossing Southbound from the Atlantic to the Pacific

April 20, 1921 -- Thomson-Urrutia Treaty signed – United States paid Colombia $25 million in return for Colombia's recognition of Panama's independence

October 2, 1941 -- El Banco Central de Emisión de la Republica de Panamá was established and authorized to issue 6 million balboas worth of paper notes, but only 2.7 million were issued

United States Panama Canal construction.

Can you find the two little guys in the lower left hand corner?[80]

October 9, 1941 -- Ricardo Adolfo de la Guardia Arango
replaced Arias as president in a coup supported by the United
States and the new government immediately closed the bank,
withdrew and burned the so-called "Arias Seven Day" notes

November 2 & 28, 1959 – Feelings of prejudicial and
discriminatory policies against Panamanians in the Canal
Zone led to pressure to fly the Panamanian flag within the
Zone and when demands to fly the flag were refused, Anti-
American riots broke out in Panama City

September 1960 – U. S. President Dwight David Eisenhower
authorized the Panamanian flag be flown alongside the U. S.
flag in designated areas of the Canal Zone

January 1963 -- U. S. President John F. Kennedy orders that
wherever a U. S. flag is flown in the Canal Zone that is not on
a U. S. military base, a Panamanian flag should be flown next
to it. This was hated by the Zonians[81] and began what are
called "The Flag Wars" exacerbating tensions between
Panamanians and the United States (After Kennedy was
assassinated, the Governor of the Canal Zone took it upon
himself to rescind the Presidential order.)

January 9, 1964 -- Anti-United States rioting broke out
and twenty-one Panamanian civilians and four United States
soldiers were killed including six Panamanian teenagers; now
celebrated as a national holiday called "The Day of the
Martyrs"

January 10, 1964 -- Panama broke off relations with the United
States and demanded a revision of the original Canal treaty

October 11, 1968 -- Panamanian President Arnulfo Arias was
ousted in a coup by General Omar Torrijos

August 10, 1977 -- United States and Panama began
negotiation for Panama Canal turnover

September 7, 1977 -- U. S. President Jimmy Carter and General Omar Torrijos signed the Torrijos-Carter Treaties abrogating the Hay-Bunau-Varilla Treaty and setting 1999 for the turnover of the Canal

April 18, 1978 -- U. S. Senate ratified the Torrijos-Carter Treaties by a vote of sixty-eight to thirty-two

October 1, 1979 -- Under terms of the 1977 Panama Canal Treaties the United States returned the Canal Zone to Panama, excluding the Canal itself

July 31, 1981 -- General Torrijos died in a plane crash

August 12, 1983 -- General Manuel Noriega assumed command of the National Guard

1985 -- Dissident leader Hugo Spadafora was decapitated – Noriega later sentenced in Panama to 20 years in prison for the murder

February 25, 1988 -- Panamanian President Eric Arturo Delvalle removed Noriega as commander and was subsequently ousted as President and Noriega took control

March 18, 1988 -- Noriega declared a "state of urgency"

April 8, 1988 -- U. S. President Ronald Reagan issued an Executive Order blocking all Panamanian interests, property, and funds in the U. S.

May 7, 1989 -- Voters rejected Noriega but Noriega refused to recognize election results

May 9, 1989 -- U. S. President George H. W. Bush in the light of "massive irregularities" in Panamanian elections called for Noriega to step down

May 10, 1989 -- Noriega nullified elections won by his opposition leader Guillermo Endara

Then CIA Director George H. W. Bush, meeting with Manuel
Noriega, the CIA's Panamanian informant.

A few days before Christmas the United States closed the Panama
Canal and invaded Panama in what was ironically called "Just
Cause."

May 11, 1989 -- U. S. President George H. W. Bush recalled U. S. ambassador and beefed up U. S. troops stationed in Panama

October 3, 1989 -- Noriega foiled attempted coup and had coup leaders executed

December 20, 1989 -- United States military invaded Panama in "Operation Just Cause" – In the early morning hours on a U. S. Military base Guillermo Endara was sworn in as President. (Endara was the "presumed winner" in a scheduled presidential election cancelled by General Noriega.)

December 24, 1989 -- Noriega took refuge at residence of Papal Nuncio in Panama City

January 3, 1990 -- Noriega surrendered to U. S. forces, was flown to Miami and arraigned in U. S. Federal District Court in Miami on drug-trafficking charges

January 18, 1991 -- United States acknowledged that the CIA and U. S. Army paid Noriega $322,226 from 1955-1986 and that Noriega began receiving money from the CIA in 1976 giving credence to the claim of Noriega's lawyers that he was the "CIA's man in Panama"

April 9, 1992 -- Noriega convicted of drug and racketeering charges, sentenced to serve forty years as a POW, entitling him to maintain his rank as a General ... of an army of one since Panama had abolished the military

1995 -- Noriega was convicted in Panama in absentia for the 1989 murder of officers involved in a failed coup

October 1, 1996 -- Fort Amador was transferred to Panama

November 1, 1999 -- United States turned over Howard Air Force Base, Fort Kobbe and other territories to Panama

December 14, 1999 -- Former U. S. President Carter

symbolically turned over Panama Canal to Panamanian
President Mireya Moscoso

December 31, 1999 -- United States officially turned over
Panama Canal to Panama

Current

2000 -- Panama was named the "#1 Retirement Destination"
and North American and European retirees began relocating
to Panama

September 1, 2004 -- Panamanian President Martin Torrijos
proposed an $8 billion expansion of the Panama Canal

October 22, 2006 -- Voters approved $5.25 billion Panama
Canal Expansion proposal by 78 percent

September 3, 2007 -- Construction began on the Panama Canal
Expansion adding a "third lane" of new locks

April 26, 2010 -- Noriega completed his U. S. prison sentence
and after a lengthy legal fight was extradited to France where
he began serving sentence for money laundering, not as POW
treated as a General, but as a common criminal

September 4, 2010 -- The one millionth ship transited the
Panama Canal, a Chinese vessel named FORTUNE PLUM,
carrying steel and crossing from the Pacific to the Atlantic

February 1, 2011 – First concrete poured for new locks in
Panama Canal expansion project

December 2011 -- United States and France agreed to let
Noriega be extradited home to Panama where he faces a 67-
year prison term. Noriega was incarcerated in El Renacer
Prison in Gamboa, next to the Panama Canal

February 2012 -- Panama introduces a one Balboa coin equal
in value to $1 U. S. because of the short lifespan and high

expense of U. S. paper $1 bills, called the "Martinelli" after Panama's President Ricardo Martinelli

November 2013 -- Panama's Metro line 1 opens, the first subway in Central America

July 2014 - Businessman Juan Carlos Varela becomes the fifth democratically elected President of Panama since the dictatorship

January 2015 - Former President Ricardo Martinelli under investigation for fraud by the new administration and denied immunity flees the country in his private jet going to Miami

August 14, 2014 --The 100th Anniversary of the Panama Canal

June 2015 the expanded Panama Canal is scheduled to go into service but due to cost overruns, contractual disputes, date is pushed to January 2016

U. S. Military Installations

Many people who served in the U. S. Military in Panama, or had relatives who served, are curious as to what happened to some of the bases that were abandoned when the United States withdrew.[82]

Name	Unit	Abandoned	Current name	Current use
Galeta Island, USN - Atlantic	CDAA (Wullenweber) radio detection	2002		
Fort Randolph, USA – Atlantic, Margarita Island	coastal defense	1999		
Coco Solo, USN – Atlantic, near Colon	submarine base	1999	Manzanillo International Terminal	container terminal
Fort De Lesseps, USA – Atlantic, Colon	coastal defense	1955		
Fort Sherman, USA – Atlantic, opposite Colon	coastal defense, Jungle Operations Training Center	1999	harbor: Shelter Bay Marina	unused, marina
France Field, USN & USAF – Atlantic, near Colon		1949	Enrique Adolfo Jiménez Airport	airfield
Gatun Tank Farm, USN – Atlantic, near Gatun Locks	underground fuel storage with oil terminal at Cristobal	1991		
Fort Gulick – Atlantic, Gatun Locks	School of the Americas	1984, 1999	Fuerte Espinar	hotel Melia

Name	Unit	Abandoned	Current name	Current use
Fort William D. Davis, USA – Atlantic, Gatun Locks	infantry, jungle warfare training, special forces training		Jose Dominador Bazan	residential area
Semaphore Hill, USN – Inland, Culebra Summit	long-range radar and communications link	1979, 1995	Canopy Tower	nature observatory
Summit, USN – Inland, Culebra Summit	Naval Communications Station Balboa, VLF (sender)			
Fort Clayton, USA – Miraflores Locks	HQ US Southern Command, communications	1999	Ciudad del Saber	academic campus, residential housing, schools
Albrook AFS, USAF - Pacific, near Balboa		1999	Albrook "Marcos A. Gelabert" Airport	regional civil airport
Arraijan Tank Farm, USN – Pacific, opposite Balboa	underground fuel storage with oil terminal at Rodham	1997		civil usage (PATSA)
Rodman Naval Station, USN – Pacific, opposite Balboa	harbor		Vasco Nuñez de Balboa, PSA Panama	Panamanian National Maritime Service, container terminal
Fort Amador, USA – Pacific, near Balboa	coastal defense	1999		recreation, new hotel (2001)
Naval Communications Station Balboa, USN – Pacific, near Fort Amador	HQ radio communications			

Name	Unit	Abandoned	Current name	Current use
Farfan, USN – Pacific, near Howard AFB	Naval Communications Station Balboa (receiver)		Radio Holland Panama	marine communications
Howard Air Force Base, USN – Pacific, opposite Balboa		1999	Panama Pacifico	real estate (development)
Fort Grant, USA – Pacific, near Balboa	coastal defense	1948	Islas Naos, Penco, Flamenco	tourism
Fort Kobbe, USA – Pacific, near Howard AFB		2000		
Transisthmian Pipeline, USN – cross Isthmus				

Panama Canal Day

Panama Canal Day: An Illustrated Guide to Cruising The Panama Canal will help you anticipate your Canal cruise and help you get the most out of your Panama Canal Day adventure. Here's everything you need to know about itineraries, bookings, the best places on the ship, and shore excursions.

David McCullough is a great historian and his book *The Path Between The Seas: The Creation of the Panama Canal, 1879-1914* is the definitive history of the Canal construction, but it only covers that period, not everything before or since.

Panama Canal Day covers it ALL which is why it has been called "the best book for cruise passengers."

Before ...
- The Bridge of Life
- New Granada
- The Dream
- A Century of Expansion
- The Panama Railroad

Path Between The Seas only covers this period

1870-1914 ...
- The French Effort
- Banana Republic
- Let The Dirt Fly

Since ...
- A Complicated Marriage
- Moving Forward
- Panama 101

Your Panama Canal Day ...
- How It Works
- It's 4:30 am
- Booking Passage
- ALL about tours
- Your Voyage
- Your Ship & Our Bill

Available in Paperback & Kindle on Amazon

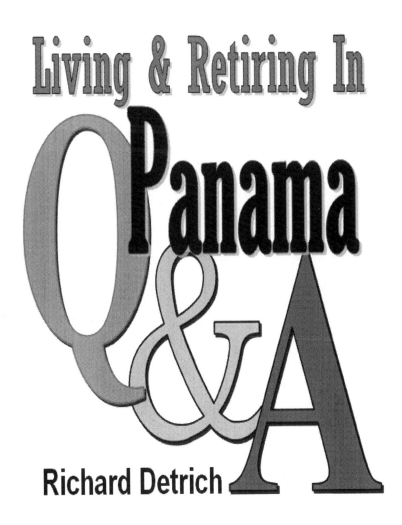

Living & Retiring In Panama Q&A

Richard Detrich

FREE! Download at

RichardDetrich.com

The New Escape to Paradise

Footnotes

---

[1] "Dear reader" … Since this book is in English, I have chosen not to use accents on Spanish names … otherwise Panama would be Panamá throughout … except when using a Spanish word, like *mañana*.. Since I don't do it for Spanish, I don't do it for other languages. I eat in restaurants other than Burger King and know entree is entrée, and Haagen Dazs is Häagen-Dazs (oh, do I know!), but since I don't use diacritical marks for Spanish, I don't use them elsewhere. I hope this explanation will save you a lot of anxiety. If not, try having some Panama rum while reading. I do enjoy getting your emails – about other things!

[2] The best book on writing the way you talk is Rudolph Flesch, *The Art of Readable Writing*.

[3] Although I prefer the term Indigenous, when Columbus first arrived in Panama he thought he was in the outer islands of India so called the people he met here Indians. Panama has seven living Indigenous cultures that were here when Columbus arrived. These people call themselves both Indians and Indigenous and both terms are used interchangeably in Panama so I, too, use the terms interchangeably.

[4] "America" and "American"… I've *struggled* throughout to be cognizant of the fact that the Americas include North, Central and South America despite the common use of "American" to refer to the United States of America..

[5] Expatriates are people from other countries, usually retaining their own citizenship, while living abroad.

---

6 Foreign Account Tax Compliance Act [FATCA] March 2010.

7 Inquiring and curious minds will want to know: The Bank of Italy was founded in San Francisco in 1904 by Amadeo Giannini and grew by a branch banking strategy to become the Bank of America.

8 Although in some Latin American countries *gringo* is a pejorative term, in Panama it is just a description of what is, namely, an *extranjero* or foreign person who does not speak Spanish, or at least does not speak it very well.

9 To set your mind at ease: Yes, in the closing days of 2013 the Panama Assembly, perhaps influenced by too much pre-holiday cheer and celebration, passed a bill into which a last-minute addendum had been stuck that would have taxed all income for persons living in Panama whether the income was generated in Panama or elsewhere. Fortunately, after the holidays, the Assembly realized what they had inadvertently approved – just like in other countries, nobody actually reads the entire bill! – and the first week of 2014 hastily killed the bill.

10 I'm delighted to report, that both Mario and his brother Renato became very responsible, hard-working family men, both great fathers. We are proud of them and thankful to have them as a part of our lives.

11 Dr. Norman Vincent Peale [1898-1993] is probably best known for his book *The Power of Positive Thinking*. A former Methodist minister, he served as pastor of the Reformed Church in America's most prestigious church, Marble Collegiate Church on Fifth Avenue in New York from 1932. He received the Presidential Medal of Freedom in 1984.

12 Dr. Robert H. Schuller was a well-known Reformed Church in America minister of Garden Grove Community Church, later the Crystal Cathedral. The "Hour of Power" program televised church services featured Schuller from 1970 to 2010.

[13] Gordon and Gladys De Pree, *The Gift*, The Zondervan Corporation, 1976.

[14] Gail Sheehy, *Passages*. New York, E. P. Dutton, 1976, PP. 20-21.

[15] Ibid.

[16] Phillip Friedman, *Grand Jury*.

[17] There is always some *gringo* in Panama who is promising a return on investment that far exceeds the going market rate. Anxious to believe what they want to hear, Incredibly, some expats invest … and inevitably lose their investment while the "financial adviser" runs off to promote yet another scam.

[18] Short-term rentals of less than 45 days require you to register with the Panama Tourist Board and to collect and report the tourist tax.

[19] *Dr. Quinn, Medicine Woman* was filmed at Paramount Ranch in Agoura Hills, CA near where we lived.

[20] Mary Ida Vandross was an amazing woman. She is the only woman with whom I have been under live fire. I was driving her home at night from a church meeting in the church van when a group of kids on a roof top had been throwing rocks at the NYPD and the police were shooting at the kids. We would later spend a few hours at police headquarters trying to identify the officers shooting at kids only to realize that there is, maybe intentionally, no way to identify a middle aged cop from his Academy graduation photo.

Luther Vandross had an amazing talent and a career that was cut short by diabetes. Mary Ida became a spokesperson for the Diabetes Association and along the way graduated from New York Theological Seminary and became an ordained evangelist. She later died of diabetes as did her daughter who was also a member of our church at Mott Haven in the Bronx.

[21] Unfortunately, I was unable to ever find out what happened to Anthony Vandross.

[22] The movie *End of The Spear* [2006] was heavily promoted in Evangelical churches until folks realized that Chad Allen, the actor who played the lead, is openly gay.

[23] In his early 90s Erito's grandfather suffered from Alzheimer's and died in his mid 90s. Only the knowledge he was able to pass on to Erito before senility has survived to benefit future generations.

[24] R.M. Koster and Guillermon Sanchez, *In The Time of The Tyrants: Panama 1968-1990*. New York, W.W. Norton & Company, 1990. P. 390.

[25]Ibid, PP. 30-39.

[26] Frederick Kemp, *Divorcing The Dictator: America's Bungled Affair With Manuel Noriega*. New York, G.P. Putnam's Sons, 1990, P. 29.

[27] Instituto Centro-Americano de Administracion de Empresas was founded in 1964 by the Central American private sector, Harvard Business School, and US Agency for International Development

[28] The concept of Felony Murder, that everyone involved in the underlying crime, regardless of their intent or if they had any knowledge of the murder before, during or after, can be convicted of murder using the "legal fiction" of the Felony Murder rule goes back to English law. England has had the good sense to abolish the law but California has not. Prosecutors love it because it is an easy way to get convictions without having to prove anything.

---

[29] Conservatively the cost of keeping Brandon in a high security California prison is about $70,000 a year, not counting the loss to taxpayers of Brandon being a productive, tax-paying citizen. For a cash-strapped State like California, Brandon's incarceration has cost the taxpayers over $1.25 million! Aside from the gross injustice, this is fiscal stupidity.

[30] For more on Brandon's case visit BrandonHein.com, a website maintained by Friends of Brandon Hein.

[31] Sons of The American Revolution.

[32] "Through long-term, mission-driven agreements with leading health providers overseas, JHI [Johns Hopkins International] leverages the expertise of Johns Hopkins specialists, and Johns Hopkins Medicine's many research, education, and health care delivery institutions, to raise the standard of health care in each affiliate's region."

[33] Mr. Toad's Wild Ride is a Disney ride, one of the few park rides that goes back to the opening of Disneyland in 1955.

[34] For a while Panama gave free medical insurance to tourists while they were visiting Panama. Sounded like a good idea, but the low cost of emergency care and the hassle of getting payment, meant most people decided the insurance wasn't worth the hassle.

[35] In fairness here, many Panamanians, culturally, have the idea that it's not healthy to shower or bathe in warm or hot water; that a hot water bath will cause you to catch cold.

[36] There is a real estate company named Panama MLS, but it is a real estate company selling their listings and not the kind of Multiple Listing Service that folks have come to expect in the US. There is no comparable MLS in Panama.

[37] "Take Care!" or "Careful!"

38 Property in Panama is priced based on a square meter, which is a little less than 11 square feet. There are 10,000 square meters in a hectare, and a hectare is about 2.5 acres.

39 *"Gringo bingo"* is the rather common, albeit illegal, practice of jacking up prices for non-Panamanians who do not speak Spanish.

40 I've never minded paying my taxes as much as the incomprehensible labyrinth of paperwork.

41 Due to the unfortunate demise of the Robert Shuller's Crystal Cathedral and Robert Schuller Ministries, the church was purchased by the Roman Catholic Archdiocese of Orange and enamed, perhaps more appropriately, Christ's Cathedral.

42 US Occupational Safety and Health Administration.

43 Locally called *"m y dos"* this is a brand name of one of several building systems used in Panama. Originally in Chiriqui homes were built of adobe which doesn't fare well in earthquakes. Once in a while in David you will still see an old adobe wall. Most homes today are concrete block covered with one inch concrete surface. M2, and similar systems are, what I derisively call "Styrofoam and chicken wire." It is a foam core with heavy steel wire grid on either side. Manufacturers claim it is faster and does well in earthquakes. My observations are that it does go up a little faster, but the required cement coat takes as long, or longer, than with block. No one knows if there are any long-term consequences of living in a Styrofoam house. Styrofoam does not decompose, but is broken down by creating ecological problems when building scrap is deposited in traditional landfills.

44 Official US Military term: "Fucked Up Beyond All Recognition."

45 My dad was also Richard, nicknamed Dick. When I was in high school people would call on the phone and ask for Dick.

My mother would ask, "Big Dick or little Dick?" So I ended up having to sit my mother down and explain why no guy in high school ever wanted to be known as "little Dick"!

[46] US Department of Agriculture.

[47] Animal and Plant Health Inspection Service, US Department of Agriculture.

[48] This term will keep popping up in the process of moving and gaining residence in Panama. If you are unfamiliar with the term, according to Wikipedia, "The Hague Convention Abolishing the Requirement for Legislation for Foreign Public Documents, the Apostille convention, or the Apostille treaty is an international treaty drafted by the Hague Conference on Private International Law. It specifies the modalities through which a document issued in one of the signatory countries can be certified for legal purposes in all the other signatory states. Such a certification is called an apostille (French: *certification*). It is an international certification comparable to a notarization in domestic law, and normally supplements a local notarization of the document.

[49] Winner is a former US Air Force cryptologist and strategic intelligence analyst with Special Forces experience throughout Latin America.

[50] Photo: Vonderjas, Wikipedia GNU Free Documentation License, Version 1.2

[51] Photo: Rodolfo Aragundi Wikipedia Creative Commons Attribution-Share Alike 2.0 Generic license.

[52] Photo: BeanZull, Wikipedia Creative Commons, Attribution-ShareAlike 3.0 Unported

[53] Andorra, Angola, Antigua y Barbuda, Arabia Saudita, Argentina, Armenia, Austria, Australia, Bahamas, Barbados, Belize, Belarus, Belgium, Botsuana, Bhutan, Brazil, Bolivia,

Bosnia y Herzegovina, Brunei Darussalam, Bulgaria, Cabo
Verde, Cambodia, Canada, Czech Republic, Chile, China,
Colombia, Comoros, Corea del Sur, Costa Rica, Croacia,
Cyprus, Denmark, Dominica, Ecuador, El Salvador, England,
Fiyi, Estonia, Finland, France, Gabon, Germany, Georgia,
Gibraltar, Granada, Greece, Guatemala, Guyana, Holland,
Honduras, Hong Kong, Hungary, Japan, Jamaica, Kenia,
Kiribati, Iceland, Italy, Ireland, Israel, Latvia, Lebanon,
Lithuania, Kuwait, Letonia, Liechtenstein, Luxembourg,
Macao, Macedonia, Madagascar, Malasia, Maldivas, Malta,
Marshall Islands, Mauricio, Micronesia, Mexico, Moldovia,
Monaco, Mongolia, Montenegro, Namibia, Nauru,
Netherlands, New Zealand, Nicaragua, North Korea, Norway,
Palaos, Papua New Guinea, Paraguay, Peru, Poland, Portugal,
Qatar, Rumania, Saint Kitts y Nevis, Saint Lucia, Salomon
Islands, Samoa, São Tomé and Príncipe, San Marino,
Seychelles, Singapore, Slovak Republic, Slovenia, South
Africa, South Korea, Spain, Sweden, Switzerland, Thailand,
Tonga, The Vatican, Trinidad and Tobago, Turkey, Tuvalu,
Ukraine, United Arab Emirates, United Kingdom, USA,
Uruguay, Vanuatu, Venezuela and Vietnam.

Nationals from Chad, Ecuador, Egypt, Philippines, Peru,
Dominican Republic and Thailand require tourist visas and
should contact an embassy or consulate before coming to
Panama.

[54] Antigua, Australia, Bahamas, Barbados, Belize, Bermuda,
Bolivia, Brazil, Canada, Chile, China, Colombia, Denmark,
Granada, Greece, Guyana, Iceland, Ireland, Jamaica, Japan,
Malta, Mexico, Monaco, Netherlands, New Zealand, San
Marino, South Korea, Suriname, Taiwan, Tobago, Trinidad,
USA, Venezuela.

[55] Andorra, Argentina, Australia, Austria, Belgium, Brazil,
Canada, Chile, Croatia, Cyprus, Czech Republic, Denmark,
Estonia, Finland, France, Germany, Greece, Hong Kong,
Hungry, Ireland, Israel, Japan, Latvia, Liechtenstein,
Lithuania, Luxembourg, Malta, Monaco, Marino, Montenegro,

Netherlands, New Zealand, Norway, Poland, Portugal, Serbia, Singapore, Slovakia, Spain, South Africa, South Korea, Sweden, Switzerland, Taiwan, United States of America, Uruguay, United Kingdom

[56] Certain professions are restricted to Panama citizens like architects, attorneys, engineers, and medical and veterinary doctors.

[57] Panama's National Holidays:
a) January 1 - New Year's Day
b) January 9 - Day of the Martyrs
c) Mardi Gras
d) Good Friday
e) May 1 - Labor Day
f) November 3 - Separation of Panama from Colombia
g) November 5 - Consolidation of the Separation of Colombia
h) November 10 – Cry of Independence in the village of Los Santos
1) November 28 - Independence of Panama from Spain
j) December 8 – Mother's Day
k) December 25 - Christmas
Presidential Inauguration Day every five years

[58] Putting things into perspective: A farm worker who made $1 an hour and retires at 62 would end up getting around $120 a month to live or around $4 a day. There are many Panamanian retired couples who are living on pensions of $100 a month.

[59] New Yorkers will remember when Chock Full o'Nuts coffee was known as "that heavenly coffee." The Chock full o' Nuts advertising jingle was sung by the owner's wife, who was also a cabaret singer, and went …

"Chock full o'Nuts is that heavenly coffee,
Heavenly coffee, heavenly coffee.
Chock full o'Nuts is that heavenly coffee,

Better coffee Rockefeller's money can't buy"

The company was forced to change "Rockefeller's money" to "a millionaire's money" by New York governor Nelson Rockefeller who owned coffee interests in Latin America. Later versions, accounting for inflation, changed "millionaire" to "billionaire."

[60] Recent presidents have chosen to remain living in their own homes and use the Presidential Palace only as an office. The palace got its name because of resident African herons brought as a gift in 1922 and so traditionally herons still freely roam the courtyard.

[61] In modern history, the Chinese first came to Panama to help build the original Panama Railroad in the mid 1800s and have been a presence and force in Panama ever since. Many of the "mini supers" or M/S stores in communities all over Panama are run by industrious Panamanian Chinese who generally live behind or above the store and as a family work long hours in the store. Locally these are called "Chino" stores.

[62] Frommers.com/destinations/chiriqui-gulf-national-marine-park/275760

[63] For the record, according to VolcanoDiscovery.com, "An *active* volcano is a volcano that has had at least one eruption during the past 10,000 years. An active volcano might be erupting or dormant. An *erupting* volcano is an active volcano that is having an eruption. A *dormant* volcano is an active volcano that is not erupting, but supposed to erupt again. An *extinct* volcano has not had an eruption for at least 10,000 years and is not expected to erupt again in a comparable time scale of the future."

[64] In 2013 the Sistema Nacional de Proteccion Civil [SINPROC], the agency responsible for dealing with national emergencies and disasters, reported 309 sismos or

earthquakes in Panama, 223 of those in Chiriqui. The largest
was 5.4 on the Richter Scale, but most of these are so small
that they are hardly felt.

[65] A few items that have gone missing: much of the Pre-
Columbian pottery at the government run museum in David,
a large multiple figure sculpture of kids playing, intended for
a new children's museum in Panama City, the remains of a
small boat carbon fourteen dated to about the time when
Columbus would have stopped in Panama, that was taken out
of the water, conserved and waiting for further study and
authentication in a government warehouse in Colon.

[66] Boquete Community Players.

[67] Restaurants, like many Boquete businesses, are started on a
whim, generally without any business plan, and so come and
go with amazing speed.

[68] Of course in my case I spend considerable time on board
cruise ships so in essence on the ship I "eat out" every night.
For me to sit at home in Boquete, in grubby clothes, with my
wife and dogs is something special.

[69] Dracula is the name of a genus of orchids.

[70] Renamed the Pacific by Magellan in 1520 because he
thought it looked so peaceful.

[71] Ayaita, Creative Commons Attribution-Share Alike 3.0
Unported license.

[72] Mark Pendergrast, *Uncommon Grounds: The History of Coffee
and How it Transformed our World*, P.6.

[73] Ibid.

[74] Ibid, P 12.

[75] Ken Davis, CoffeeReview.com, April 2001.

[76] Studies by the University of Florida, Center for Forensic Medicine have shown that decaffeination doesn't eliminate all of the caffeine, that Arabica contains about half the caffeine of the cheaper Robusta coffee and that five to ten cups decaffeinated coffee have about the same amount of caffeine as one to two cups of regular coffee.

[77] In Panama the area of a house is everything "under roof" which includes porches and garage areas.

[78] Ida Freer lives in Canada and is the author of several young adult books about the Embera in Panama: *Panama Girl, Cry of The Jaguar, In The Depths of The Darien* and *The River Weeps*. All are available on Amazon.

[79] Andrew Gwilliam, Wikipedia Creative Commons Attribution-Share Alike 2.5 Generic license.

[80] Actually *four* guys: two holding the ladder at the bottom, one holding the ladder at the top, and one climbing the ladder.

[81] "Zonians" is a term still used to describe mostly U. S. citizens who worked and lived in the U. S. Canal Zone, some military and some civilians working for the Canal. Sometimes these were people whose families had lived in the Zone for several generations.

[82] Wikipedia, based on William H. Ormsbee, Jr.

Made in the USA
San Bernardino, CA
01 December 2016